T0302159

Social Innovation Design Cases

Social innovation is an innovation whose main aim is to benefit society. There is a worldwide need for and interest in conducting innovations and social innovations. Social Innovation Design Cases: A Chronicle of Global Journeys provides an in-depth description of the design journeys of twenty social innovation cases from twelve countries around the globe in five continents. The design cases span areas ranging from promoting rural economic development to addressing climate change. The book describes in depth, citing relevant references, the design journeys of the twenty social innovations and corresponding social enterprises, following an innovation design process model. Additionally, it describes the knowledge models and meta models contributed by these cases. Each design case presents the overall business model of the social innovation and the corresponding social enterprise.

The book is for social entrepreneurs, innovators and aspiring innovators, especially those actively planning and designing social innovations in for-profit, government and not-for-profit organizations. In addition to managers, executives and mid-level staff, the book is for students and trainees who would like to understand different kinds of social innovations as well as their design and implementation. Providing details on the design and implementation of a variety of successful social innovations, the cases presented can serve as templates for future social innovations. The book can empower social entrepreneurs and innovators to develop and implement ideas for the betterment of society at large.

Social Innovation Design Cases

A Chronicle of Global Journeys

Vijay K. Vaishnavi

With Contributions from Harish C. Chandan
and Arthur Vandenberg

LONDON AND NEW YORK

First edition published 2025
by Routledge
4 Park Square, Milton Park, Abingdon, Oxon, OX14 4RN

and by Routledge
605 Third Avenue, New York, NY 10158

Routledge is an imprint of the Taylor & Francis Group, an informa business

British Library Cataloguing-in-Publication Data
A catalogue record for this book is available from the British Library

ISBN: 9781032764658 (hbk)
ISBN: 9781032755250 (pbk)
ISBN: 9781003479086 (ebk)

DOI: 10.1201/9781003479086

Typeset in Minion
by Newgen Publishing UK

To my family for their love and support
VV

"Never doubt that a small group of thoughtful, committed citizens can change the world; indeed, it's the only thing that ever has."

Margaret Mead

"Innovation—the heart of the knowledge economy—is fundamentally social."

Malcolm Gladwell

"Design is the underlying skill that activates innovation. If you want to innovate, you've got to design."

Marty Neumeier

Contents

PART III Enhancing Healthcare

PART IV Generating and/or Sustaining Employment

PART V Transforming Farming

PART VI   Addressing Climate Change

Foreword

Year 1991 was a fortunate year for me when I got introduced to Dr. Vijay Vaishnavi during the Fifth TOOLS (Technology of Object-Oriented Languages and Systems) USA conference held in Santa Barbara, California, USA. Dr. Vaishnavi was the Conference Chair, and I had a panel presentation in the conference. During our technical deliberations I was extremely impressed with Dr. Vaishnavi's width and depth of technical knowledge. I instantly became his admirer and subsequently monitored his dedicated professional path of knowledge dispersion for the betterment of society at large, the noblest act one can pursue.

Dr. Vaishnavi is an internationally recognized computer and design science researcher and educator. He is Professor Emeritus of Computer Information Systems (former Board of Advisors Professor of CIS and Professor of CS) at Georgia State University. I'm constantly intrigued with Dr. Vaishnavi's teaching and research methodology that aligns with the betterment of not only his students but also society at large. I see him not only as a challenger to his students to technically succeed but as a catalyst and change-agent to uplift society as a whole. This book on social innovation design illustrates this fact. The book specifies concise approaches and fruitful results to meet the existing and future challenges of society. The book is in continuation of Dr. Vaishnavi's dedication to knowledge dispersion for the betterment of society. Achieving a new level of ecological, health, and economical progress can undoubtedly be envisioned as the main purpose of this book.

Innovation results in the utilization of a novel idea or method and introduces fresh concepts or approaches in transforming ideas and inventions into practical products or processes that have real-world utility to transform and uplift society. I, as an innovator, educator, and business executive for the last 50 years, wholeheartedly appreciate and significantly value the role of 'idea and innovation' to overcome the hump and to keep ahead of technical and business challenges. "Innovation" is the keyword in current industrial (both large and small scale) environments, to enhance the user base with newly innovated techniques, devices, tools, etc., resulting in an increased market share and profitability. Social innovation is an important type of innovation that effectively addresses the neglected issues of society as well as realistically leads the path forward for mitigating the problems caused by unsustainable growth.

I firmly believe that this book will entice and benefit a wide spectrum of professionals in academic and industrial arenas, social reformers, and many more dealing with innovations and social innovations. I envision that this book will be a significantly valuable sourcebook not only in highly technology-oriented projects (e.g., mobility/telecom, Information technology, etc.) but will prove equally valuable for social projects within traditional areas, e.g., transforming marginal farming to a cash-crop ventures, child vaccinations and healthcare, bio-gas generation, water resource management, etc. The book will also prove to be a good resource for students in innovation, management, and design studies.

The book provides a metamodel and framework illustrating the iterative social innovation design process. Dr. Vaishnavi has himself taken an 'innovative approach' to writing this book to ensure that the book is equally valuable for its readers globally – in both developed and developing countries. The book contains twenty design case studies spanning promoting rural economic development, improving infrastructure (water management, waste management, power generation, etc.), enhancing healthcare, generating and/ or sustaining employment, transforming farming, and addressing climate change. The author has uniquely selected the use cases for both developed and developing countries having different issues, resources, and workable solutions.

I am delighted to find that the book has provided comprehensive coverage, addressing the challenges of people and their livelihoods around the globe. With my own experience working in Australia, India, Italy, Kenya, South Africa, Argentina, and the United States, I find that the book touches the lives and livelihood of common people as well as businesses, both small and large, which is near and dear to my heart. I constantly strive myself to mitigate such issues to uplift society. The book includes case studies and narrates the innovative solutions developed to meet homelessness challenges (e.g., Income-Earning Model for Homeless People), the concept of time banks which has now taken root in thirty-four countries with a major presence in the USA and UK, and reducing fossil fuel emission impacts. Johnson & Johnson's focus on reducing emissions was followed by its push beyond "business as usual" with adopting a specific energy policy and setting measurable goals. This policy applied equally to all its individual units and needed significant business commitment to realize their targeted emission reduction goal.

I felt thrilled with the writing of this Foreword as it touches the core of my heart. Undoubtedly, Dr. Vaishnavi has spent an enormous amount of time and energy in the preparation of the manuscript to make this book a treasure. I wholeheartedly believe that the book will intrigue you as much as it has intrigued me and will empower you to implement your innovative ideas for the betterment of society at large.

Madhu S. Singh, M.Tech., Ph.D., PMP, Hind Rattan
President, StarTech Global Consulting and Charity International Inc.,
USA Former Vice-President, GGI and Lead Architect,
AT&T/FirstNet Architecture & Design

Preface

Social innovation is an innovation whose main aim is to benefit society in some manner. There is a worldwide need for and interest in carrying out innovations and social innovations. Social innovations are conducted by for-profit, government, and not-for-profit organizations. While there are several books available on social innovations, these books do not include much information on how to design and implement them. There is a need for good, detailed design cases that can serve as models and templates for carrying out social innovations, but such design cases are not available. I have written this book to fulfill this need.

The book provides an in-depth description of the design journeys of twenty social innovation cases from twelve countries around the globe in five continents. The design cases span many areas ranging from promoting rural economic development to addressing climate change. The book describes in depth, citing relevant references, the design journeys of the twenty social innovations and corresponding social enterprises, following an innovation design process model. Additionally, it describes the knowledge models/metamodels contributed by these cases. For each design case, the overall business model of the social innovation and corresponding social enterprise is also described.

I started writing this book over six years ago. My interest in writing this book stems from my lifelong interest in design and my heartfelt desire to contribute to the betterment of society. My research career has focused on designing efficient data structures and algorithms, effective information systems, and the development and propagation of this type of research which is known as design science research (DSR); DSR uses design as a research method or technique. My prior book, *Design Science Research Methods, and Patterns*, includes a design science research process model (DSR cycle) to structure a design science research project. Soon after publishing this book, I adapted the DSR cycle to create a process model for designing social innovations; the adaptation was influenced by the existing work on Design Thinking. I used this process model for structuring the design of social innovations in this book.

The availability of information on many existing and on-going social innovations made it possible to write the book. The work on the book started with collecting literature on how the social innovations were or are being carried out, selecting representative social innovations in a wide variety of subject areas from countries all over the world, and categorizing them. This was followed by finding information on how the carrying out of the selected innovations has proceeded over time and structuring the design of each selected social innovation case in accordance with the developed social innovation design process model. Later, I also included information on the knowledge metamodels applicable to each design case in the book and models/metamodels contributed by each case. This was motivated by my prior book on design science research in which I had used patterns to document the knowledge models and metamodels that are used or can be used for conducting such research.

USE OF THE BOOK

The book is recommended for the use of innovators and aspiring innovators associated with the design of current and planned innovations and social innovations. Such people can be mid-level and top-level staff in for-profit, government, and not-for-profit organizations. In addition to such people, the book will be useful to any inquisitive person who would like to understand different kinds of social innovations and how they are designed and implemented. The book will be useful to such people as it provides details on the design and implementations of a variety of successful social innovations, which can serve as templates for future innovations and social innovations. The book chapters on the design cases are independent and can be read in any order.

The book is also recommended as textbook, resource book, or reference book for existing and new courses in design, innovation and social innovation design, entrepreneurship and social entrepreneurship, and management studies at graduate and senior undergraduate levels. It can aid in fulfilling the need to train students to become innovators, entrepreneurs, and social entrepreneurs.

Acknowledgements

I would like to gratefully acknowledge the contributions of Arthur Vandenberg and Harish C. Chandan to the writing of this book. Arthur (Art) Vandenberg got associated with the writing of the book soon after I did initial work on its design and structure. Art searched the literature and made recommendations on the available references for many of the design cases in the book, particularly for design cases in the second half of the book. He also wrote the first draft of the three chapters in the last part of the book (Addressing Climate Change). He worked with me on the book for over two years until February 2020.

Harish C. Chandan got associated with the book in November 2021. In addition to making several suggestions for the book, Harish contributed to briefly describing, for most chapters, elements of the last figure (business model components) and writing of the initial portion of Chapter 1 (Introduction). He also provided me with psychological support at a time when I was feeling overwhelmed by the remaining book writing work.

Author

Vijay K. Vaishnavi is Professor Emeritus of Computer Information Systems, as well as former Board of Advisors Professor of Computer Information Systems and professor of Computer Science, at Georgia State University. He holds a PhD from the Indian Institute of Technology, Kanpur and has conducted postdoctoral work at McMaster University, Canada. His research interests cover several areas including innovation design, social innovation design, design science research methods, information integration and web mining, software development, and data structures/algorithms.

1

Introduction

1.1 INNOVATION

Innovation is derived from the Latin verb 'innovate' which means to renew. In the context of organizations, innovation means improving a product, process, or service. Innovation is a mindset, process, and an outcome. Innovations are needed when the old ways of doing things don't work or for addressing new and existing problems and challenges. The four key elements of innovation include ideation, collaboration, implementation, and value creation. The economists estimate that 50 to 80% of the economic growth comes from innovation and new knowledge (Mulgan, 2010).

Innovations lead to increase in productivity and economic growth. The economic growth is determined by the physical and human capital and social institutions. The economic growth must contribute to the progress of society. Innovations must anticipate and respond to social issues. The policy makers must create new policies to enable innovation to create both economic and social value. (Young, 2011)

1.1.1 Social Innovation

Social innovation is the process of developing and deploying effective solutions to the challenging and often systemic social and environmental issues in support of social progress. These solutions often require the active collaboration of constituents across government, business, and not-for-profit organizations. An enabling policy framework is needed to fully realize the potential of social innovations. (OECD, 2021)

Social innovation has the potential to transform societies (Edwards-Schachter & Wallace, 2017; Fougère, Segercrantz, & Seeck, 2017; Grimm, Fox, Baines, & Albertson, 2013; Schubert, 2018). The European Union has adopted an *Innovation Union Strategy* to realize smart, sustainable, and inclusive growth in Europe 2020, aiming "to create an innovation-friendly environment that makes it easier for great ideas to be turned into products and services." (Europe, 2020)

Along with technological innovation, the EU uses the concept of social innovation to appreciate the social dimensions of innovation for addressing pressing societal challenges, such as climate change, poverty, lacking equity, and social justice (BEPA, 2010; Edwards-Schachter & Wallace, 2017). The Bureau of European Policy Advisors (BEPA), for example, argued that: "at a time of major budgetary constraints, social innovation is an effective way of responding to social challenges, by mobilizing people's creativity to develop solutions and make better use of scarce resources" (BEPA, 2010, p. 7).

A social innovation can be carried out by a for-profit or not-for-profit government, non-government, or private organization. It creates a business enterprise that is called a social enterprise. (Social TrendSpotter, 2018) "Some social enterprises operate as nonprofits; others are for-profits. They can make money, but the key is that they pursue a social mission rather focusing solely on profit." (Kelly, 2021)

1.1.2 Social Innovation Design Process

This book focuses on how social innovations (and associated social enterprises) are or can be created. We will use the social innovation process model shown in Figure 1.1 for this purpose. This model has been adapted from Vaishnavi and Kuechler's general process model for design science research (Vaishnavi and Kuechler, 2015) and is influenced by design thinking process model (Brown and Wyatt, 2010; Thoring and Mueller, 2011). The model describes an iterative process of problem definition, suggestion, solution development, evaluation, implementation, and knowledge flow through circumscription, followed by diffusion. Broad white arrows represent process flow and knowledge use, and narrow black arrows represent the generation of knowledge.

> *Problem Definition.* There can be multiple sources from which an awareness of the need for a social innovation may arise but empathy with the future users of the innovation is the most important among them.

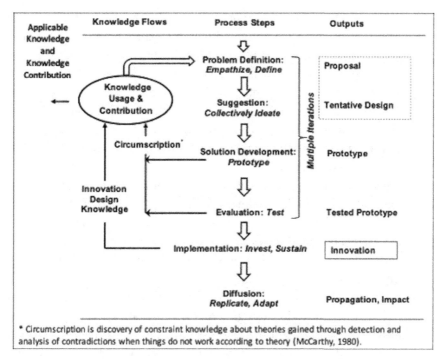

FIGURE 1.1
Social Innovation Design Process Model.

Empathy needs to be used in the definition of the problem. The output of the Problem Definition phase is a proposal, formal or informal, for an innovation design project effort.

Suggestion. This phase follows the Problem Definition phase, and its output is tentative design. Indeed, it is closely connected with Problem Definition as indicated by the dotted line around proposal and tentative design. Both the Problem Definition and Suggestion phases are likely to involve an *abductive reasoning process*. It is a reasoning process in which the designer observes the problem and then creates elements of the most likely solution (tentative design).

Solution Development. In this phase, the tentative design is further developed and prototyped. The prototyping itself is sometimes very pedestrian. That is, it may not necessarily involve novelty or originality beyond the current state-of-the-art. The novel contribution is usually present in the artifact's design rather than in its construction. Both the Solution Development and the Evaluation (next) phases involve *deductive reasoning* in deducing the artifact's material characteristics from the tentative design.

Evaluation. In the Evaluation phase, the testing results of the Solution Development phase are compared with the expectations that are either implicit or explicit in the Problem Definition and the Suggestion phases. When results embody essential deviations from expectations, we need tentative explanations to determine which further steps to follow next. These results and explanations often provide information that helps refine our understanding of the problem, the utility of the suggestion, and the feasibility of the originally imagined artifact. The output of this phase is tested prototype.

Implementation. This phase involves investment and sustenance efforts. It is only after such work that the tested prototype becomes an innovation. This requires development of a business plan and a strategy for seeking investment and for sustenance of the innovation. To preserve the investment, *reflection and abstraction* is used. The output of Implementation is innovation.

Circumscription. It is part of the major feedback loop that drives iteration cycle in the innovation design process. Innovation design is a non-linear process, not a linear process. Multiple iteration cycles involving empathy with the potential users of the innovation and use of creativity to define and solve the problem is the heart of an innovation process.

Diffusion. This phase reflects success of the innovation and is an indicator of its sustenance and impact. Here the innovation needs to be replicated to wider, possibly different, environments and may need to be suitably adapted. The output of this phase is propagation and impact.

The above process model provides a general template for designing a social innovation (and corresponding social enterprise). In this book, we, however, do not provide a detailed procedure for designing a particular social innovation and do not think that is even possible since innovation design is a highly creative process. Instead, we provide a detailed description of how each of the twenty global social innovations have been designed and describe the applicable knowledge to the innovation and the knowledge contributed by the innovation.

We structure the design of each case as a journey with one or more laps (stages) with multiple iterations within each lap (stage), in accordance with the design process model shown in Figure1.1. In some design cases, the evaluation phase is lumped with the solution development phase or is lumped with solution development and implementation phases. This is because evaluation is not conducted separately in such cases and sometimes the validity of the solution development approach is reflected by the success of the innovation itself.

In each of the design cases we also provide a section on Innovation Results followed by a section on Applicable Knowledge & Knowledge Contribution.

1.2 APPLICABLE KNOWLEDGE & KNOWLEDGE CONTRIBUTION

Any social innovation (or innovation) project, like any design science research (Vaishnavi and Kuechler, 2015) project, utilizes any available relevant knowledge including social innovation or innovation design knowledge and in turn may develop and contribute to such knowledge, which can be utilized in similar future design projects. Vaishnavi and Kuechler (2015) uses patterns as a vehicle for design science knowledge usage and contribution. In this book we instead use models to document the knowledge metamodels that are applicable to a social innovation design case and the knowledge models/ metamodels contributed by the design case. The contributed models include models for the design case that are instances of applicable metamodels. Similarly, the contributed knowledge is through model(s) that can also be abstracted to corresponding metamodel(s), which in turn can be instantiated for use in other similar social innovation design projects. The last chapter (Conclusions) summarizes and discusses the applicable metamodels and contributed models/metamodels for all the design cases in the book.

Next, we describe some of the available social innovation design metamodels that, after their instantiation, result in contributed models for one or more design cases in the book.

1.2.1 Innovation Design Models/Metamodels (from available Literature)

The following five design metamodels have been developed by Joshi and Rohrig (2014) in their SI2 framework for use in social and possibly other types of innovation:

1) *High Asset Use*: To increase the efficiency of an innovation all its assets, physical and human, need to be maximally utilized. This can be done by focusing the innovation to a niche area and through standardization.

2) *Process Re-Engineering*: An innovation involves many processes with their workflows. These workflows can be analyzed to possibly reconfigure them to improve efficiency and cost.

3) *Technology Empowerment*: An innovation can be made more effective by letting the users of the innovation use technology, particularly information technology.

4) *Price Modeling*: The prices of products and services should be broken down to smaller units to make them affordable to all segments of users.

5) *Micro-Distribution:* It is useful to have a distributed model for providing services. In this model people are given the responsibility of providing and distributing services. This increases the credibility and accessibility of the innovation.

Joshi and Rohrig (2014) have instantiated Process Reengineering and Price Modeling for Husk Power Systems (Chapter 6); High Asset Use and Process Reengineering for Waste Ventures India (Chapter 7); Price Modeling and Micro-Distribution for Safaricom's M-Pesa (Chapter 8); High Asset Use, Process Reengineering, and Price Modeling for Aravind Eye Care System (Chapter 10); High Asset Use for DesiCrew (Chapter 12); and High Asset Use and Process Reengineering for SEKEM (Chapter 16).

The following four metamodels have been defined by Hetherington (2008) as helpful to developing a social innovation:

1) *Unmet Social Need*: Fulfilling an unmet social need is what drives social innovation. Finding such a social need and then successfully addressing it can create a good social innovation.

2) *Creative Matching*: Social Innovation usually requires an out-of-the-box idea. But the idea doesn't need to be completely new. It can be simply creative matching of existing assets and resources with existing capabilities.

3) *Iterative Development*: Iterative development is needed for the creation of a social innovation or any other type of innovation. Development of a social innovation is a complex process that requires multiple iterations of trial and observation to get it right.

4) *Adaptive Organizational Forms*: To be successful, a social innovation needs to have a flexible and adaptive organizational form and structure to successfully transition through several phases of growth and evolution. The phases that a social innovation must successfully transition

through include its early advocacy and fund-raising followed by operational delivery of the innovation. These phases require different types of personnel and needed skills. This may require changes in the personnel at different levels, which may be become difficult if the innovation is growing rapidly.

The above metamodels have been instantiated by Hetherington (2008) for the following two design cases of this book: The Big Issue (Chapter 14) and WorkVentures (Chapter 15).

1.2.2 Social Enterprise Business Model Template

Osterwalder and Pigneur (2010) has defined Business Model Canvas as a description of how companies create, market, and deliver value to customers, and how this value is to be captured in profitable revenue streams. Business Model Canvas (BMC) (© Strategyzer, AG) has, over time, become a popular tool for mapping and representing business models for a wide range of industries. It is a template in the form of a visual chart that helps users to visually represent summary of the ten elements (components) of a business model. Qastharin (2015) has adapted Business Model Canvas to provide a template for summarizing the eleven elements (components) of the business models of social enterprises. Figure 1.2 shows a minor alteration of this template; we call the altered template a Social Enterprise Business Model Template. The alteration made is not to have a dashed line within the Value Proposition and Customer Segments blocks in the figure to separate co-creator and beneficiary as well as to name the last block just as Impact instead of Impact & Measurements. We use the altered template (shown in Figure 1.2) to summarize the overall business models of all the 20 social enterprises for the corresponding social innovations in the book. The descriptions of the eleven elements in this template are provided below.

Mission – Goals
Mission statement represents the high-level goals of the social enterprise and guides the overall direction of the enterprise.

Key Partners – Needed for the Social Enterprise to Work
Key partners represent external organizations that contribute crucial resources. These organizations are usually suppliers. They can include

Mission				
Key Partners	Key Activities	Value Proposition	Customer/ Beneficiary Relationships	Customer/ Beneficiary Segments
	Key Resources		Channels	
Cost Structures		Revenue Streams		
Impact				

FIGURE 1.2

Social Enterprise Business Model Template. The figure is a minor alteration of Figure 2 in Qastharin (2015), which in turn is adapted from Osterwalder & Pigneur (2010) (© Strategyzer, AG).

other types of collaborators. In some cases, competitors may also act as partners.

Key Activities – Performed for the Social Enterprise to Function

The key activities result in revenue for the social enterprise. An enterprise heavily relies on the processes that enable the production of a service/product, maintaining and developing customer/beneficiary relationships, and delivering the value proposition to its customers/beneficiaries.

Key Resources – Needed to Make the Social Enterprise Work

Key resources represent what is necessary for the production and delivery of the social enterprise services or products. These resources can be of physical, intellectual, human, or financial nature, and their mix will vary depending on the social enterprise.

Customer/Beneficiary Segments – Served by the Social Enterprise

Here the customers/beneficiaries of the social enterprise are identified.

*Value Proposition – Products and/or Services that Create Value to Customers/
Beneficiaries*
The value proposition describes the products and/or services that a social
enterprise offers to satisfy the customers/beneficiaries' needs.

Cost Structures – Costs Incurred to Operate the Social Enterprise
Business activities incur costs and different business models will have
different cost structures based on which business strategy is used; for
example, a company can choose to perform key activities in-house or
through outsourcing, or to lease machines instead of owning them. The
degree of personalized and customized services will also affect the cost
structure, as well as the channels through which they are delivered.

Customer/Beneficiary Relationships – with Customer/Beneficiary Segments
Some customers may be served in a standardized and automated way
whereas other customer segments will demand a closer, and more
customized, relationship. Generally, a complex customer/benefi-
ciary problem need will require a more personalized relationship.
Furthermore, the customers/beneficiaries' preferences will affect how
the relationship is developed.

Channels – to Interface with Customer/Beneficiary Segments
Channels can be websites, telemarketing, stores, or staff. Channels also
include after-sales activities such as customer/beneficiary support.
The main purpose of a channel is to make a customer/beneficiary
aware of the service or product. The goal of the channels is to convince
customers/beneficiaries that it is the best alternative for satisfying a certain need, as well as selling and delivering the product or service.

Revenue Streams – Cash Generated from each Customer Segment
To get the revenue, a company can apply different pricing strategies for its
products and/or services. The selling price can be fixed or dynamic. The
setting of a fixed price must consider the willingness/ability of the cus-
tomer/beneficiary segment(s) to pay for the offer, the volume that will be
delivered, as well as the functionality and quality of the offer. Examples
of dynamic pricing include direct negotiations with the customer/bene-
ficiary, auctions, and prices determined by the availability and demand
at a certain time. The travel industry often uses this strategy.

Impact
The impact of the social innovation (and associated social enterprise)
discusses the impact of the innovation in qualitative/quantitative terms.

1.3 BOOK OUTLINE

The rest of the book presents twenty social innovation design cases and their design journeys followed by the Conclusions chapter. The innovation design journey for each case is described in terms of the social innovation design process model shown in Figure 1.1. The social innovation design cases are organized into six parts as follows:

Part I: Promoting Rural Economic Development
    Chapter 2 – Honey Care Africa, Kenya
    Chapter 3 – Village of Andavadoake, Madagascar
    Chapter 4 – Buhoma Village Walk, Uganda
Part II: Improving Infrastructure
    Chapter 5 – Lufumbu Village Water Scheme, Tanzania
    Chapter 6 – Husk Power Systems, India
    Chapter 7 – Waste Ventures, India
    Chapter 8 – Safaricom's M-Pesa, Kenya
Part III: Enhancing Healthcare
    Chapter 9 – TRACnet, Rwanda
    Chapter 10 – Aravind Eye Care, India
    Chapter 11 – Rushey Green Time Bank, UK
Part IV: Generating and/or Sustaining Employment
    Chapter 12 – DesiCrew, India
    Chapter 13 – Infosys Global Education Center, India
    Chapter 14 – The Big Issue, UK
    Chapter 15 – WorkVentures, Australia
Part V: Transforming Farming
    Chapter 16 – SEKEM, Egypt
    Chapter 17 – Cotton Stripper, India
    Chapter 18 – M-Farm, Kenya
Part VI: Addressing Climate Change
    Chapter 19 – Tetra Pak, Sweden
    Chapter 20 – Elopak, Norway
    Chapter 21 – Johnson & Johnson, US

The social innovations covered in this book span the globe. They are drawn from five continents and twelve countries as shown in Table 1.1.

TABLE 1.1

Global Nature of the Social Innovation Design Cases in this Book

Continent	Originating Country	Case Name and Chapter
Africa	Kenya	Honey Care Africa (Chapter 2)
		M-Farm (Chapter 18)
		Safaricom's M-Pesa (Chapter 8)
	Madagascar	Village of Andavadoake (Chapter 3)
	Rwanda	TRACnet (Chapter 9)
	Tanzania	Lufumbu Village Water Scheme (Chapter 5)
	Uganda	Buhoma Village Walk (Chapter 4)
Asia	Egypt	SEKEM (Chapter 16)
	India	Aravind Eye Care (Chapter 10)
		Cotton Stripper (Chapter 17)
		DesiCrew (Chapter 12)
		Husk Power Systems (Chapter 6)
		Infosys Global Education Center (Chapter 13)
		Waste Ventures India (Chapter 7)
Australia	Australia	WorkVentures (Chapter 15)
Europe	Norway	Elopak (Chapter 20)
	Sweden	Tetra Pak (Chapter 19)
	UK	The Big Issue (Chapter 14)
		Rushey Green Time Bank (Chapter 11)
North America	USA	Johnson & Johnson (Chapter 21)

REFERENCES

BEPA (2010). "Empowering people, driving change. Social innovation in the European Union," *Bureau of European Policy Advisors, European Commission (2010)*, https://op.europa.eu/en/publication-detail/-/publication/4e23d6b8-5c0c-4d38-bd9d-3a202e6f1e81/language-en (last accessed on March 27, 2024)).

Brown, T. and Wyatt, J. (2010). "Design thinking for social innovation," *Stanford Social Innovation Review*, Winter 2010. https://ssir.org/articles/entry/design_thinking_for_social_innovation (last accessed on December 12, 2023).

Edwards-Schachter, M. and Wallace, M.L. (2017). "Shaken, but not stirred": Sixty years of defining social innovation," *Technological Forecasting and Social Change*, 119 (March) pp. 64–79, DOI: 10.1016/j.techfore.2017.03.012 www.researchgate.net/publication/315757282_%27Shaken_but_not_stirred%27_Sixty_years_of_defining_social_innovation (last accessed on December 12, 2023).

Europe (2020). "A Strategy for Smart, Sustainable and Inclusive Growth," *Document* 52010DC2020. https://eur-lex.europa.eu/legal-content/en/ALL/?uri=CELEX%3A52010DC2020 (last accessed on December 12, 2023).

Fougère, M., Segercrantz, B. and Seeck, H. (2017). "A critical reading of the European Union's social innovation policy discourse: (Re)legitimizing neoliberalism," *Organization*, 24 (6), pp. 819–843. www.researchgate.net/publication/312231622_A_critical_reading_of_the_European_Union%27s_social_innovation_policy_discourse_Relegitimizing_neoliberalism (last accessed on December 12, 2023).

Grimm, R., Fox, R., Baines, and Albertson, S.K. (2013). "Social innovation, an answer to contemporary societal challenges? Locating the concept in theory and practice Innovation," *European Journal of Social Science Research*, 26 (4), pp. 436–455.

Hetherington, D. (2008). "Case Studies in Social Innovation: A Background Paper," Per Capita, October 2008. https://apo.org.au/sites/default/files/resource-files/2009-01/apo-nid3 954.pdf (Last accessed on December 12, 2023).

Joshi, S. and Rohrig, E. (2014). "Moving Innovation Forward; Case Studies: 10 Sustainable and Inclusive Business Models," GIZ India, New Delhi. www.giz.de/en/downloads/giz2 014-en-moving-innovation-forward-india.pdf (last accessed on December 12, 2023).

Kelly, K. (2021). "What is the Difference between a Nonprofit and a Social Enterprise," April 28, 2021. Techsoup. https://blog.techsoup.org/posts/what-is-the-difference-between-a-nonprofit-and-a-social-enterprise (last accessed on December 12, 2023).

McCarthy, J. (1980). "Circumscription—A form of non-monotonic reasoning," *Artificial Intelligence*, 13 (1–2), pp. 27–39.

Mulgan, G. (2010). "Measuring social value," *Stanford Social Innovation Review*, 8(3), 38–43. https://ssir.org/articles/entry/measuring_social_value (last accessed on December 12, 2023)

OECD (2021). Organization for Economic Cooperation and Development. www.oecd.org/regional/leed/social-innovation.htm (last accessed on December 12, 2023).

Osterwalder, A. and Pigneur, Y. (2010). *Business Model Generation: A Handbook for Visionaries, Game Changers, and Challengers*. Chichester/GB: John Wiley & Sons. https://tudelft. openresearch.net/image/2015/10/28/business_model_generation.pdf (last accessed on August 30, 2022).

Qastharin, A.R. (2015). "Business model canvas for social enterprise," *Proceedings of the 7th Indonesia International Conference on Innovation, Entrepreneurship and Small Business* (IICIES 2015), Bandung, Indonesia, pp. 1–10. www.researchgate.net/profile/Annisa-Qastharin/publication/323393037_Business_Model_Canvas_for_Social_Enterprise/links/5aa8e20d0f7e9b0ea308294a/Business-Model-Canvas-for-Social-Enterprise.pdf (last accessed on December 12, 2023).

Schubert, C. (2018). "Social innovation; A new instrument for social change?" In W. Rammert, and A. Windeler (Eds.), *Innovation society today*. Wiesbaden: Springer VS (2018), pp. 371–391. DOI: 10.1007/978-3-658-19269-3 (last accessed on December 12, 2023).

Social TrendSpotter (2018). "What is the Difference between Social Innovation, Social Enterprise & Social Entrepreneurship?" https://socialtrendspot.medium.com/what-is-the-difference-between-social-innovation-social-enterprise-social-entrepreneurship-fe3fce7bf925 (last accessed on December 12, 2023).

Thoring, K. and Mueller, R.M. (2011). "Understanding design thinking: A process model based on method engineering," *Proceedings of the International Conference on Engineering and Product Design Education*, E&PDE'11, City University, London, UK. www.researchgate. net/publication/234065413_Understanding_design_thinking_A_process_model_base d_on_method_engineering (last accessed on December 12, 2023)

Vaishnavi, V.K. and Kuechler, W. (2015). *Design Science Research Methods and Patterns*. CRC Press, ISBN 9781498715256, 2nd edition.

Young, H.P. (2011). "The dynamics of social innovation," *Proceedings of the National Academy of Sciences Dec 2011*, 108 (Supplement 4), pp. 21285–21291. DOI: 10.1073/pnas.1100973108. www.pnas.org/doi/10.1073/pnas.1100973108 (last accessed on December 12, 2023).

Part I

Promoting Rural Economic Development

"Almost half of the population of the world lives in rural regions and mostly in a state of poverty. Such inequalities in human development have been one of the primary reasons for unrest and, in some parts of the world, even violence."

Abdul Kalam

Chapter 2: Honey Care Africa, Kenya – Promoting Honey Farming
Chapter 3: Village of Andavadoake, Madagascar – Increasing Productivity of Octopus Farming
Chapter 4: Buhoma Village Walk, Uganda – Promoting Sustainable Tourism

This part has 'Promoting Rural Economic Development' as its theme. It contains three design cases from three different countries in Africa: Kenya, Madagascar, and Uganda, dealing with rural economic development in different ways. Here are the abstracts for the three social innovation design cases:

DOI: 10.1201/9781003479086-2

2

Honey Care Africa, Kenya: Promoting Honey Farming

2.1 OVERVIEW

Traditional beekeeping is practiced widely in Sub-Saharan Africa, which includes countries such as Kenya, Tanzania, Malawi, Sudan, and Nigeria. This region has the least honey-bee disease problems mainly because of the prevalence of wild bee colonies. (The Conversation, 2020)

Beekeeping has the potential to supplement income to alleviate rural poverty in African and other countries. Yet this potential has not been fully realized due to lack of needed capital, inadequate access to the needed knowledge, and inability of the honey farmers to get a reasonable price for the honey produced. Honey Care Africa (HCA) is a bold and successful private for-profit social enterprise (social innovation) to address these problems with the overall goal of promoting beekeeping in Kenya. Honey Care Africa supports the honey farmers by purchasing their honey and maintaining high quality hives. It purchases the honey produced at fair trade prices through on-the-spot cash payment, which it processes, packs, and sells for a profit to the market. Honey Care Africa initially expanded its operations to Tanzania, and later to other countries in East Africa—Uganda, Malawi, Southern Sudan. The enterprise was founded by three Kenyan entrepreneurs—Farouk Jiwa and two of his associates, in 2000. (Honey Care Africa website, nd)

The rest of the chapter describes in detail the design of the for-profit social innovation (and the corresponding social enterprise), Honey Care Africa – Promoting Honey Farming.

DOI: 10.1201/9781003479086-3

2.2 CONTEXT

About 80% of the land in Kenya is suitable for beekeeping but the potential of beekeeping and honey production had not been fully utilized. Most of the honey consumed in the country was imported from Tanzania. (United Nations, 2008; Yale SOM, 2017)

About 75% of the people in Kenya are engaged in agriculture and a large proportion of this population have traditionally been keeping bees and extracting honey. However, beekeeping was not helping to combat rural poverty for several reasons: The farmers did not have the required infrastructure, or knowledge needed for beekeeping. The hives they were using were of the rudimentary type instead of modern—Langstroth type. They lacked the specialized knowledge in honey production. As a result, the honey produced was of poor quality. On top of that the honey produced was sold to middlemen who would provide a very low price for the honey. (Yale SOM, 2017)

2.3 INNOVATION DESIGN JOURNEY

2.3.1 Lap(s) / Stage(s)

2.3.1.1 Lap (Stage) 1 (2000–2009): Establish the For-Profit Social Enterprise

2.3.1.1.1 Problem Definition

Farouk Jiwa and his associates were keenly aware of the rural poverty (two-thirds of Kenyans living in rural areas with half of the population living below the poverty line). They were also fully aware of the inefficiency of the government in handling the rural poverty. The adult literacy rate was good, but 40% of the labor force was unemployed.

Honey production by farmers faced many problems, including not having knowledge of or access to the best honey production technology, difficulty in financing, and inability to get a good price for the honey produced. Jiwa and his associates realized that a novel solution needed to be found for how honey production could be modernized in a way that the people producing the honey economically benefit.

2.3.1.1.2 Suggestion

The idea of using a tripartite (three-way) business model for honey production and sale was mooted (Branzel and Valente, 2007; Jiwa, 2004). The three
components in the model would be: (a) A private social enterprise (PSE);
(b) Local rural communities; and (c) Funding agencies including development agencies and the private sector.

Private social enterprise (PSE) would provide the means and knowhow
for honey production to farmers, arrange necessary financing, and buy the
honey produced at remunerative price providing on-the-spot payment. Jiwa
and his associates were the private social entrepreneurs—an important part
of the model. The tripartite model would need to be fully developed.

2.3.1.1.3 Solution Development and Evaluation

Farouk Jiwa and his two associates prototyped the tripartite business model
shown in Figure 2.1 (Esper, London, and Kanchwala, 2013). They checked
if the state-of-the-art high-quality hives (Langstroth hives) (Esper, London,
and Kanchwala, 2013) could be produced at reasonable prices and how
money could be arranged or loaned for farmers to buy the hives and to provide them with the needed training in beekeeping. They also checked if the
honey collected could be purchased and then packaged and sold at prices
such that the farmers get a reasonable profit to repay the loan and to improve
their economic condition.

The details of the model were worked out and its economic feasibility
examined. It was found out that the model would work out and provide a
reasonable incentive and return to the farmers. It was decided to implement
the model.

2.3.1.1.4 Implementation

Farouk Jiwa and his two associates formed a for-profit enterprise (private
social enterprise) called Honey Care Africa (HCA) that would follow the
HCA Tripartite Business Model shown in Figure 2.1 (Esper, London, and
Kanchwala, 2013). The activities of HCA would include the following:

- Produce high quality Langstroth hives.
- Sell the hives to the farmers.
- Facilitate the farmers to get funds to purchase the hives (through
  NGOs, community-based organizations, or loans from micro-finance
  institutions).

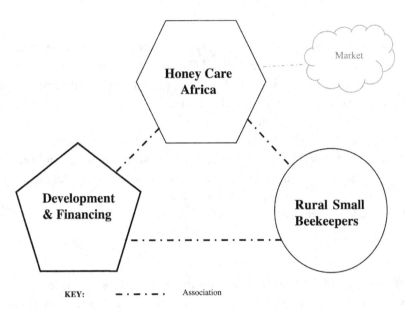

FIGURE 2.1
Honey Care Africa Tripartite Business Model.

- Provide intensive training to these farmers in beekeeping (apiculture).
- Guarantee market to the honey farmers. HCA would purchase the honey from the farmers and pay them fairtrade prices on the spot.
- HCA would process, package, and sell the honey to supermarket chains and other clients.

The necessary organizational and physical infrastructure for HCA was created. The physical infrastructure included the headquarters for HCA which was set up in Nairobi. In addition, a factory was set up to locally manufacture the Langstroth hives to be able to produce them at a cheaper price. Also, facilities were set up for the processing of honey collected from farmers, its packaging, and sales.

The activities and the operations of HCA following the HCA Balanced Dual Enablement Operations Model shown in Figure 2.2 were started. The operations of HCA had two components and needed to be given balanced attention: Hive Operations (see Figure 2.3) and Honey operations (see Figure 2.4). The Hive Operations component enabled the production of honey by the farmers. It included the manufacture of Langstroth hives and their sales to the farmers. Included in Hive Operations was hives installation at the farmer sites and their thorough regular inspections. Contacts and

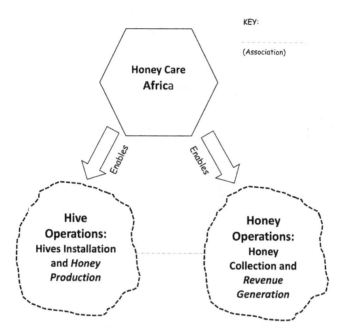

FIGURE 2.2
Honey Care Africa Balanced Dual Enablement Model.

arrangements were set up to facilitate the purchase of hives by the farmers from HCA mostly through loans from micro-finance institutions.

The Honey Operations component included the collection of honey from the farmers and its on-the-spot payment, and then its processing, packaging, and sales. The sales of the honey to supermarkets and other clients needed to be profitable after recovering the cost of the packaged honey as well as the cost of hive operations.

The innovation, Honey Care-Africa, became a reality and started functioning smoothly quickly (see Figure 2.5). It won several awards including the following:

- Equator Initiative Prize (2002)
- International Development Marketplace Innovation Award (2002)
- World Business Award (2004)
- Kenya Quality Award (2004)

The innovation needed to be monitored over time. In 2005, Farouk Jiwa (founder) stepped away from direct involvement. For the next five years (2005–2009) it was headed by several interim CEOs. Over time the

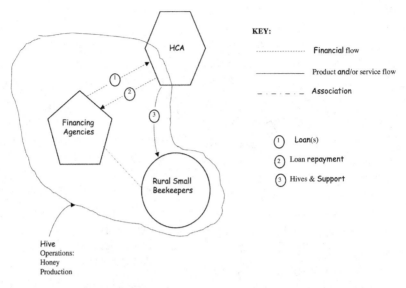

FIGURE 2.3
Honey Care Africa Hive Operations Model.

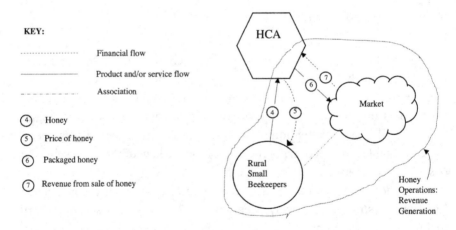

FIGURE 2.4
Honey Care Africa Honey Operations Model.

company depended mostly on donors to fund its operations. To honor the donors' preferences, the network of operations got dispersed all over Kenya resulting in the company's inability to carry out its operations effectively and efficiently. The Hive Operations component of the model started getting less attention, resulting in sub-optimal honey production. (Aspen, nd)

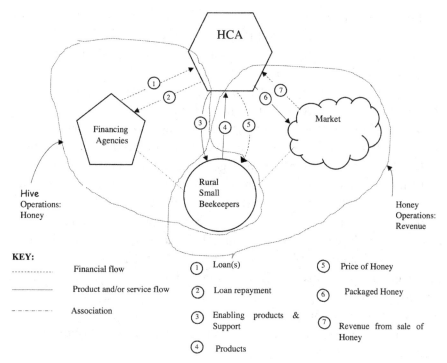

FIGURE 2.5
Honey Care Africa Detailed Operations Model.

2.3.1.1.5 Circumscription

This lap (stage) demonstrated the importance of having a balance between the two operational components of HCA—Hive Operations component (responsible for honey production) and Honey Operations component (responsibile for revenue generation)—so that there is synergy between the two components. Losing this balance by giving importance to Honey Operations at the cost of Hive Operations had adversely affected the functioning of HCA.

2.3.1.2 Lap (Stage) 2 (2010–): Overcome Financial and Logistics Problems

2.3.1.2.1 Problem Definition

While Honey Care received well deserved international praise for its social impact but by 2010 it was facing *financial problems*, which was causing *logistical problems*. This in turn was making it pay less attention to Hive Operations, causing an imbalance between the Hive Operations and the Honey Operations components of its operational model. This had damaged relations with honey farmers causing some farmers to exit the HCA network and caused reduction in the production of honey and its sale. The overall goal of this lap (stage) was to address the financial and the logistical problems to bring HCA back to health. Since there was loss of confidence in HCA there was a need for providing additional incentives to honey farmers to bring them back to the HCA fold. (Aspen, nd; Yale SOM, 2017)

Financial Problems. In the initial years, the general financing arrangement was that HCA would connect the farmers to micro-finance institutions such as Equity Bank and Milango. A good feature of this arrangement was that the farmers would own the hives, but, on the negative side, the loans involved relatively high interest rates and small windows for loan repayment. Over time HCA became more and more dependent on donations for its operations. The donors often wanted HCA to expand into new regions. This caused dispersion of operations of HCA all over Kenya. The resulting expansion of operations of HCA was good but it caused logistical problems for properly inspecting and serving the hives. There was a need to address the immediate financial problems of HCA as well as to find a better long-term solution for how the farmers can be financed for the purchase of their hives.

Logistics problems: On the one hand, the expansion of the area served by HCA meant that the farmers being served were now scattered throughout Kenya; this made it difficult to manage and serve the hives and to purchase and transport the collected honey. On the other hand, the efficiency of hive operations needed to be improved.

2.3.1.2.2 Suggestion

It was obvious that there was a need to bring a new management team that would use the original balanced Hive Operations/ Honey Operations model—giving equal emphasis to Hive Operations and Honey Operations—with additional inducements to lure back the farmers lost to HCA.

For solving the financing problems, a thorough examination of available financing arrangements and their suitability for serving the poor rural farmers was mooted. For solving the logistics problems, the examination and use and adoption of available models and technology was proposed.

2.3.1.2.3 Solution Development, Evaluation, and Implementation

In 2010, Madison Ayer was brought in as the new CEO. Being new to the honey industry, he immersed himself with HCA's operations as well as its suppliers, clients, and staff. He found out that besides the problems created by the huge honey production network, there was a fundamental problem that had been ignored—the beekeepers feared bees. He decided to seek external expertise from Open Capital Advisors to advise on revising the production model and fund-raising to overcome the immediate financial problems. (Aspen, nd).

Madison extended HCA operations to offer additional hive maintenance support to farmers. This helped in repairing relationships and improving honey production. In 2011, Alex Bezborodov was brought in as the Head of Field Operations.

The Ayer-Bezborodov team and their work in strengthening and even extending Hive Operations improved the health of HCA (Yale SOM, 2017). While the hives were sold to farmers, HCA started using professional hive technicians for hive management. The hive technicians started hive mainten-ance and harvesting of honey to obtain optimal honey yields from the hives with minimal damage to the hives while following international standards. The processes of producing and distributing as well as maintaining hives thus improved. The company started working more closely with the farmers through its inspectors. The hive technicians would regularly inspect and maintain the hives to ensure efficient honey production. In addition, they would track the hives so that the honey gets purchased and transported to the headquarters in Nairobi in a timely manner. This in turn helped produce more honey and expanded the number of farmers participating in HCA. (Aspen, nd)

Financial Problems. Open Capital Advisors helped HCA to get connected with appropriate nonprofit social investment funds to raise capital quickly. The needed fundraising was achieved with Root Capital, Lundin Foundation, and the Grameen Foundation. (Aspen, nd)

To get a better handle on the financing of hives, Alex Bezborodov started looking at alternative financing arrangements such as community-based organizations and non-government organizations. He wanted to find an arrangement that would allow for micro loans to rural farmers on easier terms and on interest rates that would be affordable to them (Yale SOM, 2017).

Kiva (Kiva, 2023), a not-for-profit, crowd funding organization that allows people to lend funds over the Internet seemed to be an attractive option. Kiva charged 0% interest and allowed a three-year payback period. HCA decided to add an interest rate of 4% to cover the overhead costs and built this interest into the loan contracts. Kiva allowed HCA to cover the loan processes including choosing the loan recipients and how the loan program would grow. HCA started transitioning to Kiva in December 2012 and Kiva became the sole financing vehicle by 2013. (Yale SOM, 2017)

Logistics Problems. The hives distributed to farmers, scattered throughout Kenya, needed to be regularly inspected and maintained to ensure efficient honey production. In addition, the company needed to track when honey from each hive was ready so that it could be purchased and transported to the headquarters in Nairobi for processing and selling. To solve this logistics problem the company employed the clustering model—Hub and Spoke model (Gaille, 2015)—pioneered in the transportation industry. Region-wise clusters were formed focusing particularly on geographically contiguous areas that were not producing much honey but were having the right environmental conditions and climate for beekeeping. Each cluster was provided a cluster manager, administrator, Kiva salesman, and several hive technicians (the number of hive technicians would depend upon the number of farmers served in the cluster). (Aspen, nd; Yale SOM, 2017)

As the number of farmers and the number of hives serviced by Honey Care Africa (HCA) increased, the efficiency of hive operations became a major issue and stumbling block (TaroWorks Team, 2015). As of 2013, HCA was servicing a total of 2,705 farmers with 6,000 hives spread over a huge area. There were just 18 hive technicians for inspecting and maintaining the hives and entering the related data. Any inspection and maintenance work on the hives had to be done at night wearing thick gloves for safety reasons, which made the entry of data (on paper) very difficult. This resulted in each hive operation needing as much as 30 minutes. On top of this, the data records needed to be delivered to the headquarters in Nairobi. The result of the inefficient hive operations was that the hive inspections were not conducted regularly and there was limitation on expanding the number of farmers (and hives) served. All this clearly pointed to the need of using technology, information and communication technology, to improve the hive operations. (TaroWorks Team, 2015)

HCA started using TaroWorks, a mobile application that works on the Salesforce Customer Relations Management platform (Taro Works Team, 2015). The app can be used to collect data on Android mobile phones, which is transmitted to Salesforce database that analyzes and reports data to the management. This made the work of data collection and correction of data entry errors easier and let the hive technicians focus on the core portion of their work. The use of TaroWorks resulted in significant improvement in hive operations and let HCA expand its operations. This is reflected in the 2015 as compared to 2013 data: increase in the number of hives—6,000 to 11,000;

decrease in the time spent on inspections—about 125 days to about 46 days. (TaroWorks Team, 2015)

2.3.2 Diffusion

HCA was expanded to Tanzania in 2005 during Lap (Stage) 1 of the innovation design and development. Honey Care Tanzania, the Tanzanian expansion, was set up and run by Jiten Chandrana. (UNDP, 2012)

By 2010, HCA expanded its operations to Uganda, Malawi, and Sudan. By this time the overall number of beekeepers under the HCA umbrella had reached more than 12,000. (UNDP, 2012)

2.4 INNOVATION RESULTS

a. Simultaneous generation of economic, social, and environmental value
b. Replicating the models in Tanzania, South Sudan, and a few other countries
c. HCA employs 50 people, helps over 9,000 small-scale beekeepers (over 38,000 direct beneficiaries) generate supplementary income of US$ 180-250 per annum ("Honey Care Africa," 2017)
d. HCA, largest producer of high-quality honey in East Africa, among the largest exporters of beeswax in the region
e. Recipient of numerous international awards

2.5 APPLICABLE KNOWLEDGE & KNOWLEDGE CONTRIBUTION

Models/Metamodels

Unmet Social Need (Hetherington, 2008; see Chapter 1)

Most parts of Kenya, like other Sub-Saharan countries, are suitable for beekeeping. Beekeeping when done well can alleviate rural poverty. But this potential has not been fully utilized because of lack of infrastructure, poor knowledge of beekeeping, and the poor returns achieved by selling the honey to middlemen. There was thus a social need to correct these problems to alleviate rural poverty. This was the need fulfilled by HCA.

Assessment of Needs, Issues, or Opportunities

Honey Care Africa used available surveys and reports in the Problem Definition phase to find out if there was under-tapped potential for beekeeping in Kenya. The assessment found that 80% of land in Kenya was suitable for beekeeping. It also found that agro-ecological, climate conditions, and land use patterns were nearly perfect for beekeeping industry.

Finding Impediments to Realizing Potential

If there was under-tapped potential for beekeeping in Kenya, then why such an industry had not already developed? Utilizing available surveys/reports, it was found that there were four impediments to realizing this potential in Kenya: (a) Lack of market knowledge in terms of demand; (b) The hives that were used for producing honey were of poor quality; (c) Small farmers in Kenya did not have enough funds to buy quality hives and to create the needed infrastructure; (d) Beekeepers were exploited by middlemen with knowledge of the market to sell their honey at low prices. In the solution development phase, Honey Care Africa provided solutions to overcoming the above identified impediments for creating a profitable beekeeping industry.

Hub and Spoke Model (Gaille, 2015)

The model was used to solve the logistics problem of inspecting and maintaining hives scattered throughout Kenya as well as purchasing their honey and transporting it to the headquarters in Nairobi. The hives located in contiguous areas were grouped together into clusters with each cluster having a cluster manager, administrator, Kiva salesman, and appropriate number of hive technicians who would be responsible for the hives in the cluster. (Yale SOM, 2017)

Creative Matching (Hetherington, 2008; see Chapter 1)

The key to the HCA innovation was to creatively combine the existing assets of farmers interested in beekeeping, current knowledge of beekeeping using Langstroth type hives, development and financing agencies, and the market while keeping the farmers insulated from both the funding agencies, and the market.

High Asset Use (Joshi and Rohrig, 2014; see Chapter 1)

The innovation focused on the niche area of beekeeping through maximally utilizing the existing assets in a manner that the beekeeping farmers get maximum profit.

Iterative Development (Hetherington, 2008; see Chapter 1)

Farouk Jiwa and his associates came up with the general model of a for-profit social innovation, but it took several iterations to get it fully ironed out and operational.

Adaptive Organizational Forms (Hetherington, 2008; see Chapter 1)

HCA turned out to be a successful innovation but over time it started having financial and logistics problems for which different type of managerial and other personnel were needed to get the innovation back on track. The innovation had the flexibility to carry out the needed changes. In 2010, a new CEO was appointed, and a new position was created for heading field operations. These needed changes were good for continued success of the innovation.

Honey Care Africa Tripartite Business Model (see Figure 2.1)

This model insulates the rural small beekeepers from the market as well as from the worries of raising money from development agencies as well as other organizations to finance the purchase of quality beehives and other infrastructure needed for producing honey. (Esper, London, and Kanchwala, 2013)

Balanced Dual Enablement Operations Models

- *Honey Care Africa Balanced Dual Enablement Operations Model* (see Figure 2.2)
  This model enables Hive Operations (hives installation and honey production) and Honey Operations (honey collection and revenue generation) in a balanced manner. (Yale SOM, 2017)
- *Honey Care Africa Detailed Operations Model* (see Figure 2.5)
  This model provides details of the HCA Balanced Dual Enablement Operations Model (Figure 2.2).
  The following are some interesting generalizations of their corresponding models:
- *Tripartite Business Model: Private Social Enterprise Tripartite Business Model* (see Figure 2.6)—generalization of Honey Care Africa Tripartite Business Model (Figure 2.1)
- Balanced Dual Enablement Operations Models
  - *Private Social Enterprise Balanced Dual Enablement Operations Model* (see Figure 2.7)—generalization of Honey Care Africa Balanced Dual Enablement Operations Model (Figure 2.2)
    - Providing needed infrastructure and knowledge for products/services development
    - Providing revenue for the delivered products/service
- *Private Social Enterprise Detailed Operations Model* (see Figure 2.8)—generalization of Honey Care Africa Detailed Operations Model (Figure 2.5)

Private Social Enterprise (PSE) Tripartite Business Model

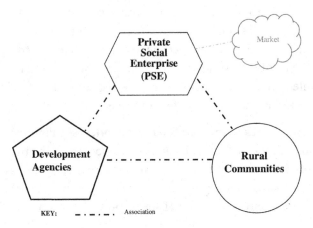

FIGURE 2.6
Private Social Enterprise Tripartite Business Model.

Private Social Enterprise Balanced Dual Enablement Operations Model

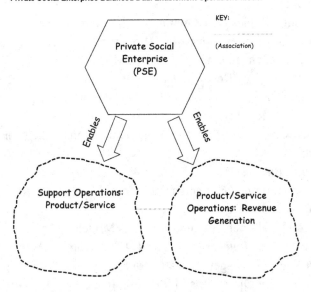

FIGURE 2.7
Private Social Enterprise Balanced Dual Enablement Operations.

The Private Social Enterprise balanced dual enablement operations model and associate models shown in Figures 2.7 and 2.8 can be used for many products that can enhance the income of rural people. Examples of such products include organic farm products and medicinal mushrooms.

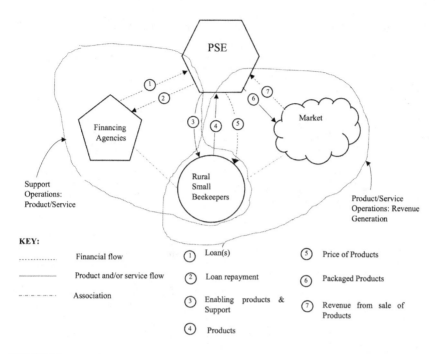

FIGURE 2.8
Private Social Enterprise Detailed Operations Model.

Social Enterprise Business Model Template (see Chapter 1, Section 1.2.2)
The model, shown in Figure 2.9, summarizes the Overall Business Model of HCA in accordance with the template provided by Figure 1.2 of Chapter 1. The eleven components of the business model are briefly described below.

Mission – Goals
The mission of Honey Care Africa is to reduce poverty in Kenya by helping rural beekeepers increase productivity in honey farming, provide financing, and ensuring good price by eliminating middlemen.

Key Partners – Needed for the Social Enterprise to Work
The key partners of the for-profit social enterprise were the rural small beekeepers, development and financing agencies, and the market. The innovation provided mechanisms for new synergistic relationship between these key partners.

Key Activities – Performed for the Social Enterprise to Function
The for-profit social enterprise helped the rural beekeepers with managing relationships with the funding agencies, provided honey farming

Honey Care Africa (Promoting Honey Farming) Overall Business Model				
Mission Design Honey Care Africa (HCA), a for-profit social enterprise, to alleviate rural poverty through honey farming.				
Key Partners • Rural small beekeepers • Development and financing agencies • Market	**Key Activities** • Hive Operations activities • Honey Operations activities **Key Resources** • High-quality hives • Training of farmers • Honey produced. • Loans from financing agencies • Revenue from honey sale	**Value Proposition** • Fair price of honey to farmers • Quality honey for consumers	**Customer/ Beneficiary Relationships** • Installation of hives and collection of honey from farmers in HCA • Hive inspections • Sale of honey to supermarkets **Channels** • Mobil app to collect data. • In-person contact with HCA honey farmers • Sales outlets	**Customer/ Beneficiary Segments** • Honey Farmers • Consumers
Cost Structures • Cost of producing hives • personnel salary cost			**Revenue Streams** • Revenue from sale of honey	
Impact • Increase in the income of HCA honey farmers.				

FIGURE 2.9
Honey Care Africa (HCA) Overall Business Model summarized in Social Enterprise Business Model Template shown in Figure 1.2.

technology to increase productivity, and eliminated middlemen to ensure farmers a good price for their product as follows. HCA produced high quality hives, ensured that farmers have high quality hives and training in beekeeping, arranged loans for farmers, and eliminated middlemen to ensure good price for the farmers for the honey they produced by buying the honey directly on cash payment.

Key Resources – Needed to Make the Business Model Work
The key resources were the high-quality hives, hive management training for farmers, honey collected from farmers, community-based and government financing agencies, and the revenue from sale of honey in the market.

Customer/Beneficiary Segments – Served by the Social Enterprise
The customer/beneficiary segments served by HCA were the honey farmers, and the HCA consumers.

*Value Proposition – Products and/or Services that Create Value to Customers/
Beneficiaries*

The products and services that created value to beekeepers were the improvement of the needed infrastructure (high-quality hives and training) and the direct purchase of honey from farmers without middlemen and offering them fair price. The consumers benefited by getting high-quality honey in the market.

Customer/Beneficiary Relationships – with Customer/Beneficiary Segments

Providing high quality (Langstroth) hives to farmers and conducting their inspections, training farmers in the use of the hives, purchasing honey from farmers at a fair price, and sale of honey to supermarkets.

Channels – to Interface with Customer/Beneficiary Segments

The interface with customer/beneficiary segments was through a mobile app to collect hive maintenance data from hive inspectors, in-person contact with honey farmers to (a) train them, (b) conduct hive inspections, (c) cash-purchase of honey, and the sales outlets for the sale of honey to supermarkets.

Cost Structures – Costs Incurred to Operate the Social Enterprise

The costs incurred to operate HCA were the cost of producing high-quality hives, and the personnel costs for managing and operating the enterprise including salaries of hive inspectors and trainers.

*Revenue Streams – Cash Generated from each Customer/Beneficiary
Segment*

The cash generated to run the enterprise was the revenue from the sale of honey.

Impact

HCA had an impact on increasing the income of the honey farmers it served through productivity enhancements, elimination of middlemen, and reasonable financing.

REFERENCES

Aspen (nd). "Case Study: Honey Care Africa, Open Capital Advisors, Root Capital, Lundin Foundation, Grameen Foundation," Aspen Network of Development Entrepreneurs. www.aspeninstitute.org/publications/case-study-honey-care-africa-open-capital-advis ors-root-capital-lundin-foundation/ (last accessed on March 27, 2024).

Branzel, O. and Valente, M. (2007). "Honey Care Africa: A Tripartite Model for Sustainable Beekeeping," Richard Ivey School of Business, The University of Western Ontario Case Study. www.globalhand.org/system/assets/9aed87d5951c7aebf1c0f2be5ecbb8842bcc3b65/original/A-Tripartite-Model-Case-Study.pdf?1363240865 (last accessed December 13, 2023).

Esper, H., London, T., and Kanchwala, Y. (2013). "Diversified Farm Income, Market Facilitation, and their Impact on Children: An Exploration of Honey Care Africa," William Davidson Institute at the University of Michigan, December 2013. https://wdi.umich.edu/wp-content/uploads/Child-Impact-Case-Study-3-Diversified-Farm-Income-Honey-Care-Africa.pdf (last accessed December 13, 2023).

Gaille, B. (2015). "Explanation of the Hub and Spoke Business Model," March 16, 2015. https://brandongaille.com/explanation-of-the-hub-and-spoke-business-model/ (last accessed on December 13, 2023).

Hetherington, D. (2008). "Case Studies in Social Innovation: A Background Paper," Per Capita, October 2008. https://apo.org.au/sites/default/files/resource-files/2009-01/apo-nid3954.pdf (last accessed on December 12, 2023).

Jiwa, F. (2004). "Honey Care Africa's Tripartite Model: An Innovative Approach to Sustainable Beekeeping in Kenya," Standing Commission of Beekeeping for Rural Development. www.fiitea.org/foundation/files/091.pdf (last accessed on December 13, 2023).

Joshi, S. and Rohrig, E. (2014). "Moving Innovation Forward; Case Studies: 10 Sustainable and Inclusive Business Models," GIZ India, New Delhi. www.giz.de/en/downloads/giz2014-en-moving-innovation-forward-india.pdf (last accessed on December 12, 2023).

Kiva. (2023). www.kiva.org (last accessed on December 13, 2023).

TaroWorks Team. (2015). "Case Study: Honey Care Africa," Taro Works, October 7, 2015. https://taroworks.org/case-study-honeycareafrica/ (last accessed on December 13, 2023).

The Conversation. (2020). "Lessons from Africa on How to Build Resilient Bee Colonies," March 19, 2020. https://theconversation.com/lessons-from-africa-on-how-to-build-resilient-bee-colonies-131478 (last accessed on December 13, 2023).

UNDP. (2012). "Honey Care Africa, Kenya," UNDP Equator Initiative Case Studies. www.equatorinitiative.org/wp-content/uploads/2017/05/case_1348161137.pdf (last accessed on March 31, 2024).

United Nations. (2008). "Innovation for Sustainable Development: Local Case Studies from Africa," https://sustainabledevelopment.un.org/content/documents/publication.pdf (last accessed on December 13, 2023).

Yale SOM. (2017). "Honey Care Africa," Yale School of Management Case Study #J13-05, September 5, 2017. http://vol11.cases.som.yale.edu/honey-care-africa/introduction/about-honey-care-africa (last accessed on December 13, 2023).

3

Village of Andavadoake, Madagascar: Increasing Productivity of Octopus Farming

3.1 OVERVIEW

Madagascar is an island country in the Indian Ocean about 250 miles off the eastern coast of Africa. Andavadoake is a small fishing village on the southwest coast of Madagascar. Fishing is the primary economic activity of a large segment of the population of the village. Andavadoake is well known for its octopus catch in the shallow waters off its coast. Its inhabitants are primarily Vezo, semi-nomadic people, who live from sea fishing. (UNDP, 2012/2017)

The social innovation, Village of Andavadoake (VoA), and the resulting not-for-profit social enterprise show what can be achieved through participation of the local community and the utilization of local community knowledge. Over time the population of local octopus off the coast of Andavadoake had been declining particularly because of commercialization of traditional fisheries. To address this problem, the village elders, with guidance from a UK-based NGO—Blue Ventures—decided to experiment in 2004 on banning octopus hunting for a period of seven months. The results of the experiment were spectacular—about 50% increase in the mean weight of octopus caught, which were confirmed by the ban in the second fishing season. This resulted in the creation of the first community-based marine reserves in the village of Andavadoake. The success of the Andavadoake experiment prompted many neighboring villages to creating their own no-take zones in their nearshore waters and 24 of these villages came together to form the Velondriake Locally Managed Marine Area for the conservation of fish and other marine organisms. (Anna, 2022; Benbow, et al., 2014; UNDP, 2012/2017)

DOI: 10.1201/9781003479086-4

The rest of the chapter describes in detail design of the not-for-profit social innovation (and the corresponding social enterprise), Village of Andavadoake – Increasing Octopus Farming Productivity.

3.2 CONTEXT

The fishing methods used in 2003 were still traditional, but with the arrival of commercial collectors and exporters the market for higher paying fresh octopus and other fish species had become available. This also suited the country as it had moved to an economy that is cash-based and driven by fisheries (United Nations, 2008). The commercialization and international-ization of the fisheries business had, however, resulted in over-exploitation of the marine resources. As a result, the population of octopus in the waters of Andavadoake had been steadily declining.

In 2003, UK-based NGO Blue Ventures Conservation in collaboration with Madagascar's Institute of Marine Sciences began monitoring the region's marine environment. By 2004 the villagers had realized that something needed to be done to improve the population of octopus and other fish reserves.

3.3 INNOVATION DESIGN JOURNEY

3.3.1 Lap(s) / Stage(s)

3.3.1.1 Lap (Stage) 1 (2003–2005): Increase Quantity and Quality of Octopus Catch

3.3.1.1.1 Problem Definition

By 2003, commercialization and exports had significantly decreased the populations of octopus and other marine resources in the shallow waters off the coast of Andavadoake. The village leaders decided that something needed to be done to increase the quantity and quality of the catch of octopus and other types of fish.

3.3.1.1.2 Suggestion

The village leaders suggested the village experiment on a relatively novel approach, to temporarily impose a seasonal ban on the hunting of octopus in a certain area to see if that increases the population of octopus and their weight. There was limited literature available on limited bans on fisheries management. Given the seriousness of the problem the village elders thought that it was worth using this approach on an experimental basis.

3.3.1.1.3 Solution Development

The details of the suggested solution needed to be developed. What would be the area in which the ban would be imposed? What would be the length and time-period of the seasonal ban on hunting octopus? How would the ban be mandated and monitored? The answers to all these questions would need to be found in a manner that was acceptable to the fishing community since there would be an economic cost of the lost catches (Benbow, et al., 2014). Therefore, the fishing community would need to be made party to the decisions made regarding the ban.

> *Area of the Ban.* The local fishing community is a reliable source of knowledge for identifying fishing sites (Ratsimbazafy, et al., 2016). The area of the ban, also called No-Take Zone (NTZ), was identified as a 200-hectare reef flat (the broadest shoreward area of the reef) at Nosy Fasy, a barrier island visible from and about three miles offshore of the village of Andavadoake (UNDP, 2012/2017).
>
> *Length and Time Period of the Seasonal Ban.* The available literature suggested that the ban would need to be with respect to the time when the females are brooding and nesting and when the young octopus are undergoing rapid growth (Benbow, et al., 2014). Based on consultations and agreement with the local fishing community it was decided to impose the first ban from November 1, 2004, until the beginning of the first tide in June 2005 (218 days).
>
> *Mandating and Monitoring the NTZ.* A dina (local law) was established to protect the site from octopus fishing, allowing fishing of other species of fish and a guardian was employed to monitor the NTZ to prevent poaching (UNDP, 2012/2017). The cost for the salary of the guards was borne jointly by Blue Ventures and the village (Benbow, et al., 2014).

3.3.1.1.4 Evaluation

The results of the experimental octopus fishing closure were very positive. The number of octopus caught increased 13 times and the mean weight increased 25 times compared to the pre-closure levels (United Nations, 2008).

3.3.1.1.5 Implementation

The results of the first closure would need to be confirmed by a second closure before the innovation is confirmed and any required action is taken to sustain it.

3.3.1.1.6 Circumscription

The very positive results of the first octopus hunting closure led to interest in replication and scaling up the model used in the closure.

3.3.1.2 Lap (Stage) 2 (2005-2006): Validate the Solution

3.3.1.2.1 Problem Definition

The first lap (stage) of the innovation indicated that a novel solution had been found for the problem of reduction in quantity and quality of octopus caught off the coast of Andavadoake. But the solution—creating a seasonal NTZ— would need to be repeated to confirm its validity.

3.3.1.2.2 Suggestion

Use the same approach for the second closure as for the first closure.

3.3.1.2.3 Solution Development

As for the first closure, knowledge of the fishing communities and their concurrence needed to be used for developing details of the solution:

> *Area of the Ban.* During the second ban, the fishing bans were concurrently implemented at two additional fishing sites (NTZs), Nosy Massay and Ampisorogna, adjacent to neighboring villages (Benbow, et al., 2014). This time the fishing bans were for all kinds of fish including octopus.
> *Length and Time Period of the Seasonal Ban.* Based on agreement among the local fishing communities the second ban on fishing was between December 15, 2005, and April 28, 2006 (135 days).
> *Mandating and Monitoring the NTZ.* A second dina (local law) was created before the second round of closures, for prohibiting fishing on any kind at the NTZs for the closure periods. Ban on the fishing of octopus in the closure period was also aided by Madagascar's southwest, region-wise octopus fishery closure for the closure period that was inspired by the first octopus fishery ban. The state's regional closure was enforced by closing commercial collection of octopus during this period (Benbow, et al., 2014).

3.3.1.2.4 Evaluation

Results of the second closure were also quite positive. Even after several months from the second closure, compared to pre-closure levels the number of octopus caught was four times and the average weight of octopus caught was more than double (United Nations, 2008).

3.3.1.2.5 Implementation

The success of the two closures has made the idea of creating No-Take Zones for banning the fishing of octopus and other fish species as a successful method for increasing the catch of octopus and other types of fish. This has resulted in the replication of the no-take zone idea along the coastline of western Madagascar. The idea has been extended and given a more formal shape as described in the next Section 3.3.2—Diffusion.

3.3.2 Diffusion

The success of creating NTZs for octopus in waters close to Andavadoake has resulted in similar closures in dozens of sites each year. These octopus' reserves have resulted in the formation of the first Locally-Managed Marine area (LMMA) Association in Madagascar—Andavadoake and twenty-four surrounding villages form the Velondriake (to live with the sea) Association charged with marine management to sustain the lifestyle of the Vezo people living in the area. (UNDP, 2012/2017)

Velondriake Association has been provided a formal structure with the creation of committees for drafting of the village laws—dina—and their enforcement. In 2010, a Madagascar decree granted Velondrriake Association and other new protected areas provisional protection, rule-making, and limited policing powers (UNDP, 2012/2017).

In addition, in 2005 the Madagascar government has created a law for seasonal closure of octopus fishing across its southwest coast (Harris, 2007).

3.4 INNOVATION RESULTS

The Andavadoake innovation of periodic closure of octopus hunting and its repetitions has provided consistent results on how positively it has impacted both the octopus catches as well as the income generated (Oliver et al., 2015).

The broad implementation of the successful innovation experiment and its enforcement through a formal framework has resulted in many benefits for marine biodiversity (UNDP, 2012/2017).

The bottom-up approach used in the conservation efforts at Andavadoake and Velondriake have also created socioeconomic impacts by making people aware of how the natural resources can be used in a sustainable manner (UNDP, 2012/2017).

3.5 APPLICABLE KNOWLEDGE & KNOWLEDGE CONTRIBUTION

Models/Metamodels

Surveys and Reports

It is the available surveys and reports that revealed fishing is the primary activity of 71% of the villagers in Andavadoake, between 2002 and 2003, octopuses' exports to France increased by 35% because of commercialization, and the work of Blue Ventures Conservation (UK based non-government organization) started in 2003, working with Madagascar's Institute of Marine Sciences, to monitor the region's marine diversity while improving livelihood.

Unmet Social Need (Hetherington, 2008; see Chapter 1)

A large percentage of the Andavadoake village were dependent on fishing and known for its octopus catch in the shallow waters off its coast. But over time the population of the local octopus started declining mainly because of commercialization of fisheries. There was a social need to do something about it and this need was fulfilled by the Andavadoake innovation.

Participatory Restrictions on Fishing

This model, *Participatory Restriction on Fishing*, imposes restrictions on how fishing is conducted to increase the quality and quantity of fish caught. Any restriction imposed is generally counter-intuitive and will not be adhered to unless the restrictions are arrived at participatively. Any such restriction should be initially followed on a pilot basis. It is only after the benefits of the restrictions are seen on a small scale that the restrictions should be used on a broader basis. (UNDP, 2012/2017)

The current case (*Andavadoake – Increasing Octopus Farming Productivity*) is a good example of the use of this model for octopus farming. In this case, restrictions were imposed on the duration and timing of catching octopus. These restrictions were arrived at participatively and utilized available experiential knowledge. The resulting guidelines on octopus farming have been replicated across the southwest coast of Madagascar.

Knowledge-Based Restricted Types of Farming

The above model (Participatory Restrictions on Fishing) is applicable to a specialized type of farming—fish farming. It can be generalized to all types of farming including organic and ocean farming resulting in the current model. In addition to increasing the quantity and quality of produce, the benefits of using this generalized model can include benefits in areas such as the environment and health of farmers as well as the people using the produce. The model has the following important attributes:

Knowledge-Based. The restrictions should be arrived at based on the best cumulative formal and informal/experiential knowledge.

Prototyping. The restrictions should first be imposed on a small area to see how it will work and to verify the benefits of using the restrictions unless the benefits of the restrictions are well established.

Example of the use of this model include the following:

Organic Farming. This is a restricted type of farming defined by United States Department of Agriculture (USDA) in which various steps are taken to maintain long-term soil health and to produce crop that is healthy to consume. Such steps include crop rotation, elimination of synthetic pesticides and fertilizers, hormones, and antibiotics. (SARE Outreach, 2022)

Regenerative Ocean Farming (Carr, 2021). It is polyculture farming of the ocean in which the whole depth of the ocean, from its surface to the seafloor, is taken advantage of in growing multiple species in an intertwined manner multiple species such as seaweeds and shellfish. It requires no inputs, has the climate benefit of sequestering carbon and rebuilding reef ecosystems. GreenWave (GreenWave, nd), a not-for-profit enterprise, is promoting this type of farming and provides support and training. The setup promoted by GreenWave, seaweed, scallops, and mussels are grown closer to the sea surface using buoys while oysters and clams are grown in cages at the seafloor. (Carr, 2021; GreenWave, nd)

Village of Andavadoake (Increasing Octopus Farming Productivity) Overall Business Model				
Mission Develop and implement the approach of seasonal ban on octopus hunting to increase the quantity and quality of octopus catch off the coast of Andavadoake.				
Key Partners • Andavadoake village elders • Local fishing community • Blue Ventures Conservation and Madagascar's Institute of Marine Sciences	**Key Activities** • Collective decision on the area of seasonal fishing ban (NTZ); its length and start/end time. • Mandating and monitoring NTZ **Key Resources** • Knowledge of the local fishing community • Andavadoake village elders for passing village law (dina) related to NTZ • Financing of NTZ by Blue Ventures Conservation and villagers	**Value Proposition** • Increase in the quantity and quality of seasonal octopus catch.	**Customer/ Beneficiary Relationships** • Village elders and the fishermen—Co-decision makers for seasonal bans • Villagers' cooperation with NTZ monitors **Channels** • Meetings between village elders, village fishermen, and people monitoring NTZ	**Customer/ Beneficiary Segments** • Andavadoake fishing community
Cost Structures • Salary of guards to monitor NTZ.			**Revenue Streams** • Revenue from sale of Octopus	
Impact • Increase in the seasonal number of octopus caught and their mean weight.				

FIGURE 3.1

Village of Andavadoake (VoA) Overall Business Model summarized in Social Enterprise Business Model Template shown in Figure 1.2.

Social Enterprise Business Model Template (see Chapter 1, Section 1.2.2)

The model, shown in Figure 3.1, summarizes the Overall Business Model of VoA in accordance with the template provided by Figure 1.2 of Chapter 1. The eleven components of the business model are briefly described below.

Mission – Goals

The mission was to design and develop a strategy for increasing the productivity of octopus hunting off the coast of Andavadoake.

Key Partners – Needed for the Social Enterprise to Work

For the innovation to work, there was a need for participation of all the influential partners: the village elders, the local fishing community, as well as Blue Ventures Conservation and Madagascar's Institute of Marine Sciences. The fact that the idea was suggested by the village elders made it easy to get buy-in from the other partners. The UK-based NGO Blue Ventures Conservation and Madagascar's Institute of Marine Sciences collaborated to monitor the region's marine environment. The Blue Ventures Conservation and the village community bore the cost of implementing the ban.

Key Activities – Performed for the Social Enterprise to Function
The key activities included deciding on the area affected by the ban (NTZ: No-Take Zone), duration, and dates for the seasonal ban on octopus hunting and how to mandate and monitor the ban. The first ban was imposed for seven months starting from November 1, 2004, until the beginning of the first tide in June 2005. (About 7 months).

Key Resources – Needed to make the Business Model Work
The key resources included the knowledge of the local fishing community, the village elders for the legal support for passing village law (dina) related to NTZ, and Blue Ventures Conservation and the village community for financing NTZ implementation.

Customer/Beneficiary Segments – Served by the Social Enterprise
The Andavadoake fishing community benefitted from the seasonal ban in terms of bigger and better catches compared to when there was no ban.

Value Proposition – Products and/or Services that Create Value to Customers/Beneficiaries
The value proposition of this social innovation was an improvement in the overall quantity and quality of the seasonal octopus catch.

Customer/Beneficiary Relationships – with Customer/Beneficiary Segments
The village elders and the village fishermen made joint decisions about the seasonal bans for octopus farming. The villagers cooperated with the people who monitored and enforced the bans for any violations.

Channels – to Interface with Customer/Beneficiary Segments
The channels included communication through meetings between the village elders, the village fishermen, and the people who monitored the ban.

Cost Structures – Costs incurred to Operate the Social Enterprise
The salaries of guards to monitor No Takeaway Zones (NTZ's) was paid jointly by Blue Ventures and the village community.

Revenue Streams – Cash Generated from each Customer/Beneficiary Segment

The sale from the bigger catches of the octopus provided overall better revenue than before the seasonal ban.

Impact

There was an overall increase in the seasonal number of octopus caught and their mean weight.

REFERENCES

Anna, S.C. (2022). "Green growth in Sub-Saharan Africa: Local innovations providing with sustainable solutions for socio-economic development," Világpolitika és Közgazdaságtan, 1. évfolyam, 2. szám, 2022. https://unipub.lib.uni-corvinus.hu/7849/1/VILPOL20220207.pdf (last accessed on December 13, 2023).

Benbow, S.L.P., Humber, F., et al. (2014). "Lessons learnt from experimental temporary octopus fishing closures in South-West Madagascar: Benefits of concurrent closures," African Journal of Marine Science, 36 (1), March 2014, 31–37. www.researchgate.net/publication/262179321_Lessons_learnt_from_experimental_temporary_octopus_fishing_closures_in_south-west_Madagascar_Benefits_of_concurrent_closures (last accessed on December 13, 2023).

Carr, G. (2021). "Regenerative Ocean Farming: How can Polycultures help our Coasts?" Student Blog, School of Marine and Environmental Affairs, University of Washington, March 15, 2021. https://smea.uw.edu/currents/regenerative-ocean-farming-how-can-polycultures-help-our-coasts/ (last accessed on December 13, 2023).

GreenWave (nd). www.greenwave.org (last accessed on June 19, 2023).

Harris, A. (2007). "To live with the sea, development of the Velondriake community – Managed protected area network, Southwest Madagascar," Madagascar Conservation & Development, 2 (1), November 2007, pp. 43–49. www.researchgate.net/publication/26589494_To_live_with_the_Sea_Development_of_the_Velondriake_Community_-_Managed_Protected_Area_Network_Southwest_Madagascar (last accessed on December 13, 2023).

Hetherington, D. (2008). "Case Studies in Social Innovation: A Background Paper," Per Capita, October 2008. https://apo.org.au/sites/default/files/resource-files/2009-01/apo-nid3954.pdf (last accessed on December 12, 2023).

Oliver, T.A., Oleson, K.L.L., Ratsimbazafy, H., Raberinary, D., Benbow, S., Harris, A. (2015). "Positive catch & economic benefits of periodic octopus fishery closures: Do effective, narrowly targeted actions 'catalyze' broader management?", PLoS ONE, 10 (6), June 17, 2015, e0129075. DOI:10.1371/journal.pone.0129075. https://journals.plos.org/plosone/article/file?id=10.1371/journal.pone.0129075&type=printable (last accessed on December 13, 2023).

Ratsimbazafy, H.A., Oleson, K.L., Roy, R., et al. (2016). "Fishing site mapping using local knowledge provides accurate and satisfactory results: Case study of octopus fisheries in Madagascar," Western Indian Ocean Journal of Marine Science, 15 (2), December 2016, pp. 1–7. www.researchgate.net/publication/316787968_Fishing_site_mapping_using_local_knowledge_provides_accurate_and_satisfactory_results_Case_study_of_Octopus_fisheries_in_Madagascar (last accessed on December 13, 2023).

SARE Outreach. (2022). "Transitioning to Organic Production," Sustainable Agriculture and Research (SARE), Outreach, 2022. www.sare.org/publications/transitioning-to-organic-production/what-is-organic-farming/ (last accessed on December 13, 2023).

UNDP. (2012/2017). "Village of Andavadoaka, Madagascar," UNDP Equator Initiative Case Studies (2012). www.equatorinitiative.org/wp-content/uploads/2017/05/case_134826 1589_EN.pdf (last accessed on December 13, 2023).

United Nations. (2008). "Village of Andavadoaka, Madagascar: Marine Reserves for Octopus." In *United Nations Innovation for Sustainable Development: Local Case Studies from Africa.* https://sustainabledevelopment.un.org/content/documents/publication.pdf (last accessed on December 13, 2023).

4

Buhoma Village Walk, Uganda: Promoting Sustainable Tourism

4.1 OVERVIEW

Bwindi Impenetrable National Park (BINP) is an UNESCO-designated World Heritage site located in southwestern Uganda (a landlocked country in East-Central Africa). It was established and opened for tourists in 1991; it combines the Impenetrable Central Forest Reserve with the Mgahinga Gorilla Reserve and the Rwenzori Mountains Reserve. The park (nearly 300 square miles in area) is accessible only on foot. It is a sanctuary for the colombus monkeys, chimpanzees, and many types of birds. It is most notable for a type of endangered mountain gorilla called Bwindi gorillas. Half of the world's population of these gorillas live in this park. (Achieve Global Safaris, 2023)

Buhoma is the most accessible section of the park where gorilla-tracking first started in Uganda (in 1993) and Buhoma is a village adjacent to the park. A limited number of tourists are allowed inside the park every day after they pay a small park entrance fee, 20% of which is shared with the people living in areas adjacent to the park. The tourists are charged an additional fee for tracking one of the three groups of gorillas. Prior to the establishment of BINP, the local communities living in Buhoma, and other villages depended on forest products for their living. After its designation as a national park the people in the area were barred from removing such materials except that 10% of people living in selected areas have access to certain portions of the park for limited harvesting of some products. This affected the livelihood of people living in Buhoma and other nearby villages. (Gorilla Tracking Uganda, nd)

Buhoma Village Walk (BVW) is a small-scale eco-friendly not-for-profit *social/community enterprise (social innovation)* just outside the Bwindi Impenetrable National Park to generate additional income to the local people living in the Buhoma area and to promote conservation of the park. It was created by the

DOI: 10.1201/9781003479086-5

villagers with the support of Bwindi Mgahinga Conservation Trust, The Food and Agriculture Organization, and the Uganda Wildlife Authority, and implemented between 2001 and 2004. The three-hour Village Walk in the company of a guide provides tourists with very informative exposure to the people living adjacent to the Bwindi Impenetrable Forest and their culture. This successful sustainable project has been or is being replicated in other regions of Uganda. (FAO/United Nations Foundation, nd; United Nations, 2008)

The rest of the chapter describes in detail the design of the not-for-profit social innovation (and the corresponding social enterprise), Buhoma Village Walk (Promoting Sustainable Tourism).

4.2 CONTEXT

With very little income from sharing of the entrance fee revenue and the loss to the normal livelihood of people in the Buhoma village, the village people wanted to economically benefit from developing some form of BINP-related tourism product. The Food and Agriculture Organization of the United Nations Foundation (FAO/UNF) and the local Uganda Wildlife Organization as well as the non-government organization, the Bwindi Mgahinga Conservation Trust (BMCT) were eager to help develop such a community-based product. It would have the additional benefit of providing an incentive for conserving the biodiversity of the Bwindi Impenetrable National Park (BINP) World Heritage site. The local community would need to participate in the design and management of the tourism services to benefit them directly. The poor infrastructure of the area was a constraint that needed to be dealt with. (FAO/United Nations Foundation, nd; United Nations, 2008)

4.3 INNOVATION DEVELOPMENT JOURNEY

4.3.1 Lap(s) / Stage(s)

4.3.1.1 Lap (Stage) (2001–2006): Develop Buhoma Village Walk

4.3.1.1.1 Problem Definition

How to develop and implement the Buhoma Village Walk as a high-quality community-based tourism product for tourists visiting the Bwindi

Impenetrable National Park? On the one hand, the Walk should provide the tourists a direct exposure to the culture and activities of the local people in the area. On the other hand, it should provide additional income to the local households in a way that the environment is not harmed, and strategic alliances are built between community organizations, government institutions, and private sector companies. (FAO/United Nations Foundation, nd)

4.3.1.1.2 Suggestion

Use simplicity and full participation of the local community as guiding principles for all phases of the innovation design. Utilize the assistance provided by FAO/United Nations, the Bwindi Mgahinga Conservation Trust (BMCT), and the Uganda Wildlife Authority (UWA).

4.3.1.1.3 Solution Development and Evaluation

There was a need to identify viable small-scale enterprises that are based on the available natural resources just outside BINP. This would achieve the dual goal of generating income for the local community and conserving the biodiversity of the park. Starting June 2001, a methodical FAO/UNF market analysis and development process was used to achieve this objective. The process was kicked off with a village workshop attended by representatives from villages neighboring BINP, local staff of Uganda Wildlife Authority, and private lodge owners in the area. The workshop was followed by meetings and feasibility surveys. Based on this work, the guided Buhoma village walk that includes sites such as birdwatching and a handicraft workshop was selected as the tourism product to be developed. To guide further work and to provide local expertise and knowledge of the local culture, a village walk "enterprise group" was created that included eight guides from the local community and several households that would manage the sites where the tourists would stop during the walk. (FAO/United Nations Foundation, nd)

Three organizations, the Bwindi Mgahinga Conservation Trust (BMCT), the Food and Agricultural Organization, (FAO), and the Uganda Wildlife Authority (UWA), agreed to provide support to the community in developing and implementing this tourism product. (FAO/United Nations Foundation, nd)

Between 2001 and 2002, several surveys were conducted to investigate the potential of developing the tourism activities identified earlier. In 2002 a workshop was organized to identify the goals and objectives of the project. About twenty sites for the Walk were identified and a selection process resulted in the finalization of nine sites. The selection utilized the community's local knowledge of the conditions and terrain. (United Nations, 2008)

The selected sites for the Walk included unique natural and cultural attractions such as a handicraft center, a waterfall, tea plantations, butterfly pool on Munyaga River where hundreds of multi-colored butterflies can be found, banana brewing, the local gin distillery, the traditional healer, and a community school. (Kabiza Wilderness Safaris, 2022; United Nations, 2008)

"A community initiative was created as a host institution with all members of the community participating in the election of its officers." The trail for the Walk was designed by the owners of the nine identified sites along with BMCT (Bwindi Mgahinga Conservation Trust) and UWA (Uganda Wildlife Authority). A management team was formed that would also coordinate with UWA. The team "decided to meet fifth day of every month" along with the guides "to discuss management issues of the trail." (United Nations, 2008)

4.3.1.1.4 Implementation

"The community defined a formula for sharing monthly proceeds from the Walk admission fees—30% for the guide; 5% for stationery and brochure printing; 5% for the Walk coordinator; 20% for the Buhoma Community Campground (to support community development projects); the remaining 40% distributed as: 70% for the private site owners and 30% for the households of the Batwa forest people who perform their cultural dance." (United Nations, 2008)

The cost of the project remained limited—"less than US$ 900 for the design of the trails, labor, construction of small crossing bridges, and construction of steps on slopes, and resting stools. Radio handsets were purchased for US$ 1,060. Additionally, a hut and a shed were built for the traditional healer." (United Nations, 2008)

The project (Buhoma Village Walk) was initiated in 2004. The running costs for the Walk were met from the revenue generated from the Walk. "The revenues included US$ 51.42 contributed by the site owners each month to maintain the trail and to rehabilitate the steps and bridges. Each site in the trail was maintained by its respective owner." (United Nations, 2008)

"In 2006. The income generated by the Walk amounted to US$ 13,163 which was distributed according to the agreed upon formula. The Batwas (forest people) earned US$ 1,500 in 2006 (United Nations, 2008)." In 2007, 1,789 tourists were recorded in Buhoma Village generating US$ 15,789 in income. (United Nations, 2008)

4.3.1.1.5 Circumscription

The simple project seems to be a great success. However, as Laudati (2010) points out, "Far from improving the overall welfare of rural peoples, eco-tourism often translates into greater state control and increasing pressure from outside forces on people's day-to-day lives." Greater care needs to be taken to be sensitive to how the attitudes of the local people towards biodiversity conservation are promoted while providing the economic alternatives.

4.3.2 Diffusion

"The Walk has been replicated at the Nkuringo gate in the BINP (Bwindi Impenetrable National Park) Kisoro district. Guides have gone there to provide advice on site selection." (United Nations, 2008)

The simplicity of the Walk is attracting other groups such as those from the Queen Elizabeth National Park and the Kibale National Park for the establishment of similar walks. (United Nations, 2008)

4.4 INNOVATION RESULTS

The project has resulted in the creation of a simple tourist product that has been successful. It has resulted in the creation of additional income to the residents of Buhoma village and adjoining areas.

The creation of the Village Walk has resulted in conserving the biodiversity of Bwindi Impenetrable National Park. This is a big benefit for conservation of natural resources.

An important result of the planning and development of this project has been the creation of a model for developing such products in Africa and other regions of the world.

4.5 APPLICABLE KNOWLEDGE & KNOWLEDGE CONTRIBUTION

Models/Metamodels

Unmet Social Need (Hetherington, 2008; see Chapter 1)

People living in the Bwindi Impenetrable National Park area used to remove forest products for their living before its designation as a national park. This changed after its designation as a national park in 1991; after the national park designation, only a small percentage of people living in selected areas were given access to certain portions of the park. This affected the livelihood of people living in the area. This created a social need to do something to generate additional income for these people while promoting conservation of the park, resulting in the Buhoma Village Walk innovation.

Participatory Development of Needed Tourism Infrastructure by a Village Community

The most important attribute of this model is the involvement of the local population (potential beneficiaries) and their representatives in the planning and development of the tourism product. The development of the infrastructure project was guided by external agencies, but its successful implementation and acceptance was solely because of the participation of the local village people. In 2002, with the support of the Bwindi Mgahinga Conservation Trust (BMCT), the Food and Agriculture Organization (FAO), and the Uganda Wildlife Authority (UWA), the villagers agreed to develop a high-quality simple community tourism product in the form of a Village Walk. (United Nations, 2008)

The model was used to create the Buhoma Village Walk but it can be used in creating similar other tourism products in the Buhoma region as well as other regions of Africa and the world.

Creative Matching (Hetherington, 2008; see Chapter 1)

The current case, Buhoma Village Walk, is a simple innovation that involves using nine existing sites of the Buhoma village in a three-hour guided tour. It thus uses existing assets such as the handicraft center, tea plantation, and butterfly pool in a creative manner. The work involves designing and implementing the details of the walk.

Social Enterprise Business Model Template (see Chapter 1, Section 1.2.2)

The model, shown in Figure 4.1, summarizes the Overall Business Model of BVW (Buhoma Village Walk) in accordance with the template provided by Figure 1.2 of Chapter 1. The eleven components of the business model are briefly described below.

Mission – Goals

Create a small-scale eco-friendly community enterprise that promotes sustainable tourism while generating additional income to the local people living in the Buhoma area and promoting conservation of Buhoma Impenetrable National Park.

Buhoma Village Walk (Promoting Sustainable Tourism) Overall Business Model				
Mission Design and implement Buhoma Village Walk (BVW), a not-for-profit social/community enterprise, that promotes sustainable tourism and generates additional income to people of Buhoma area while preserving the biodiversity of Buhoma Impenetrable National Park (BINP).				
Key Partners • Buhoma village people • BMCT • Food and Agriculture Organization of the UN Foundation • Uganda Wildlife Authority	**Key Activities** • Design and implementation of BVW • Conducting guided three-hour Village Walk	**Value Proposition** • Small-scale eco-friendly income-generating enterprise	**Customer/ Beneficiary Relationships** • Co-participation by the local Buhoma community in design and management of BVW	**Customer/ Beneficiary Segments** • Buhoma village community • Tourists visiting BINP.
	Key Resources • BINP • People living adjacent to BINP and their culture. • BVW admission fees		**Channels** • Surveys • Workshop • Meetings	
Cost Structures • Fixed Cost: Design of trails; labor cost; construction of small crossing bridges; construction of steps and slopes; resting stools; radio handsets; construction of hut and shed for the traditional healer. • Running Cost: Guide salary; stationery and brochure printing; walk coordinator salary; contribution to Buhoma Community Campground; payment to private site owners and households of cultural dancers.			**Revenue Streams** • BVW admission fees	
Impact • Additional income to Buhoma village community • Conservation of BINP				

FIGURE 4.1
Buhoma Village Walk (BVW) Overall Business Model summarized in Social Enterprise Business Model Template shown in Figure 1.2.

Key Partners – Needed for the Social Enterprise to Work
The key partners included the villagers in the Buhoma area, Bwindi Mgahinga Conservation Trust (BMCT), the Food and Agriculture Organization, the Uganda Wildlife Authority, and the United Nations.

Key Activities – Performed for the Business to Function
The key activities include developing and implementing the Buhoma Village Walk as a high-quality community-based tourism product for tourists visiting the Bwindi Impenetrable National Park and conducting guided three-hour Village walks for the tourists.

Key Resources – Needed to make the Business Model Work
The key resources included the following: 1. The Tourism and Culture Development Committee of the Buhoma community as a host institution

with all members of the community participating in the election of its officers. 2. The nine Buhoma Village Walk sites – a handicraft center, a waterfall, tea plantations, butterfly pool on Munyaga River, traditional washing of clothes at the Mayunga river, banana brewing, the local gin distillery, the traditional healer, and a community school. 3. The owners of the nine identified sites, BMCT (Bwindi Mgahinga Conservation Trust) and UWA (Uganda Wildlife Authority). 4. A management team to coordinate with UWA.

Customer/Beneficiary Segments – Served by the Social Enterprise
The Buhoma Village Walk serves the people of the Buhoma village community.

Value Proposition – Products and/or Services that Create Value to Customers/ Beneficiaries
Buhoma Village Walk is a small-scale eco-friendly tourist product that generates value to both the Buhoma Village community and the tourists visiting Buhoma Impenetrable National Park.

Customer/Beneficiary Relationships – with Customer/Beneficiary Segments
The customer-beneficiary relationship is that of co-participation by the local Buhoma community in the design and management of Buhoma Village Walk.

Channels – to Interface with Customer/Beneficiary Segments
Surveys, workshop, and meetings were used as an interface with the Buhoma village community. Surveys were used to identify the tourism activities that will be included in the project. A workshop was organized to identify the goals and objectives of the project. Meetings were and are used for the running and management of the project.

Cost Structures – Costs Incurred to Operate the Social Enterprise
The costs incurred to run the project include a fixed cost to design and implement the Buhoma Village Walk and an ongoing running cost that is incurred to run the Walk. The fixed cost includes the cost of designing the trails, labor cost, cost of constructing small crossing bridges, cost of constructing steps and slopes, cost incurred for purchasing resting stools and radio sets, and cost of constructing the hut and shed for the traditional healer. The running cost includes the salary of guides, cost of stationery and brochure printing, salary of the walk coordinator, contribution to Buhoma Community Campground, and payment to private site owners and households of cultural dancers. The

running cost is distributed as 30% for the guide, 5% for stationery and brochure printing, 5% for the Walk coordinator, 20% for the Buhoma Community Campground, 28% for the private site owners, and 12% for the households of the Batwa forest people who perform their cultural dance.

Revenue Streams – Cash Generated from Each Customer/Beneficiary Segment

The only source of income for the project is from the income generated from tourist admission fees.

Impact

The impacts of the project include the income it generates for the Buhoma village community, the conservation it provides to the Bwindi Impenetrable National Park (BINP), and an additional useful attraction it provides to the BINP tourists.

REFERENCES

Achieve Global Safaris (2023). "Bwindi Impenetrable National Park." www.bwindinationalpar kuganda.com (last accessed on December 13, 2023).

FAO/United Nations Foundation. (nd). "Community-Based Tourism – A Case Study from Buhoma, Uganda." www.fao.org/3/j7201e/j7201e.pdf (last accessed on March 29, 2024).

Gorilla Tracking Uganda. (nd). "Buhoma Section of Bwindi Impenetrable National Park." www.gorilla-tracking-uganda.com/why-gorillas-in-buhoma-bwindi-np-trekking (last accessed on December 13, 2023).

Hetherington, D. (2008). "Case Studies in Social Innovation: A Background Paper," Per Capita, October 2008. https://apo.org.au/sites/default/files/resource-files/2009-01/apo-nid3 954.pdf (last accessed on December 12, 2023).

Kabiza Wilderness Safaris. (2022). "Buhoma Community Village Walk—Bwindi Impenetrable Forest." https://kabiza.com/kabiza-wilderness-safaris/buhoma-community-village-walk/ (last accessed on December 13, 2023).

Laudati, A. (2010). "Ecotourism: The modern predator? Implications of gorilla tourism on local livelihoods in Bwindi Impenetrable National Park, Uganda," *Environment and Planning D: Society and Space*, 28, pp. 726–743. www.researchgate.net/publication/ 248881603_Ecotourism_the_modern_predator_Implications_of_gorilla_tourism_on_ local_livelihoods_in_Bwindi_Impenetrable_National_Park_Uganda (last accessed on December 13, 2023).

United Nations. (2008). "Innovation for Sustainable Development: Local Case Studies from Africa." https://sustainabledevelopment.un.org/content/documents/publication.pdf (last accessed on December 13, 2023).

Part II

Improving Infrastructure

"You and I come by road or rail, but economists travel on infrastructure."
Margaret Thatcher

Chapter 5: Lufumbu Village Water Scheme, Tanzania – Offsetting Shortage in Water Infrastructure
Chapter 6: Husk Power Systems, India – Environmentally Friendly Electricity Generation
Chapter 7: Waste Ventures India – Integrated Waste Management
Chapter 8: Safaricom's M-Pesa, Kenya – Mobile-Based Financial Services

This part of the book has 'Improving Infrastructure' as its theme. It contains four design cases from three different countries, India, Tanzania, and Kenya. These cases improve different types of infrastructure. Here are the abstracts for the four social innovation design cases:

DOI: 10.1201/9781003479086-6

5

Lufumbu Village Water Scheme, Tanzania: Offsetting Shortage in Water Infrastructure

5.1 OVERVIEW

Lufumbu is a small poor village in southwest Tanzania, lying in an arid to semi-arid region. The village community mostly lives on the income generated from agriculture that is affected by the lack of adequate rainfall. (One World – Nations Online, 2023)

In 1992, the Tanzanian Government conducted a survey to find the villages that required government funding for constructing water supply infrastructure. Lufumbu unfortunately was not included in the list. This prompted the villagers to raise their own resources to establish a water supply scheme relying on the simple gravity principle, which was designed by the villagers and water technicians. The scheme was funded mostly by the villagers and the United Nations Development Program and was completed in just four and a half months. (United Nations, 2008)

Lufumbu Village Water Scheme (LVWS) is a not-for-profit social innovation (social enterprise). It has been a great success producing benefits including increasing agricultural productivity and decreasing the incidence of water borne diseases in the community. The innovation exemplifies how a community can pool its resources and develop a solution to solve the community's problem(s). (United Nations, 2008)

The rest of the chapter describes in detail design of the not-for-profit social innovation (and the corresponding social enterprise), Lufumbu Village Water Scheme (Offsetting Water Infrastructure Shortage).

DOI: 10.1201/9781003479086-7

5.2 CONTEXT

Villages like Lufumbu suffer from water scarcity largely because of their location in an arid to semi-arid region. The livelihood of the villagers depends largely on agriculture (Ndunguru and Lameck, 2011). As of 1992 the average income of the villagers was less than US$ 1 a day. The major reason for the low income was the shortage of water that affected agricultural output—food crops (maize, legumes) and cash crops (coffee, banana). The lack of road infrastructure and the poor access of the village to roads was also affecting income from the agricultural produce. (United Nations, 2008)

Despite the water scarcity in Lufumbu, it was not selected in 1992 in the Tanzanian Government Survey to determine the villages in greatest need of water and thus in need of Government-funded water projects (Love, 2016) due to budgetary constraints. This was a great disappointment for the village community, and it wanted to do something about it.

5.3 INNOVATION DESIGN JOURNEY

5.3.1 Lap(s) / Stage(s)

5.3.1.1 Lap (Stage) 1 (1992–1993): Develop Village Water Scheme

5.3.1.1.1 Problem Definition

The government's decision meant that the government would not fund a water supply project for Lufumbu despite the village's severe water shortage. The villagers met and discussed and ranked their infrastructure deficiencies that were affecting their life and health. Lack of water infrastructure was decided to be their topmost problem. The main problem was the lack of funds for solving the problem. They decided to do something about it.

5.3.1.1.2 Suggestion

The village elders decided to develop and implement a simple water infrastructure project. Despite their meagre resources, they decided to raise some initial funds for the project and to seek additional funds from charitable and development organizations. In addition, they would utilize their own labor to implement the project. (Ndunguru and Lameck, 2011)

5.3.1.1.3 Solution Development, Evaluation, and Implementation

A simple water supply system for the village based on the principle of gravity was designed by the villagers with the help of water technicians. A water reservoir would be constructed at a higher elevation, which was possible given the topography of the area. This would allow the reservoir to supply the water needs of the village. Water would need to be collected for the reservoir by collecting water from drawing points and using water mains to draw the water into the reservoir.

The detailed design envisaged the construction of a 60,000-liter reservoir. Water would be drawn from 56 drawing points and 10 kilometers of water mains would be laid to collect water for the reservoir. To save money, locally available materials—stones and iron sheets—would be used. To keep the cost down the villagers would provide all the needed labor for the construction. The total cost of the project was estimated to be US$ 50,000. (Love, 2016; United Nations, 2008)

An elaborate scheme was developed for how the village community would participate in the construction. All adult men would participate in the entire construction work—collecting sand and stones, constructing the reservoir tank and its intake water pipes, and laying down the water mains to the reservoir as well as the mains for water distribution. The adult women would do all the construction auxiliary work—collecting and ferrying building materials and water. Older people and children would do the support work such as the cooking food for the workers. (Love, 2016; United Nations, 2008)

Sufficient funds were collected from the village community and the construction project was started. Efforts were initiated to seek additional funds from the Roman Catholic Church and the United Nations Development Program, which were successful. The United Nations Development Program contributed 42% and the Roman Catholic Church contributed 10% of the needed funds. This supplemented the funds raised by the community—48% of the total cost. The project was quickly finished, in just four and a half months. The project was successful in achieving its goal of providing water supply for the village community and even achieved some unanticipated results as discussed in the Results section. The innovation was noteworthy for the way it was implemented and managed. The project was divided into seven segments, each of which was managed by an elected committee. The ongoing management and maintenance of the water infrastructure project is being done by an elected committee (Village Water Management Committee) with members from the village who have undergone the required training. (Love, 2016; United Nations, 2008)

5.3.1.1.4 Circumscription

The project was a great success and fulfilled the existing water supply requirements for the village.

5.3.1.2 Lap (Stage) 2 (2004–2005): Extend the Water Scheme

5.3.1.2.1 Problem Definition

Over time the demand for water in the village increased because of increase in population and expanded settlements. The project needed to be expanded to cater to the additional demand.

5.3.1.2.2 Suggestion

Expand supply lines to reach out to areas with inadequate distribution lines.

5.3.1.2.3 Solution Development, Evaluation, and Implementation

The Lufumbu Village Council sought additional funds from United Nations Development Program. A grant of US$ 20,090 was approved for the project. The new project was started in July 2004 and completed in six months. (UNDP, 2012) The project extension was successfully completed and consolidated with the original successfully implemented and validated project.

5.3.2 Diffusion

The success of the Lufumbu Village Water Project innovation has had a wide-ranging positive effect in the entire region for the community-based nature of the innovation as well for its design. The innovation has made people confident that projects initiated and implemented through community-participation can be successful and has therefore provided encouragement for other community-based projects. (United Nations, 2008)

The design of the Lufumbu water project also has been noted for its low cost and short time of implementation. As a result, the district government has adopted this design—use of stones and corrugated iron sheets—as the standard for the design of all community-based water infrastructure schemes. (Love, 2016; United Nations, 2008)

5.4 INNOVATION RESULTS

The innovation has had several direct and indirect benefits, some of which were not anticipated at the time of designing the innovation:

Direct Benefits: (United Nations, 2008; The Royal Academy of Engineering, 2010; Love, 2016)

  a. The access to tap water has become possible. This has resulted in dramatically improving the health of the community because of reduction in water borne diseases such as diarrhea, cholera, and typhoid.
  b. The agricultural productivity has increased. This has encouraged the villagers to expand coffee farming.
  c. The availability of water has made the production of house bricks possible. This has resulted in the construction of modern brick houses— more than 300 such houses have been built around Lufumbu.

Indirect Benefits: (United Nations, 2008; Love, 2016)

  a. Availability of water has encouraged villagers to plant trees in the valleys and hills in the area. A result of this afforestation and reforestation has been the creation of greenery that has attracted birds, insects, and small wild animals. An additional benefit of the plantation of trees has been the retention of water in the catchment area for water feeding the constructed water reservoir.
  b. The quality of life of women living in the village has improved. The innovation has decreased the workload of women—no need for fetching water from long distances, less work on caring for the sick.

5.5 APPLICABLE KNOWLEDGE & KNOWLEDGE CONTRIBUTION

Models/Metamodels

Unmet Social Need (Hetherington, 2008; see Chapter 1)

Lufumbu, like many other areas in the region, suffered from water scarcity, which affected the livelihood of its community that largely depends on agriculture. Correcting the water scarcity was thus a social need that Lufumbu Village Water Scheme addresses.

Creative Matching (Hetherington, 2008; see Chapter 1)

The Lufumbu Village Water Scheme social innovation was an out-of-the-box idea of constructing a water reservoir at a higher elevation, collecting water into the reservoir, and then supplying water to the village using water mains. However, carrying out this innovation creatively utilized available resources including manpower of the village and their savings, locally available materials, and funding agencies—UN Development Program and the Church.

Adaptive Organizational Forms (Hetherington, 2008; see Chapter 1)

For the project to be successful, it needed to have organizational structures that would adapt to the different needs of the project as it transitioned through its different phases—design, implementation, and ongoing management and maintenance.

High Asset Use (Joshi and Rohrig, 2014; see Chapter 1)

The limited human and physical resources available to the village community needed to be maximally utilized for the project to be carried out efficiently. This was done by electing committees for different phases and segments of the project.

Participatory Development and Implementation of Needed Water Infrastructure Project (Love, 2016; United Nations, 2008)

The salient features of this model are:

1. *Bottom-up Development.* Realization of the need for water infrastructure by the village community and its decision to fulfill this need through its own efforts.
2. *Full Participation.* Participation of the entire village community in the planning, design, implementation, and management of the project as well as the financing of the project.

Participatory Development and Implementation of Infrastructure Project by a Village Community

This is a generalization of the above model (*Participatory Development and Implementation of Needed Water Infrastructure Project*) to any needed infrastructure project and to any village community. The success of the Lufumbu Village Water Scheme in Tanzania leads to this model with the following features:

1. All village communities, including those from developing countries, can take the initiative in the realization of a needed infrastructure in their villages.
2. The key to success of such effort is the leadership of the village community to harness the human and financial resources of the community. Full participation of all the people according to their abilities and capacities brings energy and excitement to the project. External financial resources can be sought but having a base of funds raised locally increases the confidence of any development agency in the successful completion of the project.
3. The participation of the local community in assessing the infrastructure needs and, in the design, and development of the project ensures the completion of the project and its full utilization when it is completed.

Social Enterprise Business Model Template (see Chapter 1, Section 1.2.2)
The model, shown in Figure 5.1, summarizes the overall business model of LVWS in accordance with the template provided by Figure 1.2 of Chapter 1. The eleven components of the business model are briefly described below.

Mission – Goals
Design and implementation of a water supply scheme (LVWS) for the Lufumbu village in Tanzania that offsets water shortage in the village without government assistance.

Key Partners – Needed for the Social Enterprise to Work
The key partners were elders of Lufumbu village, adult men and women, older men and women and children, water technicians, Roman Catholic Church, and the United Nations.

Key Activities – Performed for the Business to Function
The key activities of the project were collecting funds from the village community, United Nations, and the Roman Catholic Church; designing a gravity-based water supply system; constructing a water reservoir and water mains for collecting water for the reservoir and supplying water to the village; and management and maintenance of LVWS.

Key Resources – Needed to make the Business Model Work
The key resources for the project were the village community, water technicians, the United Nations, and the Roman Catholic Church.

Lufumbu Village Water System (Offsetting Water Infrastructure Shortage) Overall Business Model				
Mission Design and implement the not-for-profit Lufumbu Village Water System (LVWS), for establishment of a water supply scheme by Lufumbu villagers to offset water infrastructure shortage.				
Key Partners • Lufumbu village people • Water technicians • United Nations Development Program (UNDP) • Roman Catholic Church	**Key Activities** • Design and construction of water supply scheme • Management and maintenance of LVWS **Key Resources** • Lufumbu village people • Water technicians • UNDP • Roman Catholic Church	**Value Proposition** • Water reservoir and water supply scheme • Supply of clean water • Supply of water for irrigation	**Customer/ Beneficiary Relationships** • Community participative design and construction of LVWS • Supply of water to the community **Channels** • Village elders • Elected committees. • Village community	**Customer/ Beneficiary Segments** • People of Lufumbu village and surrounding areas. • Benefited in: o Getting water supply o Agricultural productivity o Reducing water borne diseases
Cost Structures • Fixed Cost: Material and labor expenses • Running Cost: Zero or minimal cost due to collective participation in management and maintenance			**Revenue Streams** • None in cash	
Impact • Availability of safe drinking water; reduction in water-borne diseases, brick houses • Improvement in agricultural productivity • Improved ecosystem, forestation, and reforestation • Reduction in workload of women				

FIGURE 5.1
Lufumbu Village Water Scheme (LVWS) Overall Business Model summarized in Social Enterprise Business Model Template shown in Figure 1.2.

Customer/Beneficiary Segments – Served by the Social Enterprise
The beneficiary segments of the project included the people of Lufumbu village as well as the surrounding areas. They benefitted in terms of getting water supply, increasing agricultural productivity and reduction of water borne diseases.

Value Proposition – Products and/or Services that Create Value to Customers/ Beneficiaries
The water reservoir plus the water mains for drawing water into the reservoir and supplying it to the village from the reservoir constitute the products that are valuable to the village community. Regular supply of

clean water to the village community constitutes a valuable service to the community that also reduces water borne diseases. Supply of water for irrigation improves agricultural productivity.

Customer/Beneficiary Relationships – with Customer/Beneficiary Segments
The project had relationships with the village community at two levels. The people were involved in participatively designing and implementing the project. After the water supply scheme was implemented, the village people were the beneficiaries of getting regular home supply of clean water and getting water for irrigation from the water supply scheme.

Channels – to Interface with Customer/Beneficiary Segments
The project interfaced with the village people through village elders and elected committees for designing, implementing, managing, and maintaining the water supply scheme. The project also interfaces with the village community for regular supply of clean water to them.

Cost Structures – Costs Incurred to Operate the Social Enterprise
The fixed costs incurred by the project were the cost of the materials used in the project; the labor did not incur any cost as it was provided by the villagers. The running cost of the project was zero or minimal due to collective participation of the village community in the management and maintenance of the water scheme.

Revenue Streams – Cash Generated from Each Customer/Beneficiary Segment
There was no cash revenue for running the water scheme as all the services for running the project were provided by the village community free of charge and in turn the community was getting clean water supply and water for irrigation free of charge.

Impact
The Lufumbu water scheme had many measurable impacts for the people of the Lufumbu village and adjoining areas. These included enhancement in the overall quality of life; availability of safe drinking water; reduction in water-borne diseases resulting in improved health; improvement in agricultural productivity; enabling the manufacture of bricks leading to the construction of brick houses; improved ecosystem, forestation, and reforestation; and reduction in workload of women who traditionally had the responsibility of gathering water needed for daily living.

REFERENCES

Hetherington, D. (2008). "Case Studies in Social Innovation: A Background Paper," Per Capita, October 2008. https://apo.org.au/sites/default/files/resource-files/2009-01/apo-nid3 954.pdf (Last accessed on December 12, 2023).

Joshi, S. and Rohrig, E. (2014). "Moving Innovation Forward; Case Studies: 10 Sustainable and Inclusive Business Models," GIZ India, New Delhi. www.giz.de/en/downloads/giz2 014-en-moving-innovation-forward-india.pdf (last accessed on December 12, 2023).

Love, M. (2016). "Water Works in Lufumbu," June 7, 2016, https://sustainablejourneys.net/ page/2/ (last accessed on December 13, 2023).

Ndunguru, M.J. and Lameck, W.U. (2011). "Community Participation." In J. Itika, K.D. Ridder, and A. Tollenaar (Eds.), *Theories and Stories in African Public Administration*. African Public Administration and Management series, Vol. 1. African Studies Centre, University of Groningen, Mzumbe University, pp. 63–74. https://pure.rug.nl/ws/portalfi les/portal/10755124/APAM-1-manuscript.pdf (last accessed on December 13, 2023).

One World – Nations Online. (2023). "Tanzania." www.nationsonline.org/oneworld/tanzania. htm (last accessed on December 13, 2023).

The Royal Academy of Engineering. (2010). "Global Water Security—An Engineering Perspective," April 2010. www.indiaenvironmentportal.org.in/files/Global_Water_Secu rity_report.pdf (last accessed on March 28, 2024).

UNDP. (2012). "Expansion of Lufumbu Community Water Supply Scheme," SGP: The GEF Small Grants Programme. https://sgp.undp.org/spacial-itemid-projects-landing-page/ spacial-itemid-project-search-results/spacial-itemid-project-detailpage.html?view= projectdetail&id=7179 (last accessed on December 13, 2023).

United Nations. (2008). "Innovation for Sustainable Development: Local Case Studies from Africa." https://sustainabledevelopment.un.org/content/documents/publication.pdf (last accessed on December 13, 2023).

6

Husk Power Systems, India: Environmentally Friendly Electricity Generation

6.1 OVERVIEW

As of 2010, 1.4 billion people worldwide including 400 million people living in 125,000 villages of India had no access to electricity; 85% of these people in India lived in the state of Bihar. By 2016, the number of people without access to electricity fell to less than 1.1 billion, a major portion of this improvement happened in India. By April 28, 2018, all villages in India have been electrified and, as of January 4, 2019, nearly 100% of the rural and urban households in India have been provided with electricity. By 2020, 99% of people in India have access to electricity (The World Bank Data - India, 2023).

Electricity is mainly generated using coal and natural gas, but they are also most responsible for greenhouse gas emissions. In addition to hydro and nuclear, solar and biomass are environmentally friendlier resources for electricity generation and are increasingly being promoted and used. Producing electricity from sunlight or biomass such as crop waste is particularly attractive for remote rural areas. As an example of the availability of crop waste, 1.8 billion kilograms (4 billion pounds) of rice husks are estimated to be produced from rice processing per year in the state of Bihar in India. Utilizing such crop waste, Husk Power System is a startup private (for profit) company in Bihar, India, established in 2008 by Gyanesh Pandey, Manoj Sinha, and Ratnesh Yadav (Rai, 2011/2018).

Husk Power Systems (HPS) efficiently produces electricity from rice husks (a waste product of the rice hullers that separate the husks from the rice) as well as corn cobbs and cotton stalk and distribute it to thousands of rural families. Using a technology developed by the company, HPS lets a biomass

DOI: 10.1201/9781003479086-8

gasifier use rice husks as input to let the output of the gasifier fuel a generator generate 25 to 100 kilowatts of electricity, creating a mini power plant for supplying electricity to a village on a metered basis. Each mini power plant supplies electricity to a hamlet or village up to two miles away after it is properly wired (Sinha, 2011). As of 2011, the company served 150,000 people through its 60 systems in villages of the states of Bihar, Tamil Nadu, and West Bengal in India. (Husk Power Systems, nd)

Over the years, the needs, and aspirations of the customers of the company as well as the energy environment have evolved and the company too has evolved (HPS Website; Goodier, 2018; Dewan, 2019). At the time HPS was founded, the goal was to provide 6–8 hours of electricity per day to rural households utilizing rice husk available in abundance. But over time with changes on multiple fronts, the new goal became to provide 24x7 electricity to rural households and agricultural as well as commercial customers utilizing both solar energy and energy produced from biomass sources such as rice husk, corn cobbs, and cotton stalks. (Goodier, 2018)

In 2014, the company developed a hybrid system that uses both solar power and biomass power that can generate 24x7 power and can serve both households and commercial customers. The company expanded to Tanzania in 2015. By 2017, the company had installed mini power plants with a total capacity of 2 MW. As of 2018 the company operated 75 mini grids in India and five in Tanzania. (Goodier, 2018)

The rest of the chapter describes in detail design of the for-profit social innovation (and the corresponding social enterprise), Husk Power Systems (Environmentally Friendly Electricity Generation).

6.2 CONTEXT

Gyanesh Pandey and Ratnesh Yadav from the state of Bihar in India were childhood friends. Gyanesh Pandey did his B.Tech. in Electrical Engineering from Banaras Hindu University, India, and master's degree in Electric Power and Power Electronics Engineering from Rensselaer Polytechnic Institute, USA and started working in the Power management Semiconductor industry in the U.S.; Ratnesh Yadav did his Bachelor of Arts from Delhi University, India and had agricultural experience including the bio-diesel area (Agarwal and Satish, 2013).

Both Pandey and Yadav were acutely aware of the need for rural economic development in India, particularly in Bihar that was among the poorest states of India. Both had grown up facing acute shortage of electricity and knew that reliable availability of electricity in villages was necessary for economic development.

Yadav was working in Patna, Bihar and Pandey was working in Los Angeles, USA. One day in 2002 they had a casual telephone conversation on how they could contribute to Bihar's economic development and, on how the rural electricity problem could be solved in an environmentally friendly manner. It took more than five years for a solution to the problem to be developed and the launching of a sustainable company to offer a solution. The decision of Pandey to return home (Bihar) for good in late 2006 prompted him to seriously seek a solution to the problem initially that he and Yadav had touched on in their 2002 casual conversation.

6.3 INNOVATION DEVELOPMENT JOURNEY

6.3.1 Lap(s) / Stage(s)

6.3.1.1 Lap (Stage) 1 (2008–2012): Produce Electricity for Rural Areas in Environmentally Friendly Manner

6.3.1.1.1 Problem Definition

The problem was, how to produce electricity in rural and remote areas of India in an environmentally friendly way.

6.3.1.1.2 Suggestion

After Pandey was back in India, he, along with Yadav, started looking for possible ideas for solving the rural electrification problem. They examined the solution strategies in the horizon but rejected them on different grounds. The extension of the central electricity grid would be too costly and wasteful to serve remote villages. Rice husk was available in abundance but producing electricity in the dual-fuel mode—using the gas produced from rice husk in conjunction with diesel fuel to power an electric motor was inefficient and not good for the environment; Yadav was very environmentally conscious. This gave rise to the idea of powering an electric motor by only using the gas produced by a biomass gasifier—operating the electric motor in a single-fuel mode. But this required work on modifying the electric circuitry of an electric motor, developing a prototype and testing it. (Sinha, 2011)

6.3.1.1.3 Solution Development

Gyanesh Pandey and Dr. S. K. Singh, a scientist at India's Ministry of New and Renewable Energy, developed in less than five months a gasifier system working in a single-fuel mode for producing electricity (Sinha, 2011). They constructed a prototype for the system by modifying the circuitry of a compressed natural gas engine and using it to fuel an electric generator; this is an example of technological change. (Bornstein, 2011)

6.3.1.1.4 Evaluation

Gyanesh Pandey and his team needed to test whether the developed prototype could be used for electrifying a small village. To do that they assembled a crude power distribution network for supplying electricity to the village of Tamakuha (literally meaning 'fog of darkness') for the first time. The experiment was successful—Tumkuha was lit in August 2007. To move further on realizing the vision of electrifying hamlets and villages Pandey and Yadav needed to develop a business model and business strategy. This is where Manoj Sinha entered the scene. (Bornstein, 2011)

6.3.1.1.5 Implementation

Both Manoj Sinha and Gyanesh Pandey had their college education from Banaras Hindu University, India. Sinha did his B.Tech. in Electronics Engineering and MS in Electrical & Computer Engineering from the University of Massachusetts Amherst, USA and master's in business administration from the Darden Graduate School of Business Administration, University of Virginia, USA (Agarwal and Satish, 2013). Pandey and Sinha were college friends while at Banaras Hindu University. He was aware of the work that Pandey and Yadav had done. While he was doing his MBA at Darden Graduate School of Business, he used this knowledge to build a business plan and strategy for converting the prototype developed by Pandey and others for electrifying a village into a sustainable business. Sinha was assisted in this work by his classmate Charles Ransler. The business plan won US$ 60,000 from a social innovation competition sponsored by Darden and University of Texas. Based on the business plan, Husk Power Systems was founded in 2008. (Sinha, 2011)

6.3.1.1.6 Business Model

Most of the units developed by HPS generate 32 kilowatts of electricity per hour from 50 kilograms (110 pounds) of husk, enough to provide the basic electricity needs (6–8 hours per day) of a village of about 500 households or 50 shops. HPS has the capability to manufacture single-fuel gasifier based 25 kW-100kW mini power plants based on its propriety design. The company would enter a contract with rice mills and farmers for buying rice husk and other farm waste at a fixed cost. The company would produce electricity using the feedstock and supply it to each village household or business using a direct point-to-point wiring system. HPS developed pricing packages for households and businesses. The package for a household would, for example, supply enough power to operate two 15-watt compact fluorescent lamps and a fan for 6–8 hours a day and to charge cell phones. The pricing packages were significantly cheaper than competing alternatives such as kerosene lanterns and diesel electricity generators. Each household or business would pre-pay HPS based on the pricing package. (Bhattacharyya, 2014; Sinha, 2011)

HPS uses one of three models to conduct its business. In the typical (BOOM—Build, Own, Operate, Maintain) model, HPS would manufacture the appropriate capacity single-fuel gasifier and build the local power distribution network (owning both), operate them, and maintain them; collecting the electricity fees from the served community. In the second (BOM—Build, Own, Maintain) model, the company would hand over the operations of the biomass gasifier to an agent for a fee, who would also collect the electricity charges and hand them over to HPS; HPS would build the gasifier and power distribution network. In the third (BM—Build, Maintain) model, HP would only build the gasifier and maintain the power distribution network; the agent would buy and operate the gasifier and the distribution network. (Sinha, 2011)

In addition to the revenue generated by electricity consumers, HPS generates revenue from carbon credits it generates and for selling the waste (rice husk char) produced at each at each mini power plant. Each power plant of HPS saves 125–150 CO_2 per year by not using fossil fuels for generating electricity. This generates up to 10% of the company's revenue. For rice husk char, the company has created a process to convert it into unscented incense sticks that it gets sold in the market. (Sinha, 2011)

Preventing or at least drastically reducing the electricity theft in the power distribution system was a major problem for HPS for its sustainability. The company has devised a strategy that has both managerial and technology aspects to overcome the problem. On the managerial front, HPS has decided to get the buy-in of the village served and participation of the villagers in various decisions. The company let the village have their say in the location of the mini power plant and timing of its operations. Another way the company gets the village buy-in is by recruiting and training local village people as employees to run the operations, which also generates local economic activity. On the technology front, HPS has developed a cheap pre-paid smart meter that is installed at the household or business to monitor the electricity usage. The two-pronged strategy has helped HPS to lose less than 5% of electricity to theft and leakage (which is a fraction of the average loss due to theft and leakage). (Sinha, 2011)

Financing HPS: Husk Power Systems did not have any initial funding to start the company. It instead focused on finding and developing a good solution for providing electricity to rural people and small businesses using the principle that funding would follow a good solution. Given the very early stage of the innovation, it would need self-financing, awards, and grants. The initial research and experimentation were funded by the personal savings and the founders did not draw any salary for over 20 months after the successful experimentation of electrifying Tumkuha village, and the US$ 60,000 competition award. After the company was formed, in 2009 HPS won US$ 250,000 from Draper Fisher Jurvetson and Cisco Systems based on an inaugural business plan competition for improving the basic technology that the company had developed. In 2008 itself, HPS entered a multiyear grant funding partnership with the Shell Foundation. In addition to the funding requirements, the partnership helped HPS to gain credibility. By 2009, HPS had matured enough to seek commercial funding. By this time, HPS had eight power plants and was serving 30 villages. It received financing from Acumen Fund, Bamboo Finance, LGT Philanthropy, DFJ/CISCO, and International Finance Corporation. It formed a board of directors and offered one seat to each of the investors. (Bornstein, 2011; Sinha, 2011)

6.3.1.1.7 Circumscription

HPS had successfully gone through the initial phases of creating a successful company around the innovation of single-fuel gasifiers. However, starting 2013, multiple factors—sociological, technological, political—were making further progress difficult. The company needed to adapt to the new realities.

6.3.1.2 Lap (Stage) 2 (2013-): Adapt to New Realities

6.3.1.2.1 Problem Definition

Setting up Husk Power Systems by the four founders in 2008 was a great idea. It developed a clean technology for electrifying small villages in remote areas of India, particularly in the state of Bihar. At that time the people there had small electricity needs—getting about seven hours of electricity in the evenings—and HPS fulfilled those needs without pinching the purse. But the three factors—sociological, technological, political—and the organizational issue had created a storm that HPS needed to surmount to survive and thrive. What were these problems and issues?

Sociological Factors. For the last many years India had gone through a phase of high economic growth with the GDP rising at around 8% per year. This gave rise to higher expectations for electricity even among village people. They now wanted 24x7 power and were aspiring to own television sets, refrigerators, and other appliances. The mini grids of HPS were not fulfilling these needs. (Goodier, 2018)

Technological Factors. The price of solar power had dropped sharply. The price of solar equipment in Bihar dropped from US$ 5-US$ 6 in 2008 to US$ 1 per watt in 2013 (Goodier, 2018). This made gasifier power less attractive. However, solar power had its own drawbacks: it was available only during daytime hours and people had to depend on the costlier option of using battery power at other times. (Goodier, 2018)

Political Factors. The political campaign for the Indian general election in 2014 picked up steam in 2013. The political parties, especially the Bhartiya Janta Party (BJP) started promising total electrification. The new BJP dominated government led by Narendra Modi in 2014 started fulfilling this promise: As of 28 April 2018, 12 days ahead of the target date, all Indian villages "a total of 597,464 census villages were electrified" (Electricity Sector in India, 2022). This statement refers to villages having access to electricity but is different from the village households getting power connections; however, even this latter objective is getting fulfilled quickly—as of 2020, only 18,734 households (0.07%) remain to be electrified (Saubhagya, 2022).

Organizational Issue. The CEO of HPS, Gyanesh Pandey resigned in 2013 "shortly after they had raised money in 2012" (Dewan, 2019); Ransler had left in 2010 and Yadav left in 2014 (Goodier, 2018). According to Goodier (2018), Manoj Sinha said, "Slowly, everyone started leaving," This was a depressing situation coupled with the fact that "Investors pulled back the money since they were not getting the confidence" (Dewan, 2019). The three factors discussed above were obviously contributing to this situation.

6.3.1.2.2 Suggestion

The leadership vacuum needed to be filled immediately. HPS needed to adapt to all the changes (the three factors discussed above). HPS needed to persevere and integrate its technology with the solar technology.

6.3.1.2.3 Solution Development, Evaluation, and Implementation

In 2013, Manoj Sinha, the only founder who was continuing to be actively associated with the company, left his job in the USA, and joined HPS as the CEO. With a business education background he had the ability to steer the company in a new productive course as renewable energy company. In 2015, HPS developed hybrid technology that integrates solar photovoltaic system and biomass gasification along with a unique smart metering technology. Aided in this work was HPS's strategic partnership with First Solar, one of the largest solar panel manufacturers in USA and SparkMeter, a startup company that produces smart meters for mini grids. In 2015, HPS decided to expand to Tanzania because of the similarity in energy needs for households in Tanzanian and Indian villages that are not served by the electricity grid or need to supplement the electricity supplied by the grid. (Goodier, 2018) It has also "partnered with Diamond Development Initiative (DDI) in Nigeria and Technology Management Group in Ghana" (Water and Energy for Food, 2023).

HPS, through multiple innovations, has pioneered a hybrid powerplant system that seamlessly integrates the use of solar power and biomass gasification. It has innovated the gasification process to eliminate any use of clean water. As a result, HPS has become a company that builds, owns, and operates the lowest cost hybrid power plant and distribution network in India and Africa. Using a smart metering system, the company can offer its customers a grid-compatible and theft-proof flexible system that can be customized to the user needs. (Husk Power Systems, nd).

According to the HPS website (Husk Power Systems, nd), HPS is operating "over 75 plants in India and Tanzania serving 15,000 households and businesses", is offering "World's lowest [cost] grid compatible system of less than US\$ 2.35 per watt or US\$ 300 per connection," and has forged "strategic global partnerships: First Solar, Cummins and Vodafone." In 2021, Husk Power Systems expanded to Nigeria through agreements with Nigeria Electrification Project, which is funded by the World Bank and African Development Bank (Economic Times Energy World, 2021).

For its growth and expansion in India, HPS needed investments. In 2018, it raised a "\$20 million Series C round of equity funding" from

"Shell Technology Ventures LLC," "Swedfund International", and "ENGIE Rassembleurs d'Energies." This is in addition to the "Series A funding in October 2012" and "Series B funding in August 2014." (Mallya, 2018)

6.3.2 Diffusion

Husk Power Systems (HPS) needed to adapt with the changing times and technology right from its inception. It started with producing electricity from agricultural waste but soon adapted to developing and operating hybrid mini grids using electricity produced from both agricultural waste and solar energy.

HPS continues to consolidate its operations in India and has also expanded to Tanzania and Nigeria. Currently it has over 120 sites in India producing 3.6 MW of power, eight sites in Tanzania producing 0.32 MW of power, and six sites in Nigeria producing 300 KW of power. (Husk Power Systems, nd)

HPS has had an impact of various types—economic, social, and environmental. The economic impacts have been on households, cutting their use of kerosene by 6 to 7 liters per month. The economic impacts have been on businesses, providing them better quality lighting and providing electricity for use in new businesses such as cyber-cafes photocopying shops. HPS has also benefited rice mills by providing them with extra income for their waste rice husk. The social impact of HPS has been in providing good quality reliable lighting in remote rural areas, in reducing exposure to smoke and fumes from kerosene lamps, and in increasing the ownership and use of mobile phones. The environmental impacts have been in cutting greenhouse gas emissions. (Sevea Consulting, 2013/2016)

6.4 INNOVATION RESULTS

The innovation results of Husk Power Systems (HPS) can be summarized as (Sevea Consulting, 2013/2016):

a. Creating its proprietary gasification technology that directly converts agricultural waste into electricity.
b. Creation of low-cost mini-plant monitoring systems via the Internet.

   c. Development of in-house information management that are customized for distributed operations.

   d. Use of local and low-cost materials for developing failsafe, needed infrastructure, and local electrical networks.

Through its innovations and entrepreneurship, HPS has become the market leader in mini-grid technology, creating over 100 mini-grids in Asia and Africa and serving over 5,000 small business customers. HPS is the first company to introduce 100 solar mini grids (Mishra, 2021; Smart Energy International. 2022).

6.5 APPLICABLE KNOWLEDGE & KNOWLEDGE CONTRIBUTION

Models/Metamodels

Unmet Social Need (Hetherington, 2008; see Chapter 1)

As of 2010, nearly 30% of people worldwide had no access to electricity. Eighty-five percent of these people lived in 125,000 villages of the state of Bihar. There was thus an acute social need to do something about providing electricity to people living in such villages. Husk Power Systems (HPS) set about addressing this need. Over the years there was big progress in connecting a very large percentage of Indian people to the electric grid. HPS evolved to continue to remain a viable option for providing electricity to remote areas of Bihar and other areas.

Process Reengineering (Joshi and Rohrig, 2014; see Chapter 1)

Husk Power Systems has undergone major changes in how electricity is produced and distributed over the years. Initially, the consumers were mainly rural households, the electricity was produced in small power stations that used agricultural waste, electricity was used at night-time. For this profile of usage, there was an upfront charge for getting connected to electricity and a lump sum pre-consumption charge made through smart meters for lighting two cfl bulbs and charging mobile phones for 7–8 hours a day. Over time, the aspiration of people grew, the method of producing electricity evolved to hybrid between husk-produced power and solar power, the usage of electricity was by rural households and small businesses, and the availability of electricity was for 24 hours a day. In this profile, the charging was done on a pre-consumption basis using smart meters. (Sensiba, 2021)

In 2008, HPS started with the BOOM (company Builds, Owns, Operates, and Maintains) model using a technology developed by the company for directly producing 25 to 100 kilowatts of electricity from crop waste such as rice husks. In 2010, it rolled out the BOM (company Builds, Owns, and Maintains) model in which a business partner invests a small amount, operates the mini power plant, and pays about 177 to 295 Euro per month to HPS, and to the BM (company Builds and Maintains) model in which the company builds the power plant and then sells it to a business partner who owns and operates the plant while paying HPS 118 Euro for maintenance and repair per month. (Joshi and Rohrig, 2014)

The company also has re-engineered how electricity gets distributed and paid for in an environmentally friendly, cost-effective, and distributed manner. It has developed the idea of using bamboo poles for distribution of electricity to reduce the risk of theft and smart meters that are pre-paid and automatically disconnect electricity once the paid-up capacity is reached. For operating the power plants and for their maintenance and repair it needed many mechanics that the company trains through its Husk Power University. (Joshi and Rohrig, 2014)

High Asset Use (Joshi and Rohrig, 2014; see Chapter 1)
HPS maximally used all available physical assets including biomass assets— rice husks, corn cobbs, and cotton stalk. As the company evolved to create hybrid mini power plants that also used solar power. It also made maximum use of local human assets for running and managing its mini power plants.

Adaptation and Customization of Technology
The heart of the HPS innovation is the adaptation of the gasification process from rice husk and other biomass materials to produce electricity from the dual-fuel model that also uses diesel fuel, to a single fuel mode that produces electricity directly from the biomass materials. This is an example making a technological change (Ruttan, 2001)

Creative Matching (Hetherington, 2008; see Chapter 1)
In addition to developing the technology for a single-fuel gasifier for generating electricity, the company creatively used available assets and resources such as the abundantly available rice husks and local people to operate, manage, and even own mini power plants, to create a successful innovation that evolved with time.

Adaptive Organizational Forms (Hetherington, 2008; see Chapter 1)

HPS was started in 2008 and in the first phase of its innovation journey, it created a successful company driven by creating and using single-fuel gasifiers. However, in 2013 it started facing multiple challenges driven by quick changes in the aspirations of its customers, available technology, and the political environment. This, along with the fact that most of its founders started leaving the company, started to have a detrimental effect on the confidence of its investors. Fortunately for the company, Manoj Sinha, the only founder who was continuing to be actively associated with the company, left his job in USA and joined HPS as its CEO. Sinha had business education background and set about surmounting all the challenges of the company and steering it to a productive course. It developed a hybrid technology that integrated biomass gasification with solar photovoltaic system and started offering integrated mini power plants that use both solar power and biomass such as rice husks and also started using a unique smart metering technology. It also used strategic partnerships to aid it to expand within India as well as venture into Tanzanian villages.

Price Modeling (Joshi and Rohrig, 2014; see Chapter 1)

The main source of revenue to HPS is from sale of electricity to households. These households are in rural areas and have a low income. This creates the problem of default. To overcome these problems, HPS initially started charging a lump sum amount of 1.77 Euro/month/household, enough to light two CFL light bulbs and to be able to charge a mobile phone for seven to eight hours daily for a month. In addition, HPS charged 1.18 Euro to acquire a power connection and to get a power cable to be able to connect the house to the main power line. This served as a security that the households would get electricity from the company and continue to use it in future. As the company evolved, it started offering its customers pre-paid customized options that used smart metering systems. (Joshi and Rohrig, 2014)

Technological Intervention (Ruttan, 2001)

HPS is based on intervening through technology to create a company that addresses the electricity needs of small rural communities and businesses. Salient features of the technological intervention are:

1. Creation of an innovation—Single-Fuel Biomass Gasifier—that acts as a technological intervention between local biomass—rice husks—and the electricity needs of small rural communities.

2. Manufacturing of biomass gasifiers that convert rice husks produced as waste by rice mills into combustible gas used by generators to produce electricity.
3. Developing local small power distribution networks that are used to supply the produced electricity to small local communities.
4. Integrating the single-fuel biomass gasifiers with solar photovoltaic systems and smart metering technology.

Husk Power Systems Business Models: BOOM, BOM, and BM (Sevea Consulting, 2013/2016)
HPS uses three related business models:

1. BOOM: HPS builds the biomass gasifier and local power distribution network, owns them, operates them, and maintains them; collects the electricity fees from the served rural community.
2. BOM: HPS hands over the operation of the biomass gasifier and the power distribution network to an agent for a fee who collects the electricity charges and returns them to HPS; HPS continues to build the biomass gasifier and the power distribution network.
3. BM: HPS builds the biomass gasifier and the local distribution network which are bought by an agent who also operates them while HPS still maintains them.

Social Enterprise Business Model Template (see Chapter 1, Section 1.2.2)
The model, shown in Figure 6.1, summarizes the overall business model of HPS in accordance with the template provided by Figure 1.2 of Chapter 1. The eleven components of the business model are briefly described below.

Mission – Goals
Production of electricity in rural and remote areas of India in an environmentally friendly way, using solar power and rice husks as a fuel to run an electricity generator, to create local mini power plants (25 to 100 kilowatts) to supply for profit electricity 24x7 to villages.

Key Partners – Needed for the Social Enterprise to Work
The key partners of HPS are:
   a. The rice mills as suppliers of the biomass waste, rice husk, village households and businesses.
   b. Village farmers.

Husk Power Systems (Environmentally Friendly Electricity Generation) Overall Business Model				
Mission: Design and develop the for-profit social enterprise, Husk Power Systems, to run a hybrid power generation system that uses both solar energy and biomass for environmentally friendly electricity generation.				
Key Partners • Rice mills • Farmers • Agents • Village people	Key Activities • Design and manufacture of gasifiers. • Building and maintenance of power distribution networks. • Collection of electricity fees • Collecting income from carbon credits. • Selling waste from mini power plants. • Converting rice husk char into unscented incense sticks.	Value Proposition • 24X7 power • Removing and Utilizing crop waste	Customer/ Beneficiary Relationships • Supply of metered electricity • Training and employment of local village people	Customer/ Beneficiary Segments • Rural households • Agricultural customers • Commercial customers
	Key Resources • Self-financing, commercial funding. • Biomass and solar energy resources. • Biomass gasifiers and photovoltaic systems • Hybrid mini-power plants • Agents and trained operators • Strategic business partners		Channels • Meetings	
Cost Structures • Fixed Cost: Materials and labor, solar batteries, equipment • Running Cost: Cost of converting crop waste and solar power into electricity		Revenue Streams • Electricity fees from consumers • Carbon credits • Revenue from selling rice husk char		
Impact • Availability of 24X7 electricity in remote villages and hamlets • Environmentally friendly production of electricity • Rural economic development				

FIGURE 6.1
Husk Power Systems (HPS) Overall Business Model summarized in Social Enterprise Business Model Template shown in Figure 1.2.

> c. Agents managing some or all the areas of business operations—building, owning, operating, maintaining—the power plants.
> d. The rural communities as customers as well as partners in the running and management of the power plants.

Key Activities – Performed for the Business to Function
The key activities of HPS are:
> a. Design and manufacture of gasifiers; building and maintenance of power distribution networks; and collection of pre-paid electricity fees.

b. Collection of about 10% of the revenue from the generated carbon credits and selling the waste (rice husk char) produced at each mini power plant.

c. Converting the rice husk char into unscented incense sticks and selling them to increase revenue.

Key Resources – Needed to make the Business Model Work

The key resources of HPS are:

a. Self-financing and equity funding from "Shell Technology Ventures LLC," "Swedfund International", and "ENGIE Rassembleurs d'Energies"

b. Biomass resources from agriculture and the free solar energy

c. Biomass gasifiers and photovoltaic systems

d. Hybrid mini-power plants

e. Agents and trained operators for running and maintaining the power plants

f. Strategic business partners for running and expanding HPS

Customer/Beneficiary Segments – Served by the Social Enterprise

The customers served by HPS are the rural households and businesses, its agricultural customers, and its commercial customers.

Value Proposition – Products and/or Services that Create Value to Customers/ Beneficiaries

The products and services provided by HPS to its customers:

1. Making electricity available to villages, 24x7 for households and agricultural as well as commercial customers

2. Removing and utilizing crop waste such as rice husk; it is attractive particularly for remote rural areas.

Customer/Beneficiary Relationships – with Customer/Beneficiary Segments

HPS has relationships with its customers at two levels:

a. Supply of metered electricity.

b. Training, and employment of local village people in local businesses.

Channels – to Interface with Customer/Beneficiary Segments

The company's interface with its customer segments is through face-to-face and online meetings.

Cost Structures – Costs incurred to Operate the Social Enterprise

As with any business, HPS has fixed costs and running costs. The fixed costs include those incurred for purchasing needed materials and the cost of equipment such as the photo-voltaic batteries. The running cost is the cost of converting crop waste and solar energy which includes the labor cost and other types of operational costs.

Revenue Streams – Cash Generated from each Customer/Beneficiary Segment

The cash generated by HPS from its customer segments includes the electricity fees it collects from its consumers, the revenue from its carbon credits (about 10% of its total revenue) and the cash it generates from selling rice husk char to incense stick factories.

Impact

There are significant economic, social. and environmental impacts and benefits of HPS. These impacts and benefits include the environment friendly production of electricity and providing it to remote rural households, agricultural customers, and businesses on a 24x7 basis leading to rural economic development; cutting of greenhouse gas emissions; reduction in kerosene usage leading to reduced exposure to smoke and toxic fumes; extra income for rice husk factories; ability to charge cell phones leading to increased ownership and use of mobile phones; and development of a hybrid technology that integrates solar photovoltaic system and biomass gasification along with a unique smart metering technology.

REFERENCES

Agarwal, M. and Satish, D. (2013). "Husk Power Systems: Lighting up the Indian Rural Lives," oikos Case Collection. https://oikos-international.org/wp-content/uploads/2013/11/oikos_Cases_2013_Husk_Power.pdf (last accessed on December 13, 2023).

Bhattacharyya, S.C. (2014). "Viability of off-grid electricity supply using rice husk: A case study from South Asia," *Biomass and Bioenergy*, 68, September 2014, pp. 44–54. www.researchgate.net/publication/263076555_Viability_of_off-grid_electricity_supply_using_rice_husk_A_case_study_from_South_Asia (last accessed on December 13, 2023).

Bornstein, D. (2011). "A Light in India." *New York Times*, January 10, 2011. https://archive.nytimes.com/opinionator.blogs.nytimes.com/2011/01/10/a-light-in-india/ (last accessed on December 13, 2023).

Dewan, N. (2019). "Generating Electricity for Millions; Husk Power bolsters Modi's Dream of Power to All." *Economic Times*, March 1, 2019. https://economictimes.indiatimes.com/small-biz/entrepreneurship/generating-electricity-for-millions-husk-power-bolsters-modis-dream-of-power-to-all/articleshow/68213635.cms?from=mdr (last accessed on December 13, 2023).

Economic Times Energy World. (2021). "Husk Power Systems Enters Nigeria; To Set Up 7 Solar Mini-grids," September 29, 2021. https://energy.economictimes.indiatimes.com/news/power/husk-power-systems-enters-nigeria-to-set-up-7-solar-minigrids/86616446 (last accessed on December 13, 2023).

Goodier, R. (2018). "Inevitable Change: How Husk Power Embraced Adaptability," *Demand*, Spring 2018 Issue. https://medium.com/impact-engineered/inevitable-change-how-husk-power-embraced-adaptability-1b10a5a1c41a (last accessed on December 13, 2023).

Hetherington, D. (2008). "Case Studies in Social Innovation: A Background Paper," Per Capita, October 2008. https://apo.org.au/sites/default/files/resource-files/2009-01/apo-nid3954.pdf (last accessed on December 12, 2023).

Husk Power Systems. (nd). www.huskpowersystems.com/about-us/ (last accessed on December 13, 2023).

Joshi, S. and Rohrig, E. (2014). "Moving Innovation Forward; Case Studies: 10 Sustainable and Inclusive Business Models," GIZ India, New Delhi. www.giz.de/en/downloads/giz2014-en-moving-innovation-forward-india.pdf (last accessed on December 12, 2023).

Mallya, H. (2018). "Husk Power Systems Raises $29M from Shell, Others to Scale Renewable Mini-grids in Africa and Asia," TECH, 16th January 2018. https://yourstory.com/2018/01/husk-power-systems-series-c-expansion?utm_pageloadtype=scroll (last accessed on December 13, 2023).

Mishra, A. (2021). "Innovator Takes Rural India and Africa "Mini" with New Grid Technology," February 22, 2021. *Forbes*. www.forbes.com/sites/ankitmishra/2021/02/22/innovator-takes-rural-india-and-africa-mini-with-new-grid-technology/?sh=7541447869d6 (last accessed on December 13, 2023).

Rai, U. (2011/2018). "Bihar's Husk Power," *The Hindu Business Line*, published on March 10, 2011; updated on March 12, 2018. www.thehindubusinessline.com/news/variety/bihars-husk-power/article20108183.ece1 (last accessed on December 13, 2023).

Ruttan, V.W. (2001). *Technology, Growth, and Development: An Induced Innovation Perspective.* New York and Oxford: Oxford University Press.

Saubhagya. (2022). Rural Electrification Corporation Limited: Saubhagya. www.recindia.nic.in/saubhagya (last accessed on December 13, 2023).

Sensiba, J. (2021). "Husk Power Systems Provides Clean Energy for Rural People in Developing Countries," CleanTechnica, November 22, 2021. https://cleantechnica.com/2021/11/22/husk-power-systems-provides-clean-energy-for-rural-people-in-developing-countries/ (last accessed on December 13, 2023).

Sevea Consulting. (2013/2016). "Husk Power Systems: Power to Empower." Case Study, 2016. www.seveaconsulting.com/wp-content/uploads/2016/02/Case_study_HPS.pdf (last accessed on December 13, 2023).

Sinha, M. (2011). "Seeking an end to energy starvation," *Innovations Case Study: Husk Power Systems, Innovations*, 6 (3), pp. 71–83. www.mitpressjournals.org/doi/pdf/10.1162/INOV_a_00083 (last accessed on December 13, 2023).

Smart Energy International. (2022). "Manoj Sinha: Building a Culture on Trust, Collaboration and Learning." www.smart-energy.com/industry-sectors/distributed-generation/manoj-sinha-building-a-culture-on-trust-collaboration-and-learning/ (last accessed on March 28, 2024).

The World Bank Data – India (2023). https://data.worldbank.org/indicator/EG.ELC.ACCS.ZS?locations=IN (last accessed on December 13, 2023).

Water and Energy for Food. (2023). "Husk Power Systems: Biomass and Solar PV Hybrid Mini-grids for Off-Grid Farming Communities," Water and Energy for Food. https://we4f.org/innovators/husk-power-systems (last accessed on December 13, 2023).

7

Waste Ventures India: Integrated Waste Management

7.1 OVERVIEW

Waste management deals with all activities needed to manage waste including its collection, transportation, and final disposal. Disposing waste in landfills has historically been the most common way for waste disposal but this practice is dangerous to human life and the environment. With the growth economic prosperity in emerging countries, the waste volumes are increasing but with the right approach the waste can be turned into income while at the same time improving the environment (Engel, et al., 2016).

India generates 62 million tons of waste (containing both recyclable and non-recyclable waste) every year with an average annual growth rate of 4% (PIB, 2016; Swaminathan, 2018). A significant portion (40 to 60%) of this waste remains uncollected. The solid waste that is picked up is either picked up by municipal corporations in big towns or by waste pickers who scavenge and sell glass and plastic from the waste. The solid waste collected by municipal corporations goes into garbage landfills. The unpicked waste as well as that going into landfills decays and produces methane gas that is dangerous to life and the environment. The municipal garbage collection in large cities is inefficient, costly, and corrupt (Kumar, et al., 2017; PIB, 2016; Swaminathan, 2018).

Waste Ventures India (WVI) (Waste Ventures India, nd) is an innovative for-profit waste management social enterprise (social innovation) that is pushing India to use waste management models (Griha Summit, 2016) that are sustainable both environmentally and financially. WVI, founded by Parag Gupta and Roshan Miranda in 2011, was initially based in New Delhi, India. It started by providing solid waste management services to municipalities and Resident Welfare Associations in some Tier-2 and Tier-3 cities in India.

DOI: 10.1201/9781003479086-9

After facing difficulties of payment delays from municipalities and capital challenges, Waste Ventures India evolved into a waste management organization with headquarters in Hyderabad, Telengana (Inclusive Innovations, 2017) that provides waste collection services to many households in tier-3 and tier-4 cities and corporate clients (Gone Adventurin, 2017) using an app, Bintix.com, previously called Toter, Tote.com (Bintix, 2019; Gogoi, 2020; Narayanan, 2018; PitchBook, 2024).

The rest of the chapter describes in detail design of the for-profit social innovation (and the corresponding social enterprise), Waste Ventures India (Integrated Waste Management).

7.2 CONTEXT

Parag Gupta, a social entrepreneur in USA, came up with an innovative model for solid waste management in tier-3 and tier-4 cities in India. The model aims to create "a new paradigm of financially viable and environmentally sustainable waste management" (Samhita, 2012) that involves all the current stake holders (waste pickers, municipalities, resident welfare organizations) and private investors. The overarching aim of the model was to improve the standard of living of the waste pickers and to improve the environment. In 2009, Parag Gupta was given a grant of 220,766 euros by the Peery Foundation for three years for setting up a for-profit company, Waste Ventures India, and for running the learning labs for refining the new waste management model. The funding was supplemented with 36,794 Euros from Swift Foundation. He set up Waste Ventures India in 2011 with headquarter in New Delhi (Joshi, et al., 2014). He, along with Roshan Miranda and Rob Whiting, established WVI in 2013. (Team YS, 2010)

7.3 INNOVATION DEVELOPMENT JOURNEY

7.3.1 Lap(s) / Stage(s)

7.3.1.1 Lap (Stage) 1 (2009–2015): Experiment with the New Waste Management Model

This was a research, experimentation, and startup lap (stage) of the innovation. In this lap (stage) the funding was mostly through grants, selling of compost and processed recyclables. The solid waste management model was tried for some tier-2 and tier-3 cities.

7.3.1.1.1 Problem Definition

"India generates 62 million tons of waste every year, of which less than 60% is collected and around 15% processed" (Joshi and Rohrig, 2014; Swaminathan, 2018). The municipalities in Indian towns and cities are mandated by national Municipal Solid Waste Act 2000 (revised in 2016) (PIB, 2016; Vikaspedia, 2016) to collect, segregate, transport, and suitably dispose-off solid waste. With the huge volume of solid waste, the municipalities barely cope with collecting and dumping waste in landfills. The service does not generate any revenue to the municipalities. This waste management system creates bigger and bigger filthy garbage dumps which produce methane gas that is toxic to human health and the environment. The wage pickers, at the lowest end of the system, barely make one to two US dollars a day—below poverty wages—for their services and for selling any recyclable materials—plastic and glass—they can separate from the waste. This system needs to be drastically changed to make it into an efficient environment-friendly system that generates money and pays living wages to the waste pickers.

7.3.1.1.2 Suggestion

Design an integrated solid waste management system that starts with using the existing waste pickers to pick solid waste door-to-door and ends in the sale of processed recyclables and compost. This strategy should provide stable income to millions of waste pickers and increase their wages multifold. (*Economic Times*, 2014; Talsma, 2013)

7.3.1.1.3 Solution Development, Evaluation, and Implementation

The outline of the model envisioned by Gupta is to collect, compost, recycle and reuse waste. The waste pickers are trained to separate the waste into organic and non-organic waste. They are also trained to compost the organic waste to produce manure. Waste that is paper, plastic, or glass is recycled. The waste pickers are organized into cooperatives who would negotiate their services with municipalities. The model needed to be implemented to find its workability. (Samhita, 2012)

Operations Model Details. Waste Ventures India (WVI) acts on a balanced dual enablement operations model (see Figure 7.1) that ensures that the waste collectors earn good wages, and the solid waste is processed and handled in a manner that is environmentally friendly. On the one hand, it enables raw waste

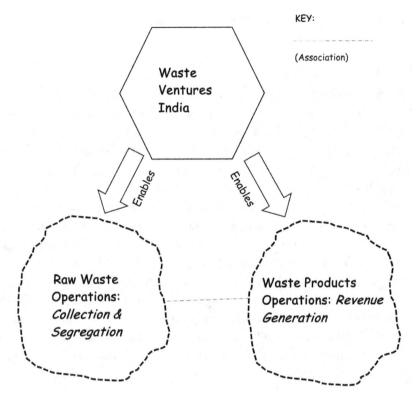

FIGURE 7.1
Waste Ventures India Balanced Dual Enablement Operations Model.

operations to collect and segregate the waste into organic and non-organic waste. On the other hand, it enables the processing and appropriate handling of the waste products without harming the environment and in the process also generates revenue. The two types of operations are given equal emphasis because they have a direct bearing on each other. The overall approach of WVI is not to replace existing arrangements and facilities—municipal garbage collection, waste processing plants—but to work with them.

Raw Waste Operations. There are two kinds of towns served by Waste Ventures India (WVI) for garbage collections and segregation—towns with municipalities that hire waste pickers for this purpose and those where this work is not currently done through municipalities. For the towns with municipal garbage collection, WVI organizes waste pickers into cooperatives to negotiate their wages and trains them to segregate waste into organic and inorganic waste. For towns where garbage collection and segregation are not done by municipalities, WVI conducts household collection on payment of a monthly fee and the collected waste is processed through anaerobic compositing. (Sharma, 2014)

7.3.1.1.4 Circumscription

The initial idea of working with the municipalities did not work out well because of payment delays and the challenges of raising the needed capital. So, a change was needed to the overall model of Waste Ventures India (WVI).

7.3.1.2 Lap (Stage) 2 (2016-): Create a Self-sustaining Waste Management System

In this lap (stage) of the innovation, Waste Ventures India (WVI) utilized the knowledge gained in the first lap (stage) to move to a self-sustaining social enterprise that fulfills the overall goal of creating an integrated solution of garbage collection and disposal that is environmentally friendly.

7.3.1.2.1 Problem Definition

Working with municipalities was tried in the first lap but it did not work out well because of payment delays and difficulties in making WVI self-sustaining. A change in the operations model of WVI was needed building upon the compositing process learned in the first lap.

7.3.1.2.2 Suggestion

Start partnering with the private sector as well as provide service directly to households mainly in tier-3 and tier-4 cities, working directly with the waste pickers. (rePurpose, 2019)

7.3.1.2.3 Solution Development, Evaluation, and Implementation

The new strategy implemented was to provide waste management services to the private corporations, to provide household level waste pick-up and recycling service for some tier-3 and tier-4 cities, and to create and manage a decentralized compositing center. It would benefit the waste pickers directly in raising their standard of living and create an environmentally friendly waste management system. (Kumar, et al., 2017)

The company was shifted to Hyderabad, Telangana, and the implementation was boosted by some key people joining the company for its operations: Rob Whiting from the US who was a co-founder of WVI; Roshan Miranda, also a co-founder of WVI; Mathangi Swaminathan. Abdul joined as the product manager of the startup and built its technology platform. The company launched Tote.com, Hyderabad's first household level recyclable pickup service (Shalini, nd), later renamed as Bintix.com (Bintix, 2019; Gogoi, 2020; South Asia Fast Track, 2018).

In general, the strategy followed in this stage of the innovation development has been to partner with the private sector instead of the municipalities, and to empower the waste pickers by providing them fair wages and following fair labor practices. (rePurpose, 2019)

Utilizing the knowledge gained about composting in the first Lap (Stage), WVI has moved to a model for solid waste management that is both financially and environmentally sustainable. The company now provides a single-point technology driven service for both individual households and corporate clients. It trains and employs waste pickers who pick-up garbage from households for a fee. The waste is purchased on a cash payment basis. The organic waste is composted and converted into organic fertilizer. All the non-organic recyclable garbage is sold to certified up-cyclers. (Inclusive Innovations, 2017; Isaac, 2016; Singh, 2016)

Waste Ventures India has developed and implemented an inclusive, decentralized, and holistic model for waste management in India. It is currently based in Hyderabad with branch offices in Delhi and Chennai. It offers many services including those for dry waste collection, organic waste processing, extended producer responsibility and plastic offsets, and waste audits and certification. The new strategy and operations model for waste management seems to be successful but needs to be expanded to cover additional cities.

7.3.2 Diffusion

Waste Ventures India is consolidating its business in India with a plan to expand to other emerging economies. It is integrating technology to make its services accessible and user-friendly.

This for-profit social enterprise is expanding while having a major impact on the country's waste disposal system. At the same time, it continues to focus on waste-pickers, providing them training and living wages. (Sandhu et al., 2017)

7.4 INNOVATION RESULTS

WVI has provided a professional and reliable waste collection, processing, and recycling service to thousands of households and a large number of corporate clients. The social enterprise startup company, WVI, is now serving about 25,000 households and corporate campuses such as Coca Cola, Flipkart, Infosys, Hindustan Unilever. It provides employment with equitable pay to more than 1,200 waste pickers, avoiding child labor. It has averted more than 4,000 tons of waste and more than 11,000 tons of carbon dioxide. (Naveena, 2017; Pirzer and Endeva, nd; Shalini, 2018; Waste Ventures India, nd)

7.5 APPLICABLE KNOWLEDGE & KNOWLEDGE CONTRIBUTION

Models/Metamodels

Unmet Social Need (Hetherington, 2008; see Chapter 1)

Waste is growing in India and other emerging economies with the growth of economic prosperity. Managing it in a way that improves the environment and improves the standard of living of wage pickers has been a very important social need that WVI is trying to address.

Exploration and Experimentation (Malouf, 2018)

Exploration and Experimentation is done to empirically discover answers to questions (Malouf, 2018). Waste Ventures India started with the idea of exploring and experimenting on the creation of a new model for waste management by a for-profit company that does waste management in an environmentally friendly manner as well as raise the living standards of the waste pickers. The initial model envisioned letting the waste pickers create cooperatives and negotiate with municipal corporations in tier-2 and tier-3 cities. It was tried but did not work because of payment delays and the investors losing interest. The model was then revised and experimented mainly on some tier-3 and tier-4 towns, and corporate clients. The revised model seems to be successful.

High Asset Use (Joshi and Rohrig, 2014; see Chapter 1)

Household and corporate waste is a nuisance that needs to be dealt with in an efficient manner, but it also can be viewed as an asset that can be productively utilized. Waste pickers constitute another asset that needs to be fully utilized. Waste Ventures India (WVI) makes use of existing networks of waste pickers through a model that recovers 90% of household and corporate waste through recycling, composting, and creating new products using waste products. WVI trains waste pickers to segregate waste at the time of collection from households into dry non-organic recyclable waste and organic waste. The dry non-organic waste is sold to certified up-cyclers and the organic waste is composted and converted into organic fertilizer. The company is currently focusing on household and corporate clients mainly in tier-3 and tier-4 cities of India to provide an economically and environmentally sustainable model and blueprint for waste management that raises the wages of waste pickers and converts waste into cash while protecting the environment. (Joshi and Rohrig, 2014).

Innovative Learning

The company created a model for waste management on paper, which seemed to be an attractive model. But doing waste management in an economically friendly manner and fulfilling other social objectives is complex. To make progress on creating a good model that is practical had to tried on the ground and finalized through innovative learning. This is what was done through multiple small-scale waste management projects in tier 3 and 4 cities and three learning labs (in Indore, Damanjodi, and Motihari). This is an example of innovative learning to discover the right model for waste management since we do not have all the answers.

Process Reengineering (Joshi and Rohrig, 2014; see Chapter 1)

Traditional waste management in India has been done in a manner that is harmful to the environment and not providing living wages to the waste pickers. In large towns, it has been done by municipalities creating waste dumps. Waste Ventures India (WVI) needed to do process re-engineering of the existing process to experiment on a model that is both economically and environmentally sustainable while increasing the wages of the waste pickers. The company broke the entire process into modular components and started experimenting on how to design the process; the experiment is still on-going. Initially, the company started working in tier-2 and tier-3 towns, working with existing municipalities but it did not work out well from a financial standpoint. It then shifted to corporate clients and households in tier-3 and tier-4 towns and started providing a technology driven service to corporate clients and households. The waste pickers are employed on fair wages and trained by WVI. Households are provided information by waste pickers to segregate waste into two types, biodegradable and non-biodegradable and it is purchased by the waste pickers on a cash basis. Waste pickers further separate waste into recyclable, biodegradable, and inert waste. The organic waste (about 60% of waste) is processed in decentralized thermophilic aerobic composting centers and the resulting compost is sold. The recyclable waste—plastics, glass, metal, etc.—is sold to the recycling industry. The remaining (about 10% of the waste) is deposited in landfills. (Joshi and Rohrig, 2014)

Promotion of Innovation Culture

Waste Ventures India promoted innovation culture during the development of a good model for waste management. They worked with an engineer from MIT to design a cart for garbage collection that avoids slippage during its movement. This resulted in the collection of 40% additional garbage. They also explored ways to monetize decentralized conversion of biogas from organic waste for cooking or electricity generation. Promotion of innovative culture is a known desired goal of an organization.

Creative Matching (Hetherington, 2008; see Chapter 1)

Waste Ventures India is a successful for-profit social innovation that developed a successful model for waste management that departs from the traditional method of waste management creating a process that contributes to the environment and raises the living standards of the waste pickers. It creatively matches existing assets and resources with existing capabilities.

Balanced Dual Enablement Operations Model: Waste Ventures India Balanced Dual Enablement Operations Model

This model (shown in Figure 7.1) is very similar to the Honey Care Africa Dual Enablement Operations Model (Figure 2.2) discussed in Chapter 2 and an instantiation of the metamodel, Private Social Enterprise Balanced Dual Enablement Operations Model, shown in Figure 2.8.

In this model Private Social Enterprise enables two types of operations, Raw Waste Operations and Waste Products Operations are conducted in a balanced manner:

Raw Waste Operations (Collection and Segregation)

    a. Waste Ventures India (WVI) enables the collection and segregation of raw waste.
    b. WVI raises awareness for waste segregation.
    c. WVI trains and pays municipal workers—waste pickers—to collect and segregate household waste.

Waste Products Operations (Revenue Generation)

    a. Waste Ventures India (WVI) enables the creation of saleable products from waste and sells them.

    b. WVI segregates bio-degradable and non-biodegradable waste.

    c. WVI creates compost out of bio-degradable waste and sells it to farmers.

    d. WVI further segregates non-bio-degradable waste and sells it to recycling companies.

Social Enterprise Business Model Template (see Chapter 1, Section 1.2.2) The model, shown in Figure 7.2, summarizes the overall business model of WVI in accordance with the template provided by Figure 1.2 in Chapter 1. The eleven components of the business model are briefly described below.

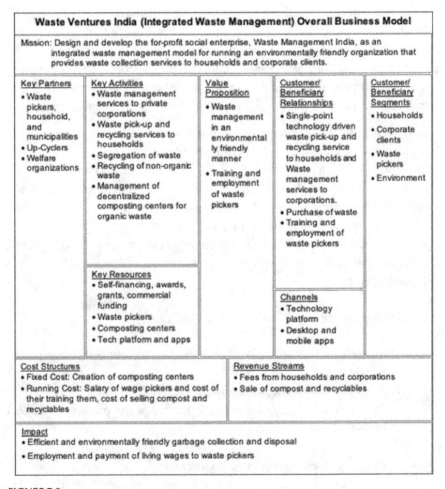

FIGURE 7.2

Waste Ventures India (WVI) Overall Business Model summarized in Social Enterprise Business Model Template shown in Figure 1.2.

Mission – Goals

Creation of a model for establishing a self-sustaining for-profit social enterprise for integrated waste management for households and corporate clients, that is environment-friendly and that improves the standard of living of the waste pickers.

Key Partners – Needed for the Social Enterprise to Work

The key partners of WVI are Waste pickers, households, municipalities, private investors, Up-Cyclers who purchase non-organic recyclable garbage, and Welfare organizations such as the Indian Grameen services.

Key Activities – Performed for the Business to Function

The key activities are providing waste management services to private corporations, waste pick-up and recycling services to households, management of decentralized anaerobic composting centers, separating the waste into organic and non-organic waste, composting the organic waste to produce manure, and selling of all the non-organic recyclable garbage (including paper, plastic, and glass) to certified up-cyclers.

Key Resources – Needed to make the Business Model Work

The key resources of Waste Ventures India are self-financing, awards, grants, and commercial funding, waste pickers, composting centers, technology platform, desktop, and mobile apps.

Customer/Beneficiary Segments – Served by the Social Enterprise

The customer/beneficiary segments of WVI are households, corporate clients, waste pickers, and the environment because of the following: The company provides a single-point technology driven service for both individual households and corporate clients for profit, employing and training waist pickers, fewer items going into waste dumps, resulting in less methane pollution in the environment.

Value Proposition – Products and/or Services that Create Value for Customers/Beneficiaries

The products and services that create value for the customers are waste management in an environmentally friendly manner, which includes door-to-door garbage collection from households and garbage collection from corporate clients, production of organic composted manure, providing training and employment to waste pickers with better wages.

Customer/Beneficiary Relationships – with Customer/Beneficiary Segments

Waste Ventures India has a relationship with its customers (households and corporations) and beneficiaries (waste pickers) through single-point technology driven waste pick-up, recycling service, and purchase of waste; training and employment of waste pickers; and environmentally friendly disposal and recycling of waste.

Channels – to Interface with Customer/Beneficiary Segments
WVI has developed a technology platform, desktop, and mobile phone apps to interface with its customers.

Cost Structures – Costs Incurred to Operate the Social Enterprise
The fixed cost includes creation of composting centers, and the running cost includes the salary of waste pickers, cost of training them, and the cost of selling organic compost manure and recyclables.

Revenue Streams – Cash Generated from Each Customer/Beneficiary Segment
The revenue streams for the company are the fees collected for picking up garbage from households and corporations, and the funds realized from the selling of organic fertilizer from the composted organic waste and the non-organic recyclable garbage to certified up-cyclers.

Impact
The impact of Waste Ventures India (WVI) are efficient and environmentally friendly garbage collection and disposal, reduction of waste going into solid waste dumps reducing methane pollution, and the employment, training, and increased salary of waste pickers.

REFERENCES

Bintix (2019). Bintix – Your Dry Waste Collection Partner. www.bintix.com/home (last accessed on December 13, 2023).

Economic Times (2014). "Start-ups Using Technology to Deal with India's Garbage Crisis," July 21, 2014. https://economictimes.indiatimes.com/biz-entrepreneurship/start-ups-using-technology-to-deal-with-indias-garbage-crisis/start-ups-dealing-with-garbage-crisis/slideshow/38791917.cms (last accessed on December 13, 2023).

Engel, H., Stuchtey, M., and Vanthournout, H. (2016). "Managing Waste in Emerging Markets," McKinsey & Company, February 2016. www.mckinsey.com/business-functions/sustainability/our-insights/managing-waste-in-emerging-markets (last accessed on December 13, 2023).

Gogoi, A. (2020). "Junk to Value: Hyderabad Startup Will Collect Waste from Your Doorstep and Pay You!" The Better India, January 30, 2020. www.thebetterindia.com/212289/bintix-waste-management-recycle-payment-startup-hyderabad-doorstep-collection-ang136/ (last accessed on December 13, 2023).

Gone Adventurin. (2017). "Toward Circularity of Post-consumer Flexible Packaging in Asia," November 2017. https://assets.ctfassets.net/f7tuyt85vtoa/Zt4soYnJWUKoWC i8uu8iW/a48a9e1b94a28e2c0e52c6f89fa32363/2017-11-20-Flexibles-Report.pdf (last accessed on December 13, 2023).

Griha Summit. (2016). "Waste Ventures India." www.grihaindia.org/grihasummit/tgs2 016/presentations/17feb/innovations/Mathangi_Swaminathan.pdf (last accessed on September 5, 2022).

Hetherington, D. (2008). "Case Studies in Social Innovation: A Background Paper," Per Capita, October 2008. https://apo.org.au/sites/default/files/resource-files/2009-01/apo-nid3 954.pdf (Last accessed on December 12, 2023).

Inclusive Innovations. (2017). "Business Models for Integrated Waste Management," World Bank Group. April 2017. www.innovationpolicyplatform.org/www.innovationpolicyp latform.org/system/files/4%20Integrated%20Waste%20Manangement_Apr6/index.pdf (last accessed on September 5, 2022).

Isaac, C. (2016). "A Solution to Waste Woes," *Deccan Chronicle*, 21 September 2016. www.decc anchronicle.com/lifestyle/health-and-wellbeing/210916/a-solution-to-waste-woes. html (last accessed on December 13, 2023).

Joshi, S. and Rohrig, E. (2014). "Moving Innovation Forward; Case Studies: 10 Sustainable and Inclusive Business Models," GIZ India, New Delhi. https://www.giz.de/en/downlo ads/giz2014-en-moving-innovation-forward-india.pdf (last accessed on December 12, 2023).

Kumar, S., Smith, S.R., Velis, C., Kumar, S.J., Arya, S., Rena, Kumar, R., and Cheeseman, C. (2017). "Challenges and Opportunities associated with Waste Management in India," *Royal Society Open Science*, 2017 March, 4 (3), 160764. www.ncbi.nlm.nih.gov/pmc/ articles/PMC5383819/ (last accessed on December 13, 2023).

Malouf, D. (2018). "Exploration over Experimentation." https://davemalouf.medium.com/expl oration-over-experimentation-cdc590863a62 (last accessed on December 13, 2023).

Narayanan. (2018). Neelambari Home Blog, December 1, 2018. https://neelambari.home. blog/2018/12/01/bintix-waste-ventures-and-recycling/ (last accessed on December 13, 2023).

Naveena. (2017). "Startup Interview Series – Waste Ventures India – Toter," Telegu 360. www. telugu360.com/startup-interview-series-waste-ventures-india-toter/ (last accessed on December 13, 2023).

PIB. (2016). "Solid Waste Management Rules revised after 16 years; Rules now extended to Urban and Industrial Areas," Press Information Bureau, Government of India, 05 April 2016). http://home.iitk.ac.in/~anubha/H15.pdf (last accessed on December 13, 2023).

Pirzer, P and Endeva (nd). Waste Capital Partners (nd). "Case Study, Business Call to Action." Uploaded August 2015. http://endeva.org/wp-content/uploads/2015/08/bcta_casestu dy_wastecapital.pdf (last accessed on December 13, 2023).

PitchBook WPI (2024). Waste Ventures India. https://pitchbook.com/profiles/company/115 341-85#funding (last accessed on March 29, 2024).

rePurpose. (2019). "Waste Ventures India is rethinking solid waste management," July 10, 2019. https://repurpose.global/letstalktrash/managing-solid-wastes/ (last accessed on June 22, 2020).

Samhita. (2012). "Waste Ventures." www.samhita.org/social-organisation/waste-ventures-india-pvt-ltd/ (last accessed on December 13, 2023).

Sandhu, K., Burton, P., and Dedikorkut-Howes, A. (2017). "Between hype and varacity; pri-vatization of municipal solid waste management and its impacts on the informal waste sector," *Waste Management*, 59, January 2017, pp. 545–556. www.sciencedirect.com/science/article/abs/pii/S0956053X16305670 (last accessed on December 13, 2023).

Shalini, B. (nd). "Waste Ventures India: Toter – City's first digitally enabled recycling service." http://startuphyderabad.com/waste-ventures-india-toter-citys-first-digitally-enabled-recycling-service/ (last accessed on December 13, 2023).

Sharma, K. (2014). "Waste Ventures Solving India's Garbage Problem," IndianWeb2. www.indianweb2.com/2014/07/21/waste-ventures-solving-indias-garbage-problem/ (last accessed on May 27, 2019).

Singh, T. (2016). "How one organization in Hyderabad is helping people manage waste in a responsible and scientific way," The Better India, September 13, 2016. www.thebett erindia.com/67697/how-one-organization-in-hyderabad-is-helping-people-manage-waste-in-a-responsible-scientific-way/ (last accessed on December 13, 2023)

South Asia Fast Track. (2018). "Q&A with Mr. Roshan Miranda. Co-Director & Director, Waste Ventures India." https://southasiafasttrack.com/2018/07/17/addressing-twin-obj ectives-to-make-hyderabad-better-city-roshan-miranda-waste-ventures-india-expla ins/ (last accessed on December 13, 2023).

Swaminathan, M. (2018). "How Can India's Waste Problem See Systemic Change?" *Economic & Political Weekly*, 53 (16), 21 Apr. 2018. www.epw.in/node/151565/pdf (last accessed on September 5, 2022).

Talsma, T. (2013) "Waste Ventures: Creating Green Livelihoods. Changemakers. www.chang emakers.com/economicopportunity/entries/waste-ventures-creating-green-liveliho ods)last accessed on March 3, 2020).

Team YS. (2010). "Earth Day Special: Parag Gupta talks about Waste Ventures, a 2010 Echoing Green Finalist," YourStory, April 22, 2010. https://yourstory.com/2010/04/earth-day-special-parag-gupta-talks-about-waste-ventures-a-2010-echoing-green-finalist (last accessed on December 13, 2023).

Vikaspedia. (2016). "Solid Waste Management Rules." https://vikaspedia.in/energy/environm ent/waste-management/solid-waste-management-rules (last accessed on December 13, 2023).

Waste Ventures India. (nd). https://wasteventures.com (last accessed on December 13, 2023).

8

Safaricom's M-Pesa, Kenya: Mobile-Based Financial Services

8.1 OVERVIEW

Mobile banking services enables the conduct of financial services using mobile devices. Before 2010 they were most often performed using SMS (Short Message Service) and called SMS mobile banking. Mobile payment service was the earliest form of mobile financial service; the first patent filed for such service "Mobile Payment System" was filed in 2000. Mobile payment service has been a way to extend financial service to the "unbanked" or the "underbanked" community that was estimated to be 50% of the world adult population as of 2009. (Barnes and Corbitt, 2003; Narayan, 2013; Sorbet, 2022)

M-Pesa is an SMS mobile banking system of Safaricom (largest Kenyan mobile network operator) that allows users to deposit and withdraw money through a network of M-Pesa agents operating in small shops. It allows menu-based transactions, through PIN-secured SMS messages, to transfer money to other M-Pesa users and non-users, to pay bills, to buy airtime, and to transfer money between the service and a bank account (in certain markets). Users are charged a small fee for sending and withdrawing money using the service. The service was started in 2007 by Vodaphone in Kenya through its subsidiary, Safaricom. It has expanded quickly to many countries including Afghanistan, South Africa, India, Romania, and Albania, making the company a successful mobile-based financial service company. It has contributed to making the carrying out of business and increasing productivity easy. (Barnet, 2017; Joseph, 2017; Joshi and Rohrig, 2014; Kumar et al., 2010; Maya, 2016, McGath, 2018; Ndung'u, 2021; Proudly Made in Africa, 2014)

DOI: 10.1201/9781003479086-10

The rest of the chapter describes in detail design of the for-profit social innovation (and the corresponding social enterprise), M-Pesa (Mobile-Based Financial Services).

8.2 CONTEXT

In 2007, Kenya had high literacy levels (90% for males and 80% for females) and 80% of the people had a mobile phone but 38% of them did not use any form of financial service and only 12% of them had bank accounts. At the same time, prior to 2007, there was not a fast, easy, and safe way to 'send money home' (for people working in towns to send money home to their families in villages). Safaricom was a leading mobile operator in Kenya. (Barnett, 2017; International Finance, Corporation, 2009)

To assess the idea of using mobile phones in the microfinance sector of Kenya for transferring money, a simple application, M-Pesa, was developed. M-Pesa was tested in a 6-month pilot study, funded by the UK government's Department for International Development, that ended in May 2006. The study used eight agent stores and had 500 customer participants distributed in three geographical areas of Kenya. Initially the transactions in the study were limited to loan repayments but the transaction volumes increased immediately after the participant customers were allowed to buy airtime using M-Pesa. Even after the pilot study ended the participants continued to use the service which indicated its success and acceptability. This encouraged Safaricom to launch M-Pesa as a for-profit social enterprise commercially. (Joshi and Rohrig, 2014; Shadbolt, 2014)

8.3 INNOVATION DEVELOPMENT JOURNEY

8.3.1 Lap(s) / Stage(s)

8.3.1.1 Lap (Stage) 1 (2007–2010): Launch M-Pesa as an Electronic Money Transfer Service

8.3.1.1.1 Problem Definition

The problem M-Pesa was trying to address was how to let Kenyan people remit money within the country in a fast and easy manner.

8.3.1.1.2 Suggestion

Based on the available technology and results of the pilot study conducted, the obvious idea was to let the mobile operator, Safaricom, commercially launch M-Pesa, a SMS-based system that enables users to deposit, send, and withdraw funds using their mobile phones. The success of the innovation would depend upon how well it is fully developed and implemented.

8.3.1.1.3 Solution Development, Evaluation, and Implementation

M-Pesa platform was developed by Vodafone and was commercially launched in Kenya through its affiliate, Safaricom. The user interface of the platform was kept simple and the use of M-Pesa services was made intuitive and straightforward. The customer would not need to have a bank account, a smart phone, or a high-speed internet connection. The customer would need to register for an M-Pesa account with a Safaricom agent (dealer)—there was a large network of Safaricom agents spread throughout the country. (Mas and Radcliffe, 2010; Mas and Ng'weno, 2010; Maya, 2016)

M-Pesa offers a simple payment and money transfer system. It allows the customers to deposit money in their phones and to remit funds (from a minimum of 100 KShs (Kenyan Shillings) to a maximum of 35,000 KShs for M-Pesa users as well as non-users that can be withdrawn at Safaricom agents. It also allows them to make bill payments. The M-Pesa transactions are secure; they are PIN-protected and supported by Safaricom customer service. (Maya, 2016).

The registration of M-Pesa accounts and deposit of money in the phones are free. The customers are charged a flat fee of 30 KShs for each money transfer or bill payment to a registered user and 1 KSh for balance enquiries. Money transfer to unregistered users incur a higher fee varying from 75 KShs to 400 KShs. While there is no withdrawal fee for a non-registered user, the fee varies from 25 KShs to 170 for a registered user. The rates did not change for the first three years of operation despite inflation. Customers' accounts are maintained through a Vodafone server. Their deposits are maintained at commercial banks. They are not paid any interest on their account balances, instead this interest is deposited into a not-for-profit trust fund maintained by Safaricom. (International Finance Corporation, 2009; Mas and Radcliffe, 2010; Mbiti and Weil, 2011)

M-Pesa quickly became a very successful innovation. It attracted 10 million customers in three years, which grew to 14 million customers at the end of four years. People could deposit and withdraw funds at 28,000 Safaricom agents (retail stores), nearly half of them are in rural areas. M-Pesa earned

USD 94 million in FY2010, which was 9% of Safaricom's revenue. (Mas and Radcliffe, 2010)

M-Pesa's market success can be attributed to: (i) A conducive environment and a lack of competition for the service provided; (ii) A good design of the service; and (iii) A good business plan and execution strategy. There was a huge latent demand for an inexpensive, secure, and efficient service for remitting funds from people working in urban areas to their families in villages. There was hardly a competition for this service. Coupling this service with buying and sending airtime, storing funds for later use, and paying bills made a strong portfolio of unmet needs. The Central Bank of Kenya provided a conducive environment for providing these types of services outside the banking system. (Mas and Radcliffe, 2010)

The 6-month pilot study before the commercial launch of M-Pesa provided a good pulse on what the focus of the service needs to be and how the system for providing this service should be designed. Sending money home was identified as the key service. The desirability of having a simple interface for the service was obvious given that the service would be needed by even people who may not be very proficient and knowledgeable in using technology.

The business model used by M-Pesa is to leverage the mobile phone technology to provide an agent-based SMS-based service that starts with providing a simple, safe, and secure, and inexpensive method of remitting money and providing additional services such as buying airtime and payment of bills. Having a network of commission-based agents to deliver the service was a backbone of the innovation. As the customer base and the number of agents increased, there was a need to have a structure for managing the agents. The Hub and Spoke model (Gaille, 2015) was used as a model for this structure. The agents were organized as just agents and super agents. Agents would deal with the customers for providing them the various types of service. They would in turn be managed by their corresponding super agents who would also interface with Safaricom.

8.3.1.1.4 Circumscription

The first lap or stage of the innovation was very successful and was ready for expansion to include features that were not available. The customers of M-Pesa at this stage included many people who did not have any bank account. But it also included people who had one or more bank accounts. An obvious expansion of the service was to provide an ability to transfer funds between a bank account and the corresponding M-Pesa account.

8.3.1.2 Lap (Stage) 2 (2010–2014): Link Bank Accounts with M-Pesa

8.3.1.2.1 Problem Definition

The problem addressed at this stage was to provide an ability to transfer funds back and forth between an M-Pesa account and the corresponding bank accounts(s).

8.3.1.2.2 Suggestion

The obvious method to start addressing the problem would be to link an M-Pesa account and its corresponding bank account(s) if any.

8.3.1.2.3 Solution Development, Evaluation, and Implementation

Earlier, the problem for providing the linkage of mobile money with banks was the unavailability of an appropriate regularity environment because the banks objected to this linkage. But the problem was solved in 2009 when the Treasury of Kenya issued a statement that legalized mobile money. In 2010, Equity Bank, the largest retail bank in Kenya, and Safaricom jointly launched a mobile product, M-Kesho. M-Kesho allowed Equity Bank customers to link their bank accounts with their M-Pesa accounts. This successfully achieved the goal of this lap (stage) of the innovation. (Cook and McKay, 2017; Ngugi, et al., 2010; Ndung'u, 2017, Proudly Made in Africa, 2014)

8.3.1.2.4 Circumscription

With a successful linkage of bank accounts with corresponding M-Pesa accounts for the M-Pesa account holders with bank accounts, a new vehicle for assessing credit worthiness became available. This could be utilized for giving them loans for opening small and medium enterprises.

8.3.1.3 Lap (Stage) 3 (2015-): Let Lenders Tap Mobile Technology

8.3.1.3.1 Problem Definition

Now that the M-Pesa accounts had been linked to the respective bank accounts for those M-Pesa account holders who had bank accounts, the M-Pesa account usage generated data that should be used by the banks to determine creditworthiness.

8.3.1.3.2 Suggestion

The large amount of data generated from the use of M-Pesa can be used to generate credit scores, which can used to make decisions on giving uncollateralized loans for setting up small and medium size enterprises.

8.3.1.3.3 Solution Development, Evaluation, and Implementation

Given all the needed information, a new avenue for giving loans opened. In 2015, Kenya Commercial Bank (KCB), the largest commercial bank in Kenya, started collaborating with M-Pesa to derive credit scores to its M-Pesa linked customers to consider giving them uncollateralized loans. KCB started considering applications for such loans. The acceptance rate for such applications was rather high—80%. KCB started giving them an average loan of KShs 4,000. The default rate of such loans was low—2%, which confirmed the usefulness of M-Pesa derived credit data and thus successfully achieved the goal of this lap (stage). (Ndung'u, 2017; Ndung'u, 2021)

8.3.2 Diffusion

M-Pesa started expanding its services to other countries soon after it was started in Kenya. In 2008, M-Pesa was launched in Tanzania and Afghanistan. In 2010, M-Pesa was launched in South Africa but as of 2015 it had not expanded its customer base in other countries partly because 70% of the people already have at least one bank account. In 2011, M-Pesa was launched in India in close collaboration with ICICI bank. In 2014, M-Pesa was launched in Romania with the aim of expanding to other countries in Eastern Europe. It was launched in Albania in 2015 but was shut down in 2017. (Good Returns, 2021; Sen, 2014)

Impact: M-Pesa has had a major impact on mobile money services and a broad range of resulting financial services in Kenya and many other countries. It also has had an environmental impact, being a part of Safaricom that is actively engaged in reducing greenhouse gas emissions. (Ngugi, et al., 2010; Suri, et al., 2012)

8.4 INNOVATION RESULTS

M-Pesa, launched in 2007, has been a major disruptive innovation for mobile money—mobile phone-based electronic funds storage and transfer—service in Kenya. It has resulted in a wide financial services revolution (Ndung'u, 2021; Ng'weno, 2010), as summarized below:

a. M-Pesa had become the world's first major mobile money service. As of June 2020, it had over 98% of Kenya's registered mobile money subscriptions. Using over 230 thousand agents it processes over 4.8 million transactions per day. Mobile money service has now spread to large number of developing countries facilitated by enabling regulatory frameworks.

b. The mobile money growth in Kenya spurred by M-Pesa has led the banks to link their accounts with mobile money micro accounts resulting in building customer deposits.

c. M-Pesa led mobile money services has enabled commercial banks to assess credit worthiness of clients and to disburse loans.

d. M-Pesa technological platform has enabled international remittances.

e. M-Pesa has started collaborating with mobile money firms in providing a broad range of financial services.

8.5 APPLICABLE KNOWLEDGE & KNOWLEDGE CONTRIBUTION

Models/Metamodels

Unmet Social Need (Hetherington, 2008; see Chapter 1)
People working in towns of Kenya did not have a reliable, fast, and safe way to send money to their families living in villages. This was a major social need that M-Pesa met. In addition, it started meeting other financial services needs of the people living in Kenya.

Technology Empowerment (Joshi and Rohrig, 2014; see Chapter 1)
This innovation is a good example of letting people use information and communication technology for their benefit. This innovation let people of Kenya use SMS (Short Message Service) mobile banking system.

Price Modeling (Joshi and Rohrig, 2014; see Chapter 1)
Safaricom has made its services available to the poor while keeping them economically sustainable. It charges a fee that ranges from 0.74 euro to 3.69 euro for small transactions (about 8–12% of its transactions). This small amount of service fee is still cheaper than the service fee for money transfer from other providers. In addition, the service of Safaricom is more reliable.

Safaricom does not pay any interest on M-Pesa deposits that are treated as wallets; the interest earned by Safaricom is used for charity and community-based services. (Joshi and Rohrig, 2014)

Micro Distribution (Joshi and Rohrig, 2014; see Chapter 1)
A special feature of Safaricom is the use of its distributed service model. It uses the large number of its M-Pesa cash agents to provide its services. This helps it to reach even the remotest villages. The cash agents are provided commissions based on the number of transactions they make and thus have the incentive to increase the number of transactions. (Joshi and Rohrig, 2014)

Promotion of Positive Environmental Impact
M-Pesa is engaged in reducing greenhouse gases emission—many trans-receiver stations are run on wind and solar energy. The use of solar powered cell phones has additional beneficial environmental impact.

Creative Matching (Hetherington, 2008; see Chapter 1)
M-Pesa cleverly uses existing assets of Safaricom's mobile network service and their large network of agents to create a new needed service through the development of a simple and intuitive interface.

Agent-Centric Model (United Real Estate, nd)
Safaricom's M-Pesa uses an agent-centric model. Safaricom recruits and trains M-Pesa agents. The agents support customers for cash withdrawal, and money transfer, which has resulted in expansion of the customer base of Safaricom. They are paid commission and in turn they provide additional revenue to Safaricom through the fees paid by the customers for cash withdrawal and money transfer. Agent-centric models are well known in the real estate business (United Real Estate, nd).

Hub And Spoke Model (Gaille, 2015)
With the large increase in the customer base of M-Pesa, the number of M-Pesa agents became large. To manage the large number of agents, Safaricom used the Hub and Spoke model (Gaille, 2015). They created super agents to manage the agents. Safaricom would thus deal with super agents while agents would deal with customers.

Social Enterprise Business Model Template (see Chapter 1, Section 1.2.2)
The model, shown in Figure 8.1, summarizes the overall business model of M-Pesa in accordance with the template provided by Figure 1.2 in Chapter 1. The eleven components of the business model are briefly described below.

Safaricom's M-Pesa (Mobile-Based Financial Services) Overall Business Model				
Mission: Design and develop the for-profit social enterprise, Safaricom's M-Pesa, a mobile-based financial services company that serves the needs of the unbanked and underbanked communities in Kenya.				
<u>Key Partners</u> • Safaricom • Safaricom agents • Participating banks	<u>Key Activities</u> • Maintenance of the M-Pesa app • Recruitment and training of agents • Payment and money transfer activities • Transfer activities between M-Pesa accounts and corresponding bank accounts • Assessment of credit worthiness of M-Pesa customers <u>Key Resources</u> • Safaricom • Participating agents • Banks needing credit worthiness service.	<u>Value Proposition</u> • Payment and money transfer services • Enabling loans to people without adequate credit history	<u>Customer/ Beneficiary Relationships</u> • Payment and money transfer services • Facilitation of bank loans <u>Channels</u> • Agents • M-Pesa app on mobile phones • Banks	<u>Customer/ Beneficiary Segments</u> • Unbanked and underbanked communities • Banked communities with linked M-Pesa accounts.
<u>Cost Structures</u> • Fixed Cost: Cost of developing M-Pesa system • Running Cost: Commissions to agents; M-Pesa maintenance cost		<u>Revenue Streams</u> • Fees collected by agents. • Commissions earned from banks.		
<u>Impact</u> • Making financial services available to unbanked or underbanked communities in Kenya and other countries. • Positive environmental impact				

FIGURE 8.1
Safaricom's M-Pesa Overall Business Model summarized in Social Enterprise Business Model Template shown in Figure 1.2.

Mission – Goals

Design and development of the for-profit social enterprise, Safaricom's M-Pesa, a mobile-based financial services company that provides money transfer service and other financial services through a network of agents operating in small shops accessible to unbanked and underbanked communities in Kenya.

Key Partners – Needed for the Social Enterprise to Work

Key partners of the established company are Safaricom, Safaricom agents and super agents, and the participating banks.

Key Activities – Performed for the Business to Function

The key activities of Safaricom's M-Pesa are maintenance and needed modifications of the M-Pesa app; activities related to agents such as their recruitment, training, selection of super agents from amongst the agents, management of super agents; activities related to money payment and transfer—remittance and payment of transferred funds, and transfer of funds between M-Pesa accounts and the corresponding bank accounts; and utilization of M-Pesa account activities for assessment of credit-worthiness of the account holders for the corresponding banks (if any) to give loans.

Key Resources – Needed to make the Business Model Work

For the business model of M-Pesa to work depends on the existence of the mobile network services of Safaricom and the M-Pesa app, and the customer base of Safaricom and their network of agents (some of whom act as super agents). For M-Pesa to provide credit worthiness service to banks, the bank customers need to have M-Pesa accounts and have them linked to their corresponding bank accounts.

Customer/Beneficiary Segments – Served by the Social Enterprise

The customers segments served by M-Pesa are people who have M-Pesa accounts and those who are remitted funds by anybody with an M-Pesa account. Most of these people do not have bank accounts or do not have full-service bank accounts. People having bank accounts with linked M-Pesa accounts who need loans constitute additional beneficiary segment.

Value Proposition – Products and/or Services that Create Value for Customers/Beneficiaries

The services of M-Pesa that create value to their customers is the remittances of funds and the payment of transferred funds as well as the assessment of the account holders for their credit worthiness that can be used to provide loans from the banks linked to their accounts.

Customer/Beneficiary Relationships – with Customer/Beneficiary Segments

The relationships that M-Pesa has with its customers is primarily through their accounts and the money transfer services that M-Pesa provides. With the use of data generated by M-Pesa account transactions, M-Pesa also provides a useful role in facilitating the issue of loans from the M-Pesa accounts-linked banks after helping in establishing the credit worthiness of M-Pesa account holders.

Channels – to Interface with Customer/Beneficiary Segments

M-Pesa interfaces with its customers through the M-Pesa app utilizing the mobile app services of Safaricom and the network of M-Pesa agents. It also interfaces indirectly with customers of banks who have linked their bank accounts with their corresponding M-Pesa accounts.

Cost Structures – Costs incurred to Operate the Social Enterprise

To operate M-Pesa, it needs to have incurred the fixed cost of designing and developing the M-Pesa system. The running cost of the business comprises of the cost of maintaining the M-Pesa app and the commission M-Pesa pays the agents.

Revenue Streams – Cash Generated from each Customer/Beneficiary Segment

The cash generated by M-Pesa is the money transfer fees collected by its agents and the commission it earns from banks for providing the service of assessing the credit worthiness of its account holders who have their accounts linked with their corresponding M-Pesa accounts.

Impact

M-Pesa has had a major impact on mobile money services in Kenya and other countries. It offers a simple payments and money transfer system. It allows the customers to deposit money in their phones and to remit funds for M-Pesa users as well as non-users that can be withdrawn at Safaricom agents. It also allows them to make bill payments. It thus makes financial services available to unbanked and underbanked communities in Kenya. It also provides credit worthiness data to banks so that their customers with linked M-Pesa accounts can be offered loans. M-Pesa has expanded its services to many other countries including Romania, Afghanistan, Tanzania, South Africa, and India. M-Pesa also has a positive environmental impact since it is part of Safaricom that is active in reducing greenhouse gas emissions.

REFERENCES

Barnes, S.J. and Corbitt, B.J. (2003). "Mobile banking: Concept and potential," *International Journal of Mobile Communications*, 1(3):273–288. www.researchgate.net/publicat ion/220474699_Mobile_banking_Concept_and_potential (last accessed on March 30, 2024).

Barnet, D. (2017). "M-Pesa power to the people: A cheap mobile phone is transforming the lives of East Africans." *Independent*, February 20, 2017. www.independent.co.uk/news/ m-pesa-mobile-phones-are-transforming-the-lives-of-east-africans-a7590341.html (last accessed on December 13, 2023).

Cook. W. and McKay, C. (2017). "Banking in the M-Pesa Age: Lessons Learned from Kenya." Working Paper, September 2017. Washington, D.C.: CGAP. www.cgap.org/sites/defa ult/files/Working-Paper-Banking-in-the-M-PESA-Age-Sep-2017.pdf (last accessed on December 13, 2023).

Gaille, B. (2015). "Explanation of the Hub and Spoke Business Model," March 16, 2015. https:// brandongaille.com/explanation-of-the-hub-and-spoke-business-model/ (last accessed on December 13, 2023).

Good Returns (2021). "Vodafone M PesaCash App." www.goodreturns.in/vodafone-m-pesac ash-ewlt16.html (last accessed on December 13, 2023).

Hetherington, D. (2008). "Case Studies in Social Innovation: A Background Paper," Per Capita, October 2008. https://apo.org.au/sites/default/files/resource-files/2009-01/apo-nid3 954.pdf (Last accessed on December 12, 2023).

International Finance Corporation. (2009). "M-Money Channel Distribution Case – Kenya: SAFARICOM M-PESA." https://documents1.worldbank.org/curated/en/83283150044 3778267/pdf/117403-WP-KE-Tool-6-7-Case-Study-M-PESA-Kenya-Series-IFC-mob ile-money-toolkit-PUBLIC.pdf (last accessed on March 30, 2024).

Joseph, M. (2017). "M-Pesa: The Story of How It Was Created in Kenya," Vodafone, March 6, 2017. www.vodafone.com/perspectives/blog/m-pesa-created (last accessed on December 13, 2023).

Joshi, S. and Rohrig, E. (2014). "Moving Innovation Forward; Case Studies: 10 Sustainable and Inclusive Business Models," GIZ India, New Delhi. www.giz.de/en/downloads/giz2 014-en-moving-innovation-forward-india.pdf (last accessed on December 12, 2023).

Kumar, K., McKay, C., and Rotman, S. (2010). "Microfinance and Mobile Banking: The Story So Far." Working Paper. Washington, D.C.: CGAP. www.cgap.org/sites/default/files/ CGAP-Focus-Note-Microfinance-and-Mobile-Banking-The-Story-So-Far-Jul-2010. pdf (last accessed on December 13, 2023).

Mas, I. and Ng'weno, A. (2010). "Three Keys to M-Pesa's Success: Branding, Channel Management, and Pricing," Bill & Melinda Gates Foundation, January 2010. www. findevgateway.org/sites/default/files/publications/files/mfg-en-case-study-three- keys-to-m-pesas-success-branding-channel-management-and-pricing-2010.pdf (last accessed on December 13, 2023).

Mas, I. and Radcliffe D. (2010). "Mobile Payments Go Viral: M-Pesa in Kenya," *The Capco Institute Journal of Financial Transformation*, February 2010. www.researchgate.net/ publication/227489474_Mobile_payments_go_viral_M-PESA_in_Kenya (last accessed on December 13, 2023).

Maya. (2016). "M-Pesa: When 'Mobile Money' Revolutionizes Banking in Africa." https:// rctom.hbs.org/submission/m-pesa-when-mobile-money-revolutionizes-banking-in- africa/ (last accessed on December 13, 2023).

Mbiti, I. and Weil, D. (2011). "Mobile Banking: The Impact of M-Pesa in Kenya." Working Paper 17129, National Bureau of Economic Research, June 2011. www.researchgate.net/ publication/228292847_Mobile_Banking_The_Impact_of_M-Pesa_in_Kenya/downl oad (last accessed on December 13, 2023).

McGath, T. (2018). "M-PESA: How Kenya Revolutionized Mobile Payments." *N26 Magazine*, April 9, 2018. https://mag.n26.com/m-pesa-how-kenya-revolutionized-mobile-payme nts-56786bc09ef (last accessed on December 13, 2023).

Narayan, S. (2013) "Mobile Payments," Master of Science Thesis, Stockholm, Sweden, 2013. www.diva-portal.org/smash/get/diva2:707453/FULLTEXT01.pdf (last accessed on December 13, 2023).

Ndung'u, N. (2017). "M-Pesa – A Success Story of Digital Financial Inclusion," Practitioner's Insight. www.bsg.ox.ac.uk/sites/default/files/2018-06/2017-07-M-Pesa-Practitioners-Insight.pdf (last accessed on December 13, 2023).

Ndung'u, N.S. (2021). "A Digital Financial Services Revolution in Kenya: The M-Pesa Case Study," African Economic Research Consortium. www.researchgate.net/publication/349548752_A_Digital_Financial_Services_Revolution_in_Kenya_The_M-Pesa_Case_Study (last accessed on March 30, 2024).

Ngugi, B., Pelowski, M., and Ogembo, J.G. (2010). "M-Pesa: A Case Study of the Critical Early Adopters' Role in the Rapid Adoption of Mobile Money Banking in Kenya." *Electronic Journal of Information Systems in Developing Countries*, 43 (3), pp. 1–16. www.researchgate.net/publication/228638709_M-Pesa_A_Case_Study_of_the_Critical_Early_Adopters'_Role_in_the_Rapid_Adoption_of_Mobile_Money_Banking_in_Kenya (last accessed on December 13, 2023).

Ng'weno, A. (2010). "How Mobile Money Has Changed Lives in Kenya," Bill & Melinda Gates Foundation, Global Savings Forum. https://docs.gatesfoundation.org/documents/mobile-money.pdf (last accessed on December 13, 2023).

Proudly Made in Africa. (2014). "M-Pesa: The Safaricom Story – Case Study. www.tralac.org/images/News/Documents/M-Pesa_Case_study_June_2014_synopsis.pdf (last accessed on December 13, 2023).

Sen, S. (2014). "Can Money Transfer Service M-Pesa Succeed in India?" *Business Today*, November 23, 2014. www.businesstoday.in/magazine/case-study/case-study-vodafone-mpesa-mobile-cash-transfer-service-future/story/211926.html (last accessed on December 13, 2023).

Shadbolt, P. (2014). "Generous Profit," *CFA Institute Magazine*, Jan/Feb 2014, pp. 38–41. www.cfainstitute.org/-/media/documents/article/cfa-magazine/2014/cfm-v25-n1-12.pdf (last accessed on December 13, 2023).

Sorbet, A. (2022). "History of Mobile Banking – How ItAall Started," 24 November 2022. https://finanteq.com/history-of-mobile-banking-how-it-all-started/ (last accessed on December 13, 2023).

Suri, T., Jack, W., and Stoker, T.M. (2012). "Documenting the Birth of a Financial Economy," *PNAS*, 109, June 26, 2012, p. 26. www.pnas.org/content/pnas/109/26/10257.full.pdf (last accessed on December 13, 2023).

United Real Estate (nd). "Agent-Centric Model Sparks Growth in United Real Estate." https://unitedrealestate.com/news/articles/agent-centric-model-sparks-growth-in-united-real-estate-office/230 (last accessed on December 13, 2023).

Part III

Enhancing Healthcare

"It is health that is real wealth and not pieces of gold and silver."

Mahatma Gandhi

"Of All the Forms of Inequality, Injustice in Health is the Most Shocking and Inhumane."

Martin Luther King

This part of the book has 'Enhancing Healthcare' as its theme. It contains three design cases from three different countries: Rwanda, India, and United Kingdom. These cases enhance healthcare in different ways. Here are the abstracts for the three social innovation design cases:

DOI: 10.1201/9781003479086-11

9

TRACnet, Rwanda: Fighting Pandemics Using Information Technology

9.1 OVERVIEW

Rwanda, a land-locked country, is one of the smallest and least developed countries in African mainland located in central and eastern Africa. The quality of healthcare in Rwanda has been very low. Rwanda is among the countries most hit by epidemics and pandemics such as malaria and HIV/AIDS. The three months of genocide in 1994 has added to the problems. Despite all these problems, the healthcare in Rwanda has undergone significant improvement in recent decades. Health insurance has been made mandatory for all individuals. The insurance is provided by the government through a universal healthcare system known as Mutuelle. Under this system, individuals were initially required to pay a premium of US$ 2/year; since 2011 the premium has been charged on a sliding scale with poorest citizens getting free insurance and the wealthiest individuals having to pay higher premiums. (Yarlagadda, 2022).

Healthcare was one of the priorities of its Vision 2020 development program (launched in 2000). Over the years, Rwanda has made improvements in several healthcare indicators. Disease surveillance and response using information technology has improved in response to and management of disease outbreaks. (CDC, 2019)

TRACnet is an innovative solution developed by TRAC (Treatment and Research AIDS Centre), an institution of the Ministry of Health of Rwanda. It was planned in 2003 and implemented in 2005. TRACnet is a "dynamic information technology system that is used to collect, store, retrieve, and display critical program information as well as to manage drug distribution and patient information related to the care and treatment of HIV/AIDS." TRACnet and its more recent version, Electronic Integrated Disease

DOI: 10.1201/9781003479086-12

Surveillance and Response (eIDSR) system, have helped in better management of disease outbreaks. (Kizito, et al., 2013; United Nations, 2008; World Health Organization, 2018; World Health Organization – Africa, 2021)

The rest of the chapter describes in detail design of the not-for-profit social innovation (and the corresponding social enterprise), TRACnet (Fighting Pandemics Using IT).

9.2 CONTEXT

Rwanda's quality of health and healthcare had been very low before and immediately after the 1994 genocide. The country has been under the grip of infectious diseases such as malaria as well as the HIV/AIDS epidemic. Healthcare was high on the agenda of its Vision 2020 development program launched in 2000. TRACnet was one of the initiatives launched to utilize technology to improve healthcare. (Roodenbeke, et al., 2011)

9.3 INNOVATION DEVELOPMENT JOURNEY

9.3.1 Lap(s) / Stage(s)

9.3.1.1 Lap (Stage) 1 (2003–2007): Develop Phone and Web Based Infection Monitoring System

9.3.1.1.1 Problem Definition

In the background of the over three-month long 1994 genocide in Rwanda and the fact that the country had been under the grip of infectious diseases and the HIV/AIDS epidemic, there was a need for a comprehensive healthcare solution that integrates health services using information technology.

9.3.1.1.2 Suggestion

By the early 2000s the information technology had matured, and it was possible to integrate the technology with the expanding healthcare system.

9.3.1.1.3 Solution Development, Evaluation, and Implementation

In 2003, the Treatment and Research on AIDS Centre (TRAC), under Rwandan Ministry of Health, planned and designed TRACnet, a phone-based and a web-based system that monitors infectious diseases such as tuberculosis, malaria, and HIV/AIDS and generates monthly reports. TRACnet collects, stores, retrieves, displays, and disseminates critical program information, drug distribution, and patient information related to the care and treatment of these diseases. The system was fully implemented in 2005; the software for the systems was developed by VOXIVA, Inc. (VOXIVA, Inc., 2020–22). (Kizito, et al., 2013; United Nations, 2008; World Health Organization – Africa, 2021)

The system has bilingual English and French telephone and Web interface. It leverages existing mobile networks (with free dialing) charged by solar panels, connected to standalone computers, and underlying paper record systems. The data collected by the system is transferred to CAMERWA, an independent central drugs and medical supply management system. (Frasier, et al., 2008; Kayumba, 2016; Roodenbeke, et al., 2011)

TRACnet has been successful in achieving its objectives. The system reached 60,000 patients in 2007 compared to 8,000 patients who were documented in 2004. The cost of the TRACnet project over five years was US$ 2.2 million. The project was financed by the Rwandan Government. (Kayumba, 2016; Nsanzimana, et al., 2012; Roodenbeke, et al., 2011; United Nations, 2008)

The initial results of using TRACnet were encouraging. It can be a good foundation to build upon for a system that covers a broad range of infectious diseases and is integrated with all other available systems.

9.3.2 Diffusion

TRACnet has been in operation since 2004. Building upon TRACnet, the Government of Rwanda has developed and deployed a broader system in collaboration with VOXIVA and funding from the U.S. Centers for Disease Control and Prevention (CDC) to identify and respond to disease outbreaks in the country. The system, called Electronic Integrated Disease Surveillance and Response (eIDSR) system, was completed in November 2011, and fully deployed by April 2013. "The eIDSR system is fully integrated into Rwanda's routine health reporting system, and disease surveillance and response are now standard practices across all public health facilities in Rwanda" (Kizito, et al., 2013; Rwanda Biomedical Centre, 2018; Thierry, et al., 2014)

eIDSR has been very useful for early detection and notification of disease outbreaks for quick response within Rwanda as well as across Africa in countries such as Liberia, Sierra Leone, and Tanzania. (eHealth Africa, nd; Martin, et al., 2020; Yassin, et al., 2018)

9.4 INNOVATION RESULTS

TRACnet has been a successful innovation that has made significant improvement in diagnosis and treatment of AIDS in Rwanda. The number of days between PCR (Polymerase Chain Reaction) sampling and the receipt of results at the health facility has decreased from 90 days to 5 days, which has also reduced the time for subsequent antiretroviral therapy initiation. (Kayumba, et al., 2016)

eIDSR, the system that resulted from the expansion of TRACnet, has played an important role in the identification of potential infectious disease outbreaks in Rwanda, identifying "an average of 530 probable outbreaks per year since 2015." It is "routinely capturing surveillance data on 24 diseases in near real-time." (Rwanda Biomedical Centre, 2018)

9.5 APPLICABLE KNOWLEDGE & KNOWLEDGE CONTRIBUTION

Models/Metamodels

Unmet Social Need (Hetherington, 2008; see Chapter 1)
Rwanda has faced many pandemics such as HIV/AIDS. There was a social need to have an innovative technology-driven system to manage the outbreak of such diseases. TRACnet and its recent version eIDSR fulfills this need.

Leveraging Technology for Social Good
TRACnet is a good example of a social innovation that leverages technology for social good. It leverages information technology to collect, analyze, retrieve, display, communicate, disseminate, and manage disease related information.

Iterative Development (Hetherington, 2008; see Chapter 1)
TRACnet was developed in an iterative manner and has been used as a building block to develop a broader system, eIDSR, to identify and manage disease outbreaks in the country.

Technology Empowerment (Joshi and Rohrig, 2014; see Chapter 1)
TRACnet is a dynamic information technology system that lets practitioners of HIV/AIDS and other pandemics enter health-related data and have access to vital information in real time.

TRACnet (Fighting Pandemics using IT) Overall Business Model				
Mission				
Design and develop TRACnet, a dynamic IT system, to collect, store, retrieve, and display critical information related to pandemic outbreaks and treatment of HIV/AIDS patients in Rwanda.				
<u>Key Partners</u> • Rwandan Ministry of Health • Centers for Disease Control (CDC) • VOXIVA, Inc.	<u>Key Activities</u> • Planning and design of TRACnet - a phone-based and a Web-based system to collect data to monitor infectious diseases. • Management of drug distribution. • Generation of monthly reports. <u>Key Resources</u> • Rwandan government • TRACnet software • Mobile networks	<u>Value Proposition</u> • Management of disease outbreaks • Helping care and treatment of AIDS patients	<u>Customer/ Beneficiary Relationships</u> • Early detection and notification of disease outbreaks and quick response. • Monitoring of AIDS patients and drug distribution. <u>Channels</u> • TRACnet technology user interface 　o Phone; cell phone; smart phone 　o PCs/Internet	<u>Customer/ Beneficiary Segments</u> • AIDS patients in Rwanda • People of Rwanda and neighboring African countries
<u>Cost Structures</u> • Fixed Cost: Design and development of TRACnet software • Running Cost: Salary of healthcare employees		<u>Revenue Streams</u> • Funding from Government and CDC		
<u>Impact</u> • Improvement of healthcare in Rwanda and neighboring countries				

FIGURE 9.1

TRACnet Overall Business Model summarized in Social Enterprise Business Model Template shown in Figure 1.2.

Social Enterprise Business Model Template (see Chapter 1, Section 1.2.2)

The model, shown in Figure 9.1, summarizes the overall business model of TRACnet in accordance with the template provided by Figure 1.2 in Chapter 1. The eleven components of the business model are briefly described below.

Mission – Goals

Design and development of the not-for-profit social enterprise, TRACnet, a dynamic information technology system for fighting pandemics, that manages and fights disease outbreaks in Rwanda using a phone-based and a Web-based bilingual (French/English) system to monitor infectious diseases such as tuberculosis, malaria, and HIV/AIDS, to collect, store, retrieve, and display critical program information as well as to manages drug distribution and patient information related to the care and treatment of disease outbreaks, and to generate monthly reports.

Key Partners – Needed for the Social Enterprise to Work
Rwandan Government Ministry of Health took the initiative and financed this social innovation along with the U.S. Centers for Disease Control and Prevention (CDC) and VOXIVA. The Software was developed by VOXIVA, Inc.

Key Activities – Performed for the Business to Function
The activities include planning, design, maintenance, and enhancements of TRACnet and using the system to monitor infectious diseases, managing drug distribution, and generating monthly reports.

Key Resources – Needed to make the Business Model Work
Key resources for TRACnet are the support of the Rwandan government, VOXIVA, TRACnet software, and existing mobile networks.

Customer/Beneficiary Segments – Served by the Social Enterprise
The customers and beneficiaries of TRACnet are AIDS patients in Rwanda, people of Rwanda, and neighboring African countries.

Value Proposition – Products and/or Services that Create Value to Customers/ Beneficiaries
The value proposition of TRACnet is the enhancement of the Rwandan healthcare system, management of its infectious disease outbreaks, and helping care and treatment of its AIDS patients.

Customer/Beneficiary Relationships – with Customer/Beneficiary Segments
The relationships of TRACnet with the people of Rwanda as well as with people of other countries such as Liberia, Sierra Leone, and Tanzania are early detection and notification of disease outbreaks and generating quick response to such outbreaks. The relationship that TRACnet has with AIDS patients is in monitoring their treatment and drug distribution.

Channels – to Interface with Customer/Beneficiary Segments
TRACnet interfaces with its customers and beneficiaries through phone, cell phone, smart phone, and PCs/Internet.

Cost Structures – Costs Incurred to Operate the Social Enterprise
The cost incurred to run TRACnet and its new version (eIDSR) are the fixed cost of developing the needed TRACnet/eIDSR software and the

running cost for salaries of the different types of employees including healthcare employees involved in the functioning of the system.

Revenue Streams – Cash Generated from Each Customer/Beneficiary Segment

TRACnet is a government system that gets its revenue from the Rwandan government and CDC.

Impact

TRACnet and its new version, eIDSR, are having a major impact on controlling the spread of infectious diseases and are contributing to the improvement of healthcare in Rwanda and neighboring countries.

REFERENCES

CDC. (2019). "Integrated Disease Surveillance and Response," Global Health Protection and Security, Centers for Disease Control and Prevention, December 24, 2021. www.cdc.gov/globalhealth/healthprotection/idsr/index.html (last accessed on December 13, 2023)

eHealth Africa. (nd). "Electronic Integrated Disease Surveillance & Response (eIDSR)." www.ehealthafrica.org/eidsr (last accessed on last accessed on December 13, 2023).

Frasier, H., May, M.A., and Wanchoo, R. (2008). "e-Health Rwanda Case Study," July 1, 2008. https://docs.igihe.com/IMG/pdf/rwanda_appendices.pdf (last accessed on last accessed on December 13, 2023).

Hetherington, D. (2008). "Case Studies in Social Innovation: A Background Paper," Per Capita, October 2008. https://apo.org.au/sites/default/files/resource-files/2009-01/apo-nid3 954.pdf (last accessed on December 12, 2023).

Joshi, S. and Rohrig, E. (2014). "Moving Innovation Forward; Case Studies: 10 Sustainable and Inclusive Business Models," GIZ India, New Delhi. www.giz.de/en/downloads/giz2 014-en-moving-innovation-forward-india.pdf (last accessed on December 12, 2023).

Kayumba, K., Nsanzimana, S., Binagwaho, A., Mugwaneza, P., Rusine, J., Remera, E., Koama, J.B., Ndahindwa, V., Johnson, P., Riedel, D.J., and Condo, J. (2016). "TRACnet internet and SMS technology improves time to antiretroviral therapy initiation among HIV-infected infants in Rwanda." *Pediatric Infectious Disease Journal*, 35(7), pp. 767–771. www.ncbi.nlm.nih.gov/pmc/articles/PMC4925214/ (last accessed on last accessed on December 13, 2023).

Kizito, K., Adeline, K., Baptiste, K.J., Anita, A., Agnes, B., Johnson, P., and Thierry, N. (2013). "TRACnet: A National Phone-based and Web-based Tool for the Timely Integrated Disease Surveillance and Response in Rwanda." *Online Journal of Public Health Informatics*, 5(1), p. e202. www.ncbi.nlm.nih.gov/pmc/articles/PMC3692857/ (last accessed on last accessed on December 13, 2023).

Martin, D.W., Sloan, M., Gleason, B.L., de Wit, L., Vandi, M.A., Kargbo, D.K., Clemens, N., Kamara, A.S., Njuguna, C., Sesay, S., and Singh, T. (2020). "Implementing nationwide facility-based electronic disease surveillance in Sierra Leone: Lessons learned," *Health*

Security, 18 (S1), pp. S72–S80. www.ncbi.nlm.nih.gov/pmc/articles/PMC7465552/ (last accessed on last accessed on December 13, 2023).

Nsanzimana, S., Ruton, H., Lowrance, D.W., Cishahayo, S., Nyemazi, J.P., Mahayimpundu, R., Karema, C., Raghnathan, P.L., Binagwaho, A., and Riedel, D.J. (2012). "Cell phone-based and internet-based monitoring and evaluation of the National Antiretroviral Treatment Program during rapid scale-up in Rwanda: TRACnet, 2004–2010," *JAIDS Journal of Acquired Immune Deficiency Syndromes*, 59 (2), pp. e17–e23. https://journals.lww.com/jaids/fulltext/2012/02010/Cell_Phone_Based_and_Internet_Based_Monitoring_and.20.aspx (last accessed on last accessed on December 13, 2023).

Roodenbeke, E.d., Lucas, S., Rouzaut, A., and Bana, F. (2011). "Outreach Services as a Strategy to Increase Access to Health Workers in Remote and Rural Areas: Increasing Access to Health Workers in Remote and Rural Areas," Technical Report, N. 2, World Health Organization: "ANNEX 5, eHealth in Rwanda" www.ncbi.nlm.nih.gov/books/NBK310723/ (last accessed on last accessed on December 13, 2023).

Rwanda Biomedical Centre. (2018). "Electronic Infectious Disease Surveillance and Response (eIDSR) System in Rwanda," Rwanda Health Systems Strengthening Project, Technical Highlight: March 2018. https://msh.org/wp-content/uploads/2018/06/rhss_project_eidsr_technical_highlight_may2018_final_2.pdf (last accessed on last accessed on December 13, 2023).

Thierry, N., Adeline, K., Anita, A., Agnes, B., Baptiste, K.J., Pamela, J., and Kizito, K. (2014). "A national electronic system for disease surveillance in Rwanda (eIDSR): Lessons learned from a successful implementation," *Online Journal of Public Health Informatics*, 6 (1), p. e118. www.ncbi.nlm.nih.gov/pmc/articles/PMC4050745/ (last accessed on last accessed on December 13, 2023).

United Nations. (2008). "Innovation for Sustainable Development: Local Case Studies from Africa." https://sustainabledevelopment.un.org/content/documents/publication.pdf (last accessed on last accessed on December 13, 2023).

VOXIVA, Inc. (2020–22). www.devex.com/organizations/voxiva-inc-4882 (last accessed last accessed on December 13, 2023).

World Health Organization. (2018). "Joint External Evaluation of the Republic of Rwanda. Mission Report: 14-18 May 2018." https://extranet.who.int/sph/sites/default/files/jeeta/WHO-WHE-CPI-REP-2018.22-eng.pdf (last accessed on last accessed on December 13, 2023).

World Health Organization – Africa. (2021). "Integrated Disease Surveillance," www.afro.who.int/health-topics/integrated-disease-surveillance (last accessed on last accessed on December 13, 2023).

Yarlagadda, S. (2022). "Growth from Genocide: The Story of Rwanda's Healthcare System," March 7, 2022 . *Harvard International Review*. https://hir.harvard.edu/growth-from-genocide-the-story-of-rwandas-healthcare-system/ (last accessed on April 3, 2023).

Yassin, A., Cosmas, G., Darcy, N., Sotter,H, and Joseph, J.J. (2018). "Electronic Integrated Disease Surveillance and Response eIDSR implementation in Tanzania," Conference: Global Digital Health Forum (GDHF). www.researchgate.net/publication/339480382_Electronic_Integrated_Disease_Surveillance_and_Response_eIDSR_implementation_in_Tanzania (last accessed on last accessed on September 8, 2022).

10

Aravind Eye Care, India: Hospital Network for Vision

10.1 OVERVIEW

Blindness is a major disability in the world. The major causes of blindness in the developed countries are age-related macular degeneration, glaucoma, and diabetic retinopathy. In developing countries, the major cause of blindness is cataract. (World Health Organization, 2021). Cataract is an opacification of the lens of the eye (becoming cloudy or opaque) that can eventually lead to blindness if not treated (Boyd, 2021).

Aravind Eye Care System (AECS), a social not-for-profit eye care organization, was founded by Dr. Govindappa Venkatasamy in 1976, initially known as Aravind Eye Hospitals. He created it on his retirement from the Government Madurai Medical College and the Government Erskine Hospital in Madurai, Tamil Nadu, India. Dr Venkatasamy, in his clinical work, has performed over 100,000 successful eye surgeries. Dr. Vanekatasamy's vision was to create an eye care system that provides world class treatment that is free or heavily subsidized for the poor patients, subsidized by the paying patients. He adopted the McDonald's fast food network model to the eye care system to decrease costs and increase efficiency to cope with the large number of patients. He started in 1976 with a small 11-bed hospital in Madurai and then expanded to many other cities of South India. Aravind Eye Care System is now an aggregation of eye care facilities—14 eye hospitals, 6 outpatient eye examination centers, and 108 primary eye care facilities—in South India, a postgraduate institute of ophthalmology, a management training and consulting institute for ophthalmology—Lions Aravind Institute of Community Ophthalmology (LAICO), a research foundation—Aravind Medical Research Foundation

DOI: 10.1201/9781003479086-13

that includes Aravind Eye Research Institute, a manufacturing center, and eye banks (Aravind Eye Care System, 2023; Clement, et al., 2014; Rangan, 1993/2009).

To reach more and more people in rural areas, AECS organizes Eye Care Camps that act like hospitals except that no surgery in conducted in such camps. They act as vehicles to treat patients and act as filters for identifying and recruiting patients needing cataract surgery at their hospitals (Joshi and Rohrig, 2014).

Aravind Eye Care System (AECS) has four partnership projects across three other states of India. It is also expanding to Nigeria in partnership with Chanrai Group to create the largest eye care facility in Africa. The model of AECS has been applauded and studied across the world (Artlivefree, 2012; Mishra and Rajan, 2019; Nandini and Guruprasad, 2014; Rangan and Thulasiraj, 2007).

The rest of the chapter describes in detail the design of the not-for-profit social innovation (and the corresponding social enterprise), Aravind Eye Care System (Hospital Network for Preventing Blindness).

10.2 CONTEXT

In India, the major cause of blindness, particularly in rural areas, is cataract. Out of the 39 million blind people across the world, 7.8 million are from India (Nandini and Guruprasad, 2014) and 62.6% of them are blind due to cataract (Kangarajan, et al., 2011). Cataract is a curable disease through a simple operation but can lead to blindness if left untreated. There is need for greater access to healthcare for these people so that needless blindness can be prevented. (Joshi and Rohrig, 2014)

Dr. G. Venkatasamy was on the faculty of the government Madurai Medical College, where he developed several innovative programs to deal with the problem of blindness in India such as the outreach eye care programs in 1960, a rehabilitation center for the blind in 1966, and an ophthalmic Assistants Training program in 1973. He retired in 1976 but resolved to continue his work on eye care delivery. This work included conducting rural eye camps to check eyesight, prescribe needed corrective glasses and performing cataract and other eye surgeries as needed. (Artlivefree, 2012; Prahalad, 2010; Sharma, 2014)

10.3 INNOVATION DEVELOPMENT JOURNEY

10.3.1 Lap(s) / Stage(s)

10.3.1.1 Lap (Stage 1) (1976–1991): Fortify and Extend the Aravind Eye Hospitals

This lap (stage) focuses on establishing the initial Aravind Eye Hospitals, which laid the foundation for the Aravind Eye Care System (Clement, et al., 2014; Mishra, 2014; Rangan, 1993/2009).

10.3.1.1.1 Problem Definition

There are many people who become needlessly blind because they do not undergo the needed eye surgery for their cataracts. The reason for this is lack of access to high quality eye care at reasonable cost. It is generally believed that quality and quantity are inversely related and high quality comes with high cost. But given the scale of the problem in India and the fact that a large number may not be able to afford high quality eye care, there is a need to develop a self-sustaining eye care system that counters the above maxim— an eye care system that provides high quality cataract surgeries on a large scale that is free for poor people and at a cost that is reasonable for other income segments of the population. Another problem the innovation needs to address is to provide people in rural areas access to eye care and to recruit patients for cataract surgery.

10.3.1.1.2 Suggestion

The biggest strength behind Dr. Venkatasamy's decision to tackle this social problem was his spiritual inspiration and motivation to create lasting social impact. This created the needed cultural ethos for selfless service among his family members and his team.

Dr. V (Venkatasamy) brought into play many insights and ideas to tackle the innovation design problem such as: empathy, learning by doing or experimentation, continuous improvement, Mcdonaldization, differential pricing, and self-sustenance. (Artlivefree, 2012; Krishnan, 2015)

10.3.1.1.3 Solution Development, Evaluation, and Implementation

Dr. V set about his social mission of eradicating needless blindness due to cataracts without any resources but with a strong zeal to succeed no matter what hurdles he will face. The solution would need to be fully developed and implemented to confirm its validity.

In his field extension work while he was working, he had personal knowledge of the problems in rural Tamil Nadu and knew about the scale of the problems and the reasons behind them. He knew that the people there had neither the knowledge of the reasons of their blindness nor the means to address the problem. He also knew that the people in rural areas also needed to have access to facilities where their problem can be taken care of. This work had given him a deep sense of empathy with these people, and he wanted empathy to be an integral part of how he achieves his mission. (Artlivefree, 2012; Ravilla, 2014–15)

In addition to having a strong continued focus on the purpose of eliminating needless blindness and doing so with deep empathy, Dr. V decided to follow continuous experimentation and innovation, and use of certain creative constraints in how he would achieve his mission, as described below.

Continuous Experimentation & Innovation

To fulfill its mission of eliminating needless blindness with empathy, Dr. V decided to follow continuous experimentation and innovation to remove any stumbling blocks and to improve efficiency. This would ensure that he succeeds in his mission without diluting it in any manner.

Creative Constraints

In addition to the obvious constraints such as skilled staff and access to resources, Dr. V decided to follow the following "creative constraints" (Mehta and Shenoy, 2013) in his mission to launch a private eyecare system with the purpose of eradicating needless blindness starting in his home state of Tamil Nadu:

a) Never refusing treatment of anybody
b) No compromise on quality
c) Self-reliance

The first creative constraint had its origin in Dr. V's spiritual inspiration and his deep motivation and purpose of life to cure needless blindness from the face of the earth. Thus, he would not have liked to create an eyecare system that turned away anybody who could not afford the treatment. The second constraint was based on his familiarity with the fact that quality suffered as the number of patients increased and when the care was provided free or at reduced cost such as in government hospitals. He wanted to provide cataract surgery and other eyecare treatments that maintained high quality even when the number of patients treated was large and even when the patients were treated free or at highly reduced costs. The third constraint was based on his initial failed attempts at getting loans or donations, which made him decide to take the self-reliance path. He had the strong belief that the funds would flow with maintening high quality treatment as the number of patients increased with word-of-mouth publicity. (Artlivefree, 2012; Mehta and Shenoy, 2013)

Dr. V started with a small 11-bed hospital in a rented house in Madurai, Tamil Nadu, and called it Aravind Eye Hospitals, which later came to be known as Aravind Eye Care System.

Aravind Eye Care System did not have a blueprint for its growth or a business model to act upon. However, the following *Business Model* evolved over time during *this stage and subsequent stages.*

Business Model of Aravind Eye Care System

The business model encompasses a strong and continued focus on the purpose of eliminating needless blindness and emphasis on both quality and quantity while staying self-reliant. It has the following four basic components:

a. Deep Empathy & Compassion
b. Economies of Scale
c. Cross-Subsidization
d. Vertical Integration

Deep Empathy is achieved by understanding and taking care of the real needs of the potential patients mainly through eye camps. Economies of Scale are achieved by operating in a hospital-as-a-factory mode following the McDonald's service model. Cross-Subsidization of the eye care of the poor is achieved by structuring patient fees into categories that ranged from free to premium without letting the fee categories affect the quality of service. Vertical Integration is carried out through training ophthalmic assistants, recruiting patients by conducting eye camps, and manufacturing the intra-ocular lenses. (Mishra, 2014)

Deep Empathy & Compassion: Eye Camps—Continuous
Reinforcement of Deep Empathy and Compassion

In the early days of establishing Aravind Eye Hospitals, an informal form of eye screening camps (example of Ethnographic Fieldwork) was very helpful in finding and directing patients needing cataract surgery to the eye hospitals. Groups of doctors went around Madurai in the afternoons and weekends to screen patients and offer free cataract surgery at Aravind Eye Hospitals to those who needed them. (Barone, 2020; Ravilla, 2014–15)

Dr. V pioneered massive use of eye screening camps in rural areas as an integral part of Aravind Eye Care to fulfill its mission and purpose of eliminating cataract blindness. The basic purpose of these eye camps is to reach out to rural poor to identify and bring to the base hospital those needing cataract surgery. Use of these camps reinforces among doctors and staff deep empathy with the needs of the poor people and develops compassion for them—important attributes of Aravind Eye Care as a social not-for-profit organization. The camps are usually organized in schools or public spaces and are generally sponsored by charitable trusts, local businesses, or individuals (Prahalad, 2010). "In the year ending March 2013, 2,841 camps were conducted through which 554,413 patients were screened and 90,547 patients underwent surgery" (Nandini and Guruprasad, 2014). (Rangan and Thulasiraj, 2007)

It is through the eye camps that Aravind Eye Care found that the patients needed free food and transportation, counsellors, and the prescription & dispensing of glasses to get the screened patients to undergo free cataract surgery. Food and transportation cost being a barrier to cataract surgery in rural South India was confirmed in a study by G. Brilliant and G. Venkatasamy in 1979–1980 (published in *Journal of Visual Impairment and Blindness*). Free food and transportation were provided to the poor people in the rural areas for those needing cataract surgery. The cost of doing so was borne by the local community organizations that organized the eye camps. (Ravilla, 2014–15)

It was found at the eye camps that time was needed to be spent with patients to convince them about the need for cataract surgery. This gave rise to the innovation of creating counselors as a new type of staff who would counsel patients, become their advocates, and ensure their compliance to surgery, medication, and regular follow-ups. The prescription and dispensing of glasses at the camp sites was found to be another improvement that could be made to benefit the patients and to improve their trust in Aravind Eye Care. Another innovation created was the creation of Vision Centers in rural and semi-rural communities operated by ophthalmic assistants, with consult-ation ability with ophthalmologists through telemedicine facilities. (Ravilla, 2014–15)

Aravind Eye Care utilized Geographic Information System (GIS) tech-nology to visualize neglected service areas and plan for eye camps. This reduced the distance patients needed to travel to reach the eye camps and helped in increasing the number of patients coming to the camps. (Ravilla, 2014–15)

Economies of Scale: McDonaldization of Eye Care

Given that millions of people in India were needlessly blind due to cataracts and the fact that "during the 1970s and 1980s, India had only about 12,000 ophthalmologists" (Rangan and Thulasiraj, 2007), Aravind Eye Care needed to take a bold new approach. Based on the principles behind how Mc/Donald's (and Sears) were able to serve large number of customers while maintaining a reasonable level of quality, Dr. V chose to adopt the assembly-line or hospital-as-factory format to structuring how Aravind Eye Care would conduct its cataract surgeries and even other types of eye care service. (Artlivefree, 2012; Krishnan, 2015; Rangan and Thulsiraj, 2007; Ritzer, 2013).

Cross-Subsidization: Pricing Model of Aravind Eye Care

Aravind Eye Care (AEC) followed the 'creative constraint' (discussed above) of not refusing treatment to anybody. Since most of the patients were poor, AEC conducted cataract surgeries and provided other types of eye care for these patients free of cost. Given that AEC also had to follow the 'creative constraint' of self-reliance, it had to recover the cost from other patients. It therefore created an innovative hybrid model of payments in which the payments of patients are structured into four categories—free, minimal payment, regular payment, and premium payment. This made the paying patients subsidize the treatment of patients getting free treatment. In the ini-tial years, free service was provided at the discretion of the attending doctors but by 1980 patients were given the option of self-selecting their fee category. The ratio between the number of patients in the free and highly subsidized to paying categories has been around 60:40. (Artlivefree, 2012; Mehta and Shenoy, 2013)

A very important part of the pricing model is that no differentiation is made between the paying patients and the non-paying patients; all the patients receive the same high-quality level of medical attention and service—the ophthalmologists performing cataract surgeries and providing other types of eye care service as well as the ophthalmic assistants rotate between the paying and non-paying patients. The paying patients are, however, provided some differentiation in pre- and post-operative services such as beds as against floor mats, semi-private bathrooms, and air-conditioning. (Nandini and Guruprasad, 2014)

In addition to providing the needed funding and subsidizing the non-paying and minimally paying patients, the inclusion of patients paying at the market price in the hybrid pricing model serves an additional important function. It provides a check on the quality of service. In the late 1990s, the proportion of paying patients dropped significantly and an analysis of the reasons revealed that they had not kept up with the market standards of accommodations, waiting room ambience, and other amenities such as cafeteria as well as the fact that they were not providing eye care subspecialities such as glaucoma and retinopathy. Renovation of Aravind Eye Care to correct these deficiencies brought back the nonpaying to paying patient ratio to a healthy level. (Mehta and Shenoy, 2013)

Vertical Integration

a. *Ophthalmic Assistants Program*

For the assembly-line format of conducting cataract surgeries and non-surgical eye care service, there was need to optimally utilize the ophthalmologists using a large cadre of well-trained ophthalmic assistants. Having started an ophthalmic-assistants program in 1973 while he was working at the Madurai Medical College, Dr. V was well versed with launching of such a program as part of Aravind Eye Care System. In this program 900 ophthalmic assistant trainees are trained every year (Mishra and Rajan, 2019). The preparatory work done by the qualified ophthalmic assistants makes the assembly-line model of cataract surgeries and other types of eye care service work in an efficient manner. (Rangan and Thulasiraj, 2007)

b. *Intra-ocular lenses* (their manufacture, use, and related work)

The manufacture and usage of intra-ocular lenses is discussed here but it was implemented 1992 onward. Before 1980 cataract surgery involved removing the natural lens and prescribing a high-resolution lens. The technology for the manufacture of intra-ocular lenses was developed in 1981 and their use was found to be a much better way to treat cataracts. In 1990s the use of such lenses in developing countries was debated because of their prohibitive cost. In 1990 Dr. V started exploring the possibility of buying the know-how for manufacture of these lenses. Seva Foundation provided the services of David Green who found the technology partners, IOL International, USA and Springer Technologies, Germany, who appreciated the vision of Aravind Eye Care and shared the IOL manufacturing technology at a price that Aravind Eye Care could afford. Aurolab was set up with generous support from Seva Foundation and several other agencies—Sightsavers, Combat Blindness International, CBM, and Canadian International Development Agency. Aurolab started manufacturing intra-ocular lenses in Madhurai, Tamil Nadu in 1992 with an affordable price ranging from US$ 2 to US$ 10. It now makes millions of such lenses a year and exports them to 120 countries capturing about 7% of the global market share. To help develop the skills for cataract surgery using IOL implants, Aravind Eye Care started an 8-week Microsurgery Training course in 1993. (Aurolab, 2023; Karmali, 2010; Madhavan, 2013; Natchiar, et al., 2008; Rangan, 1993/2009).

Organic Growth (Mishra, 2014; Prahalad, 2010)
The following list shows the organic growth of the eye hospitals (letting the earnings from each hospital fund the growth) starting with a 11-bed hospital, thus validating the developed solution, and fulfilling the objective of this lap (stage):

- 1976, Aravind 11-bed (expanded to 20-bed) Eye Hospital, Madurai, Tamil Nadu
- 1977, 30-bed annex to the 20-bed hospital in Madurai for providing after-surgery care
- 1978, 70-bed Free Hospital, Madurai, Tamil Nadu (exclusively for the poor)
- 1981, 250-bed Main Hospital, Madurai, Tamil Nadu
- 1985, Aravind Eye Hospital, Tirunellveli, Tamil Nadu
- 1988, Aravind Eye Hospital, Theni, Tamil Nadu

10.3.1.1.4 Circumscription
This lap achieved the objective of establishing the initial set of Aravind Eye hospitals. What remained to be done was to leverage this work to establish a broader system of eye care and get ready for future growth.

10.3.1.2 Lap (Stage) 2 (1992–1997): Leverage Existing Resources to Create Aravind Eye Care System

10.3.1.2.1 Problem Definition
Even though the initial focus was on establishing hospitals and conducting cataract surgeries, it was soon realized that a system of eye care needed to

be established that included reaching to the people who would benefit from cataract surgery and other eye care services.

10.3.1.2.2 Suggestion

Continue with and evolve the business model initiated in Lap 1.

10.3.1.2.3 Solution Development, Evaluation, and Implementation

After setting up the initial set of eye care hospitals the focus shifted to becoming a comprehensive eye care system—Aravind Eye Care System—that provides a quality and inexpensive or free eyesight to people, in addition to expanding the network of hospitals. (Mishra, 2014)

Community Outreach Programs

Dr. V was keenly aware of the need for community outreach through eye camps to overcome barriers such as poverty, fear, and suspicion. He had conducted such camps even before starting eye hospitals while he was still in government service. (Aravind Eye Care System, 2020)

Eye camps, described in Stage 1 as part of the Business Model of Aravind Eye Care System, became fully integrated in the system during this stage. According to its website, over the years the "camps have contributed 30% to the total cataract surgeries performed and over 2,500 free eye camps are now organized with the assistance of a large network of community partners." (Aravind Eye Care System, 2020)

The following summarizes additional achievements of this stage, thus successfully fulfilling the goal of this stage of the innovation:

a. Cataract surgery was made affordable by manufacturing intraocular lenses and using them. (1992, Aurolab)
b. Lions Aravind Institute of Community Ophthalmology—LAICO—was established in 1992. (Rangan and Thulasiraj, 2007)
c. An 874-bed hospital at Coimbatore, India was created in 1997 and a 750-bed hospital at Pondicherry, India was established in 2003.
d. A total of 3,649 beds consisting of 2,850 free and 799 paying beds were made available by the end of this lap (stage).

10.3.1.2.4 Circumscription

Aravind Eye Care System was well established now but it needed to work on future growth.

10.3.1.3 Lap (Stage) 3 (1998–): Sow the Seeds for Future Growth and become a Leader in Eye Care

10.3.1.3.1 Problem Definition

The work done so far needed to be fully utilized to become a leader in eye care and to facilitate future growth.

10.3.1.3.2 Suggestion

Work on conducting and facilitating eye care research, expanding eye care hospitals, and establishing collaborations inside and outside the country.

10.3.1.3.3 Solution Development, Evaluation, and Implementation

Aravind Eye Care System did the following work (Mishra, 2014) to pursue the objectives of this lap:

Eye Banks

Aravind Eye Care established eye banks. The first of such banks, Rotary Aravind International Eye Bank – Madurai was established in 1998. It was affiliated to the International Federation of Eye and Tissue Banks, which requires stringent standard of quality. This was followed by establishing high quality eye banks at Coimbatore in 1998, Tirunelveli in 2004, and Pondicherry in 2005.

New Eye Hospitals

Aravind Chennai, the largest among Aravind hospitals was established in September 2017. The Sri Venkataswara Aravind Eye Hospital, Tirupati was established in March 2019.

Partnership Projects

Partnerships were set up with Rajiv Gandhi Charitable Trust, Amethi and Lucknow, Uttar Pradesh, India; with Birla Corporation, Kolkata, Bengal, India; and with Shanghvi Trust, Amreli, Gujarat, India; and with Chanrai Group, Nigeria, Africa in 2018).

Completion of the above work successfully achieved the goals of this lap (stage) of the innovation.

10.3.2 Diffusion

Aravind Eye Care has expanded to the rest of the developing world; 275 hospitals in 27 countries have received consultancy services in eye care management. AECS has been replicated in Mexico through a Mexico City-based eye care center in 2011. (Singhal, et al., 2013)

Aravind Eye Care System has received numerous national and international awards. Some of such awards are (Aravind Eye Care System, 2023; Hilton Foundation, 2010):

a. The US$ 1.5 million Hilton Humanitarian Prize in 2010.
b. The US$ 1 million Gates Award for Global Health in 2008
c. Antonio Champalimaud Science Award by the Champalimaud Foundation, 2007

10.4 INNOVATION RESULTS

Aravind Eye Care System (AECS) is a success story of an innovation with the goal of creating a world class eye care system in India that provides high quality and affordable service and has become a major contributor to eradicating cataract related blindness in India. (Mehta and Shenoy, 2013; Mishra, 2014, Mishra and Rajan, 2019; Rangan, 1993/2009; Rangan and Thulasiraj, 2007; Sharma, 2014)

The main innovation results can be grouped in three areas:

Reaching Out

AECS is based on the principle of reaching out to patients and to treating them with deep empathy. It successfully implemented this principle with eye camps and reaching out to communities. About 2,600 eye camps are conducted every year to provide quality eye care to rural areas and to screen people for cataract eye surgery (Narendran, 2017).

Financing

Right at the start Aravind Eye Care decided to be self-sustaining and not depend on donations and loans. It used the differential model of pricing of eye care to finance AECS while providing about 50% of its patients, services either free of cost or at deeply subsidized rate.

AECS Facilities

Over time AECS has become an aggregation of eye care facilities—14 eye hospitals, 6 outpatient eye examination centers, and 108 primary eye care facilities—in South India, a postgraduate institute of ophthalmology,

a management training and consulting institute for ophthalmology—
Lions Aravind Institute of Community Ophthalmology (LAICO),
a research foundation—Aravind Medical Research Foundation that
includes Aravind Eye Research Institute, a manufacturing center, and
eye banks. (Aravind Eye Care System, 2023; Clement, et al., 2014;
Rangan, 1993/2009)

Quality and Efficiency
AECS has done McDonaldization to eye care to treat a large number
or patients at international standards of quality, without making any
distinction in eye care between patients getting the treatment free of
cost and at market rates. Over 450,000 eye surgeries or procedures are
performed at Aravind making it the largest eye care provider in the
world. (Aravind Eye Care System, 2023)

10.5 APPLICABLE KNOWLEDGE & KNOWLEDGE CONTRIBUTION

Models/Metamodels

Unmet Social Need (Hetherington, 2008; see Chapter 1)
Blindness due to not treating cataract is a major cause of blindness in
developing countries. As of 2014, India had 7.8 million blind people out of the
39 million blind people across the world and 62.6% of them were blind due
to cataract, which is treatable with cataract surgery. Thus, treating blindness
due to cataract is a major social need. This is what the mission of Aravind Eye
Care is.

Deep Empathy & Compassion and Its Continuous Reinforcement
Dr. Venkataswamy had learnt through the eye camps he used to run while he
was working in a government hospital that the rural people need to be treated
with deep empathy and compassion to make them undergo the treatment for
their preventable blindness since they not only lacked the knowledge about
their eye problem, they also did not have the means to get it treated and they
and also did not have the needed trust. Dr. V made deep empathy and compassion one of the components of the Aravind Eye Care business model and
let it be continuously reinforced through running eye camps, see Figure 10.1.
(Artlivefree, 2012; Ravilla, 2014-15)

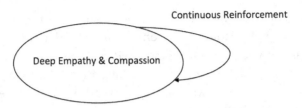

FIGURE 10.1
Deep Empathy & Compassion and its Continuous Reinforcement.

Understanding using Ethnographic Work
Through eye care camps, Aravind Eye Care realized that government alone cannot meet the healthcare needs of all because of inadequate infrastructure, growing population, and low per capita income. This understanding was achieved by working with the rural poor people and serving them. (Rangan and Thulasiraj, 2007)

Using and Expanding the Pilot Project
Aravind eye Care started modestly with a 11-bed hospital in Madhurai that conducted only cataract operations. It now has 14 eye hospitals and 108 primary eye care facilities.

Use of Creative Constraints to Spur Creativity in Innovation Design
Empathy used with the self-imposed constraints (creative constraints)—not refusing service to anybody, no compromise on quality, and self-reliance—gave rise to innovative solutions. Such sacrosanct constraints challenge creativity and give rise to new innovations. (Mehta and Shenoy, 2013)

McDonaldization (Ritzer, 2013)
The assembly-line model for food used by McDonald's was used in Aravind Eye Care to drive down the cost without compromising on quality. This was found out to be a good way to meet the creative constraint of self-reliance along with that of serving even the poor while maintaining quality. (Artlivefree, 2012; Krishnan, 2015; Rangan and Thulsiraj, 2007)

Continuous Experimentation & Innovation
Dr. V wanted to fulfill his mission of eradicating needless blindness no matter what stumbling blocks he would face. So, he decided to remove any such stumbling blocks through continuous experimentation and innovation. He wanted all the staff members to provide innovation ideas, which would be collected, and effort made to implement them within 72 hours.

High Asset Use (Joshi and Rohrig, 2014; see Chapter 1)

Aravind Eye Care achieves huge cost reduction without compromising on quality through maximal use of physical and human assets, and the use of standard procedures. It focuses on the niche area of cataract surgery. To increase the efficiency of the surgeons, it utilizes the services of mid-tier mostly women technicians who are selected from villages and trained through a two-year course. It utilizes standard procedures and has divided each surgery into subparts with specialists for each subpart. In the operation theater it has installed operation tables in such a manner that the surgeon can perform one surgery and then move immediately to perform another surgery on the adjacent table. (Joshi and Rohrig, 2014)

Process Re-Engineering (Joshi and Rohrig, 2014; see Chapter 1)

Aravind Eye Care has conducted process reengineering, resulting in the use of two methods for the improvement of its efficiency. First, it has innovatively developed a Forecasting Table that estimates the patient inflows on a particular day. This is done utilizing past patient inflows and other factors such as information on national holidays and festivals. The Forecasting Table is usually developed one year in advance and revised every month. The table helps in managing efficiently the need for surgeons and staff on a particular day. Second, Aravind Eye Care uses an integrated management system. The system monitors the amount of time a patient spends in a particular unit. The system shows a red alert if the time spent by a patient in a particular unit is more than 90 minutes. In such a case, the designated staff immediately checks the reason for the delay. This ensures that each patient is taken care of well within every unit. (Joshi and Rohrig, 2014)

Price Modeling (Joshi and Rohrig, 2014; see Chapter 1)

To make its service affordable to every segment of the society, Aravind Eye Care charges patients for its service according to their willingness to pay based on the following four pricing options. These are: free of charge (for patients coming through outreach programs), minimal fee, regular fee (market price), and premium fee (providing AC rooms, etc.). It does not require patients to show their identity to obtain free service as that can hinder their willingness to get the needed service. The free cataract operations performed by reaching patients through outreach programs are subsidized by the government of India. Every fully charged patient subsidizes the cost of delivering services of three to four patients who are treated free since they cannot pay the fees. The differential pricing model is a unique feature of Aravind Eye Care System. (Joshi and Rohrig, 2014)

In 1992, the Aravind Eye Care System started manufacturing and using intraocular (IOL) lenses manufactured at its own Aurolab that drastically reduced the cost of such lenses, bringing down the cost of cataract surgery. It now manufactures 7% of the world's IOLs used in 120 countries, thus increasing its revenues. (Mishra, 2014)

Social Enterprise Business Model Template (see Chapter 1, Section 1.2.2)

The model, shown in Figure 10.2, summarizes the overall business model of AECS in accordance with the template provided by Figure 1.2 in Chapter 1. The eleven components of the business model are briefly described below.

FIGURE 10.2

Aravind Eye Care System (AECS) Overall Business Model summarized in Social Enterprise Business Model Template shown in Figure 1.2.

Mission – Goals
Design and development of the not-for-profit social, self-reliant, and not-for-profit self-sustaining eye care organization, Aravind Eye Care System, to provide world class treatment for eradicating cataract related blindness that is free or heavily subsidized for the poor patients.

Key Partners – Needed for the Social Enterprise to Work
The key partners are the sponsors of screening eyecare camps, the subsidy it gets from fully charged patients – every fully charged patient subsidizes three-four patients, and the government subsidy it gets to partially finance free cataract surgeries.

Key Activities – Performed for the Business to Function
The activities include the following: (a) Performance of cataract surgeries, and eyecare consultations at hospitals, screening camps, and vision centers. (b) Use of the McDonald's service model to decrease costs and increase efficiency to cope with the large number of patients. (c) Training of ophthalmic assistants. (d) Recruiting of patients at eye camps. (e) Manufacture of intraocular lenses to reduce cost of cataract surgery.

Key Resources – Needed to make the Business Model Work
The key resources are eye doctors, trained ophthalmic assistants, staff, eye bank, the additional revenue from fully charged patients, and government subsidy to partially finance free cataract operations.

Value Proposition – Products and/or Services that Create Value for Customers/Beneficiaries
World class affordable cataract surgery and other types of high-quality eye care for all patients irrespective of their ability to pay as well as production of affordable interocular lenses create value to customers and beneficiaries of Aravind Eye Care System (AECS).

Customer/Beneficiary Segments – Served by the Social Enterprise
The customer/beneficiary segments of AECS are patients in India needing cataract surgery and other types of eyecare and customers of affordable interocular lenses in India and other countries.

Customer/Beneficiary Relationships – with Customer/Beneficiary Segments
The relationships of AECS with customer/beneficiary segments include performing of cataract surgeries and eye care consultations and screening patients at rural camps.

Channels – to Interface with Customer/Beneficiary Segments
The channels of AECS are eye camps to screen patients and to overcome
barriers such as poverty, fear, and suspicion; hospitals to conduct cataract surgeries; vision centers to conduct eyecare consultations; and ophthalmic assistant training programs.

Cost Structures – Costs Incurred to Operate the Social Enterprise
The fixed cost includes of setting up of hospitals and vision centers. The
running cost includes salaries of doctors and staff, plus the cost of producing intraocular lenses.

Revenue Streams – Cash Generated from Each Customer/Beneficiary Segment
The revenue of AECS comes from fees collected from patients who can
afford to pay, government subsidy for free cataract surgeries, and sale of
interocular lenses.

Impact
AECS has made major contribution to eradicating cataract related
blindness in India. The impact of AECS also includes its expansion to
Nigeria in partnership with Chanrai Group to create the largest eye care
facility in Africa.

REFERENCES

Artlivefree. (2012). "Aravind Eye-Care Systems: A Social Entrepreneurial Case Study,"
September 29, 2012. Art of Living post. September 29, 2012. https://theartoflivingfree.
wordpress.com/2012/09/29/aravind-eye-care-systems-a-social-entrepreneurial-case-
study/ (last visited, last accessed on September 8, 2022).
Aravind Eye Care System. (2023). https://aravind.org/our-story/ (last accessed, last accessed
on April 12, 2023).
Aurolab. (2023). www.aurolab.com.asp (last accessed on April 19, 2023).
Barone, F. (2020). "Ethnographic Fieldwork," Human Relations Area Files, Yale University.
https://hraf.yale.edu/teach-ehraf/an-introduction-to-fieldwork-and-ethnography/ (last
accessed on August 31, 2023).
Boyd, K. (2021). "What Are Cataracts?" American Academy of Ophthalmology, September
13, 2021. www.aao.org/eye-health/diseases/what-are-cataracts (last accessed on last
accessed on September 8, 2022).
Clement, R.C., Roy, A., Shah, R., Calderwood, J., and Burns, L.R. (2014). "The Aravind Eye
Care System." In R.L. Burns (Ed.), *India's Healthcare Industry, Innovation in Delivery,
Financing, and Marketing* (pp. 290–314). Cambridge University Press.

Hetherington, D. (2008). "Case Studies in Social Innovation: A Background Paper," Per Capita, October 2008. https://apo.org.au/sites/default/files/resource-files/2009-01/apo-nid3 954.pdf (Last accessed on December 12, 2023).

Hilton Foundation (2010). "Press Release: Aravind to Receive $1.5 million Hilton, Humanitarian Prize." www.hiltonfoundation.org/news/press-release/aravind-to-rece ive-1-5-million-hilton-humanitarian-prize (last accessed on August 24, 2023).

Joshi, S. and Rohrig, E. (2014). "Moving Innovation Forward; Case Studies: 10 Sustainable and Inclusive Business Models," GIZ India, New Delhi. www.giz.de/en/downloads/giz2014-en-moving-innovation-forward-india.pdf (last accessed on last accessed on December 12, 2023).

Kangarajan, P., Nandi, P., and Lokeshmaran, A. (2011). "Prevalence of Cataract Blindness in Rural Puducherry," Indian Medical Gazette, September 2011, 348–352. www.academia. edu/21558778/Prevelence_of_cataract_blindness_in_rural_puducherry (last accessed on last accessed on December 13, 2023).

Karmali, N. (2010). "Aravind Eye Care's Vision for India," March 5, 2010. *Forbes*. www.for bes.com/global/2010/0315/companies-india-madurai-blindness-nam-familys-vision. html?sh=6c9c68565c7e (last accessed on December 13, 2023).

Krishnan, A. (2015). "Aravind Eye-Care System – McDonaldization of Eye-Care," *Technology and Operations Management course at Harvard University. Assignment*, December 9, 2015. https://rctom.hbs.org/submission/aravind-eye-care-system-mcdonaldization-of-eye-care/ (last accessed on last accessed on December 13, 2023).

Madhavan. N. (2013). "Aurolab Has Changed the Face of Eye Care across the World," *Business Today*. www.businesstoday.in/magazine/special/story/innovation-special-aurolab-eye-care-39901-2013-06-19 (last accessed on December 13, 2023).

Mehta, P. and Shenoy, S. (2013). "The Power of Creative Constraints," DailyGood, June 10, 2013, Excerpt from the book, *Infinite Vision: How Aravind Became the World's Greatest Business Case for Compassion* by Mehta, P. and Shenoy, S., Berrett-Koehler Publishers, San Francisco, 2011. www.dailygood.org/story/442/the-power-of-creative-constraints-pavit hra-mehta-and-suchitra-shenoy/ (last accessed on last accessed on December 13, 2023).

Mishra, S. (2014). "The Arvind Eye Hospital, Madurai, India." Slides submitted to Prof. Puneet Rai, March 1, 2014. www.slideshare.net/sumammishra/arvind-eye-care-hospital (last accessed on last accessed on December 13, 2023).

Mishra, N. and Rajan, A.P. (2019). "Affordable eye care services: A case study on Aravind Eye Hospitals," *International Journal of Advance Research, Ideas and Innovations in Technology*, 5 (2), pp. 1151–1153. www.ijariit.com/manuscripts/v5i2/V5I2-1776.pdf (last accessed on last accessed on December 13, 2023).

Nandini, A.S. and Guruprasad, L. (2014). "Aravind Eye Care Systems: A Model with a Vision of Gifting Eyesight to the Needy," Conference: International Conference on Sustainable business models in the emerging global economy. October 2014. www.researchgate.net/ publication/327338745_Aravind_Eye_Care_systems_A_Model_with_a_Vision_of_gif ting_eye_sight_to_the_Needy (last accessed on last accessed on December 13, 2023).

Narendran, K. (2017). "Aravind Eye Care System," *Kerala Journal of Ophthalmology*, 29 (2), pp. 116–120, May–Aug 2017. https://journals.lww.com/kjop/Fulltext/2017/29020/Arav ind_eye_care_system.12.aspx (last accessed on December 13, 2023).

Natchiar, G., Thulasiraj, R.D., and Sundaram, R. M. (2008). "Cataract Surgery at Aravind Hospitals, 1998–2008," *Community Eye Health Journal*, 21, p. 67, September 2008. www. cehjournal.org/wp-content/uploads/download/ceh_21_67_040.pdf (last accessed on December 13, 2023).

Prahalad, C.K. (2010). "Aravind Eye Care – The Most Precious Gift." In *The Fortune at the Bottom of the Pyramid* (pp. 283–298) by C. K. Prahalad. Pearson Education. https://books.google.com/books?id=RPSG4JxAZzYC&pg=PA283&lpg=PA283&dq=Prahalad,+C.K.+"Aravind+Eye+Care+–+The+Most+Precious+Gift%22&source=bl&ots=TWrQChf5Sm&sig=ACfU3U3H5cYmqZASZxWSGeQxWs_43coIKg&hl=en&sa=X&ved=2ahUKEwjSmPz_ipvpAhUNZd8KHSaUCmgQ6AEwAXoECAoQAQ#v=onepage&q=Prahalad%2C%20C.K.%20"Aravind%20Eye%20Care%20–%20The%20Most%20Precious%20Gift%22&f=false (last accessed on December 13, 2023).

Rangan, K. and Thulasiraj, R.D. (2007). "Making Sight Affordable – Innovations Case Narrative: The Aravind Eye Care System," *Innovations*, Fall 2007, 2(4), 35–49. www.mitpressjournals.org/doi/pdf/10.1162/itgg.2007.2.4.35 (last accessed on last accessed on December 13, 2023).

Rangan, V.K. (1993/2009). "Aravind Eye Hospital, Madurai, India: In Service for Sight," Harvard Case Study, April 1993 (Revised May 2009).

Ravilla, T. (2014–15). "The Story of Innovation at Aravind Eye Care System." *L&T LDA Journal of Management*, 7, 2014–15. https://aravind.org/wp-content/uploads/2019/04/The-Story-of-Innovation-at-Aravind-Eye-Care-System.pdf (last accessed on last accessed on December 13, 2023).

Ritzer, G. (2013). *The McDonaldization of Society: 20th Anniversary Edition*. Los Angeles: Sage.

Sharma, N.R.G. (2014) "Aravind Eye Care System – Compassion in Action," *Shri Dharmasthal Manjunatheshwara Research Centre for Management Studies: Cases in Management*, 3, 1–17. http://sdmimd.ac.in/SDMRCMS/cases/CIM2014/1.pdf (last accessed on last accessed on December 13, 2023).

Singhal, M., Moe, J., and Bartlett, R. (2013). IPIHD Case Study #102, 2013: "Replicating Indian Eye Care Innovations in Mexico: The Founding and Expansion of salaUno." Published by the International Partnership for Innovative Healthcare Delivery Durham, NC (USA). www.innovationsinhealthcare.org/IPIHD%20salaUno%20case%20study%20FINAL.pdf (last accessed on last accessed on December 13, 2023).

World Health Organization. (2021). "Blindness and Vision Impairment," October 14, 2021. www.who.int/news-room/fact-sheets/detail/blindness-and-visual-impairment (last accessed on last accessed on December 13, 2023).

11

Rushey Green Time Bank, United Kingdom: Bank for Reciprocal Services Exchange

11.1 OVERVIEW

Time banks are based on the concept of a reciprocal service exchange in a community in which the service time of a person in the exchange is used as currency. Time banks can be very useful in healthcare where there is need for human support that goes beyond the treatment of medical conditions.

The time banking concept is believed to date back to the nineteenth century but for its modern incarnation, credit is given to the American civil rights lawyer, Edgar Cahn, who got an insight in 1980 on how people's service time can be valued while he was recovering from a major heart attack. The concept of time banks has now taken root in 34 countries with major presence in USA and UK. (Boyle, 2005; Boyle, 2014; Markkanen and Burgess, 2016; TimeBank Santa Cruz, 2021)

The use of time banks in healthcare in the US was pioneered by the Robert Wood Johnson Foundation in 1987 by starting six pilot projects including Member to Member program based in the health insurance company Elderplan in Brooklyn, New York City. Member to Member was an inspiration to a similar UK program, Rushey Green Time Bank (RGTB) established in 1999 as a pilot project and as a registered charity in 2004, in the surgery department of the Rushey Green Group Practice in Catford and Lewisham in Southeast London. (Boyle, 2005; Combe and Navia, 2014; Muddiman, 2013)

Rushey Green Time Bank (RGTB) provides mental and physical health support to patients of Rushey Green Group Practice by a system of volunteer time donations whereby patients can offer/receive services, such as rides to appointments, checking on patients after hospital discharge, so that both parties (service provider/recipient) receive benefits. Benefits go beyond the transaction itself, building community, helping prevent social isolation, improving the range of support options available to practice medical staff. (Combe and Navia, 2014; New Economics Foundation, 2002; Ryan-Collins, et al., 2008; Seyfang, 2002)

The rest of the chapter describes in detail design of the for-profit social innovation (and the corresponding social enterprise), Rushey Green Time Bank (Reciprocal Healthcare Services Exchange).

11.2 CONTEXT

Rushey Green Group Practice (RGGP) in Catford and Lewisham in Southeast London provides holistic care to 7,000 patients. Lewisham is a highly depressed area of London with a high level of unemployment, poverty, and ill health. Dr. Bying of this practice had observed that many patients coming for surgery were suffering from depression and isolation. He was aware of the work of Edgar Cahn on Time Banks and the pilot Time Banks started by the Robert Wood Johnson Foundation in the US. Dr. Bying got convinced of the usefulness of a Time Bank in his practice and was instrumental in starting the Rushey Green Time Bank (RGTB) in 1999, which gained charitable status in 2004. The idea of starting RGTB was to make the patients feel useful to society and connected to others who would need their services, which in turn would help them with their symptoms of depression and isolation. (Combe and Navia, 2014)

11.3 INNOVATION DEVELOPMENT JOURNEY

11.3.1 Lap(s) / Stage(s)

11.3.1.1 *Lap (Stage) (1999-): Establish Rushey Green Time Bank*

11.3.1.1.1 Problem Definition

Establish a Time Bank for the Rushey Green Group Practice.

11.3.1.1.2 Suggestion

Start with the idea of Time Bank propagated by Edgar Cahn—putting value on service time as currency ('Time Dollar') that can be used just like the regular currency.

11.3.1.1.3 Solution Development, Evaluation, and Implementation

In 1999, doctors at the Rushey Green Group Practice at Lewisham, London, attended a seminar on the Time Dollar concept of Edgar Cahn that addressed how people's service time can be valued. This clicked with the need felt by Dr. Bying and other doctors at the Practice that the patients needed some help in alleviating their isolation and depression. The result was the start of Rushey Green Time Bank (RGTB) as a successful pilot project. The initial members were recruited from patients in the waiting room of the Practice. (Muddiman, 2013)

The Time Bank was registered as a charity in 2004 with a Steering Group and a Board of Trustees with initial support from the Rushey Green Group Practice. The Bank works with volunteers and paid staff members. (Local Government Association, 2011)

Rushey Green Time Bank (RGTB) has evolved over time. It essentially facilitates the exchange of skills and experience within its community of diverse people comprising the community. It has a small team of staff members and maintains a website (www.rgtb.org.uk). The team (www.rgtb.org.uk/the-team) includes Chief Executive, Time Bank Coordinator, and Communications Support. To join the RTGB community, you must complete a short application with hOurworld (https://hourworld.org/) unless you have a referral from a partner organization; hOurworld is open software that facilitates neighbors helping neighbors. (Rushey Green Time Bank, nd)

After the application for joining the community is completed, the coordinator of RTGB calls you to find skills and interests you have and asks for two references that can vouch for your character. After the references are successfully verified, you will be invited to attend a new member group induction where you will be accepted as 'active member' and given access to hOurworld online time bank platform. The hOurworld platform will let you sign to the newsletter mailing list of RTGB. It also lets you offer a new activity based on your skill or select an existing activity or post your need for an activity. After you complete an activity, credit for the activity is awarded to your account if you have performed the activity or discounted from your account if you were the beneficiary of the activity.

11.3.1.1.4 Circumscription

The implementation of Rushey Green Time Bank provides clear benefits to individual patients and provides a way for individuals to offer services that can be exchanged for their needs. In addition, it also provides benefits to the community that includes patients and health practice providers.

11.3.2 Diffusion

The London Time Bank network containing 27-time banks was launched by the New Economics Foundation in 2001 with Rushey Green Time Bank as its kernel (Boyle, 2005). The Rushey Green Time Bank has also become part of the Time Bank Development Program, a time bank network operated under the National Health Service of Lewisham, London. (Hawaii Executive Office on Aging, 2014; New Economics Foundation, 2002)

According to research conducted by Isabel Garcia at Rushey Green Time Bank, "70 per cent of participants suffering from a combination of physical and mental problems reported some remission of their condition within six months of joining the time bank" (Boyle, 2005; Garcia, 2002). Rushey Time Bank is considered as "the most successful utilization of a time bank as a health promotion intervention" (Hawaii Executive Office on Aging 2014; Laamanen, et al., 2015; Slay, 2011).

11.4 INNOVATION RESULTS

By 2009, members of the bank had traded over 32,000 hours of exchanges (Local Government Association, 2011).

11.5 APPLICABLE KNOWLEDGE & KNOWLEDGE CONTRIBUTION

Models/Metamodels

Unmet Social Need (Hetherington, 2008; see Chapter 1)

Time banks provide a way to formalize the exchange of service time of people in a community just like currency exchange. The need for time banks in healthcare was observed to be an unmet social need in Rushey Green Group Practice. Here many patients came with symptoms of depression and isolation. They could be helped by providing a framework that increased their contact with people and make them feel useful to society.

Social Enterprise Business Model Template (see Chapter 1, Section 1.2.2)

The model, shown in Figure 11.1, summarizes the overall business model of RGTB in accordance with the template provided by Figure 1.2 in Chapter 1. The eleven components of the business model are briefly described below.

Rushey Green Time Bank (Reciprocal Healthcare Services Exchange) Overall Business Model				
Mission: Develop the for-profit social enterprise, Rushey Green Time Bank (RGTB), a comprehensive reciprocal healthcare services exchange bank, that provides mental and physical health support to patients of Rushey Green Group Practice in Southeast London				
Key Partners • Online software development Vendors	**Key Activities** • Offering of healthcare services and earning of time dollars by RGTB members. • Receiving of healthcare services by members through web hub. **Key Resources** • RGTB members • Vendor offerings additional services	**Value Proposition** • Mental and physical health support plus availability of additional related services	**Customer/ Beneficiary Relationships** • Offering and/or receiving of needed healthcare services by RGTB patients. **Channels** • Membership in RGTB • Service chits • Administrative web hub for coordination of services	**Customer/ Beneficiary Segments** • Patients of Rushey Green Group Practice
Cost Structures • Web hub creation • Administrative cost		**Revenue Streams** • No cash generated from its patients. • Donation to RGTB from local businesses and partner vendors		
Impact • Promotion of physical and mental health of time bank members				

FIGURE 11.1
Rushey Green Time Bank (RGTB) Overall Business Model summarized in Social Enterprise Business Model Template shown in Figure 1.2.

Mission – Goals
Development of the for-profit social enterprise, Rushey Green Time Bank, a comprehensive reciprocal healthcare services exchange bank, where patients volunteer their time at the Rushey Green Group Practice to receive services providing the patients an opportunity to feel useful to society that will help them with their symptoms of isolation and depression.

Key Partners – Needed for the Social Enterprise to Work
Key partners are the vendors who developed online software to connect the volunteers, patients, and staff.

Key Activities – Performed for the Business to Function
RGTB members offer services and earn time dollars. Using the earned time dollars, RGTB members can receive services through the web hub.

Key Resources – Needed to make the Business Model Work

The key resources of RGTB are its members, patient-volunteers, staff, and vendors who offer additional services through web-hub.

Value Proposition – Products and/or Services that Create Value for Customers/Beneficiaries

By volunteering, patients earn time dollars and feel useful to a society that helps them with their feelings of isolation and depression. Using their time dollars, they can receive additional related services for themselves.

Customer/Beneficiary Segments – Served by the Social Enterprise

Patients of Rushey Green Group Practice constitute the customer/beneficiary segment of RGTB.

Customer/Beneficiary Relationships – with Customer/Beneficiary Segments

The relationship of RGTB with its patients is their volunteering of services through which they earn time dollars. Using time dollars, they receive the services they need.

Channels – to Interface with Customer/Beneficiary Segments

The channels of RGTB are the record of membership in RGTB, service time records (service chits), and the web hub for coordination of services.

Cost Structures – Costs Incurred to Operate the Social Enterprise

The costs incurred to operate RGTB are the administrative cost of scheduling and keeping records of volunteering time and the cost of creation of the web hub to coordinate the offering of services to the patients.

Revenue Streams – Cash Generated from Each Customer/Beneficiary Segment

RGTB does not generate any cash from its patients. However, it does get donations from local businesses other partner vendors.

Impact

Volunteering by patients contributes to their mental health as they feel useful to society, and it reduces their depression and isolation.

REFERENCES

Boyle, D. (2005). "Sustainability and social assets: The potential of time banks and co-production," June 10, 2005. https://timebanks.org/wp-content/uploads/2011/08/Grass rootsFoundation.pdf (last accessed January 12, 2022).

Boyle, D. (2014). "The Potential of Time Banks to Support Social Inclusion and Employability," Joint Research Centre Scientific and Policy Reports. https://publications.jrc.ec.europa. eu/repository/handle/JRC85642 (last accessed December 13, 2023).

Combe, C. and Navia, F.M. (2014). *Social Innovation Case Studies:* "Rushey Green Time Bank," Social Innovation Case 3 in Chapter 6. Aviles: Spain, January 2014. Innovate Project, pp. 63–66.

Garcia, I. (2002). "Keeping the GP Away: An evaluation of the Rushey Green Time Bank," New Economics Foundation, London. www.nurturedevelopment.org/wp-content/uploads/2016/01/Keeping-the-GPAway.pdf (last accessed on March 31, 2024).

Hawaii Executive Office on Aging. (2014). "Time-banking Feasibility Study, Final Report,' June 2014. https://archrespite.org/wp-content/uploads/2022/03/LRP_2014.pdf – (last accessed April 2, 2024).

Hetherington, D. (2008). "Case Studies in Social Innovation: A Background Paper," Per Capita, October 2008. https://apo.org.au/sites/default/files/resource-files/2009-01/apo-nid3 954.pdf (Last accessed on December 12, 2023).

Laamanen, M., Wahlen, S., and Campana, M. (2015). "Mobilising collaborative consumption lifestyles: A comparative frame analysis of time banking," *International Journal of Consumer Studies*, 39 (5), pp. 459–467. https://core.ac.uk/download/pdf/33740113.pdf (last accessed April 2, 2024).

Local Government Association. (2011). "Unabridged Version: Rushey Green Time Bank," September 7, 2011. www.local.gov.uk/unabridged-version-rushey-green-time-bank (last accessed on December 13, 2023).

Markkanen, S., and Burgess, G. (2016). "Introduction to time banking and time credits," pp. 1–22, Cambridge: Cambridge Centre for Housing and Planning Research. March 2016. www.researchgate.net/publication/297696050_Introduction_to_time_banking_and_T ime_Credits (last accessed December 13, 2023), DOI:10.13140/RG.2.1.1069.7365.

Muddiman, L. (2013). "Rushey Green Time Bank," May 21, 2013. https://respondingtoget her.wikispiral.org/tiki-read_article.php?articleId=244 (last accessed on December 13, 2023).

New Economics Foundation. (2002). "Keeping the GP Away – A New Briefing about Community Time Banks and Health," February 2002. www.nurturedevelopment.org/wp-content/uploads/2016/01/Keeping-the-GPAway.pdf (last accessed on December 13, 2023).

Ryan-Collins, J., Stephens, L., and Coote, A. (2008) "The New Wealth of Time: How Timebanking Helps People Build Better Public Services," November 2008. https://neweconomics.org/uploads/files/3303e9051e1e0a62ef_rrm6bu0a4.pdf (last accessed on December 13, 2023).

Rushey Green Time Bank. (nd). www.rgtb.org.uk. Its team: www.rgtb.org.uk/the-team. New Members Journey Map: www.rgtb.org.uk/_files/ugd/7db68e_641dd26632f0407483930 754eb511591.pdf. (last accessed on December 13, 2023).

Seyfang, G. (2002). "Tackling social exclusion with community currencies: learning from LETS to Time Banks," *International Journal of Community Currency Research*, 6. https://ijccr.files.wordpress.com/2012/05/ijccr-vol-6-2002-3-seyfang.pdf – (last access on December 13, 2023).

Slay, J. (2011). "MORE THAN MONEY. Literature Review of the Evidence Base on Reciprocal Exchange Systems," November 2011. https://media.nesta.org.uk/documents/more_t han_money_literature_review.pdf (last accessed on December 13, 2023).

TimeBank Santa Cruz (2021). "TimeBanking International." https://timebanksantacruz.org/global (last accessed on December 13, 2023).

Part IV

Generating and/or Sustaining Employment

"The main target for the next years should be growth and job creation."

Mariano Rajoy

"Entrepreneurship, entrepreneurship, entrepreneurship. It drives everything: Job creation, poverty alleviation, innovation."

Elliot Bisnow

DOI: 10.1201/9781003479086-15

This part of the book has 'Generating and/or Sustaining Employment' as its theme. It contains four design cases from three different countries: India, United Kingdom, and Australia. These cases generate and/or sustain employment in different ways. Here are the abstracts for the four social innovation design cases:

12

DesiCrew, India: Business Process Outsourcing for Rural Employment

12.1 OVERVIEW

Outsourcing from an enterprise involves contracting a company (or companies) for the conduct of its activities such as its business process activities. In Business Process Outsourcing (BPO), the conduct of a selected business process is contracted to a third-party service provider. Examples of BPO are Information Technology Enabled Service outsourcing, knowledge process outsourcing, legal process outsourcing. (Eby, 2017; Time Doctor, nd)

India is a major destination of business processing outsourcing from multinational corporations, handling "56% of the world's business process outsourcing." This industry has provided jobs for nearly 75,000 Indians and is growing at an "annual growth of 50%." (OutSource2India, 2022; Ravi and Raju, 2013)

DesiCrew is an IT-enabled service company providing back-office and support services in rural areas of Tamil Nadu and Kanataka based on a vision of Prof. Ashok Jhunjhunwala at IIT Madras that the employment opportunities opened by BPOs in urban India can be replicated in rural India aided by the Internet, benefiting both the BPOs and the rural population. It was founded by Saloni Malhotra in 2007 after it was initially started in 2005 as a project in the TeNeT group and later incubated by IIT Madras and Villgro as a company within the Rural Technology & Business Incubator at IIT Madras. With seed funding from Saloni Malhotra and IIT Madras, it has received investments from Rajiv Kuchhal (angel investor), Ventureast, and ResponsAbility Ventures. (Ashwanath, nd; Deka, 2015)

DesiCrew addresses the very important problem of unemployment of educated youth in rural India, forcing them for urban migration to look for work. It creates IT-based employment in rural areas, offering world-class quality and big cost advantage to its clients. At the same time, it offers near-home jobs and higher standard of living to its employees. (Ashwanath, nd)

DOI: 10.1201/9781003479086-16

DesiCrew has over 600 employees and over 50 customers over four continents. Saloni Malhotra's work in establishing DesiCrew is being recognized; she has been nominated for Business Week's Asia's 25 Youngest Entrepreneurs list and is recipient of "FICCI's Best Social Entrepreneur Award (2009) and TiE Stree Shakti Award (2011)." (DesiCrew, nd; Saloni Malhotra, 2021)

The rest of the chapter describes in detail design of the for-profit social innovation (and the corresponding social enterprise), DesiCrew (Business Process Outsourcing for Rural Employment).

12.2 CONTEXT

Saloni Malhotra graduated in industrial electronics from Poona University in 2003; she had an ambition to do something for rural India. Soon after her graduation, she attended a lecture in Delhi, India, by Prof. Ashok Jhunjhunwala from the Indian Institute of Technology, Madras, about the large number of employment opportunities that Business Process Outsourcing (BPO) industry had created in urban India. During the lecture, Prof. Jhunjhunwala raised the question as to why there cannot be such BPOs in rural India. This question clicked with Saloni Malhotra and she soon established contact with Prof. Jhujhunwala to seek his mentorship in starting a rural BPO. Prof. Jhunjhunwala agreed to sponsor Saloni Malhotra for starting a 'rural BPO' project in TeNeT (The Telecommunications and Computer Networking) group at IIT Madras (Malhotra, et al., 2007). Saloni Malhotra quit her job and moved to Chennai to start working on the project, which developed to become DesiCrew Solutions Pvt. Ltd., India. (Ashwanath, nd; Deka, 2015; Kumar and Ganesh, 2012; Rediff News, 2007)

12.3 INNOVATION DEVELOPMENT JOURNEY

12.3.1 Lap(s) / Stage(s)

12.3.1.1 Lap (Stage) 1 (2005–2011): Develop Rural Business Outsourcing Company

12.3.1.1.1 Problem Definition

How to innovatively leverage huge untapped, educated, and employable, but currently unemployed, talent pool in rural areas of India, who do not have access to viable livelihood options?

12.3.1.1.2 Suggestion

Create a for-profit decentralized rural Business Processing Outsourcing company (BPO) with the goal of financial performance coupled with rural social development.

12.3.1.1.3 Solution Development, Evaluation, and Implementation

The first two years were spent by Saloni Malhotra working with Prof. Ashok Jhunjhunwala at IIT Madras to fully understand the social enterprise problem and to prototype a possible solution. The vision of Prof. Ashok Jhunjhunwala (mentor of Saloni Malhotra) was to have "small decentralized BPOs in the rural areas where a maximum of 15 to 20 people work, and those who work should belong to that village." Saloni Malhotra set about realizing this vision. (Deka, 2015).

Prof. Jhunjhunwala had helped in incubating a somewhat similar social enterprise—n-Logue—a sustainable network of wirelessly-connected Internet kiosks in rural India. (Jhunjhunwala, 2010) Saloni Malhotra spent the first three months in understanding people and working with Internet kiosks of n-Logue in rural areas of Tamil Nadu. She spent the next six months in understanding the actual needs of potential clients of the social enterprise she wanted to set up. Saloni Malhotra and Prof. Jhunjhunwala found that there were good number of people in rural Tamil Nadu who were employable in such a rural BPO, but it would take longer to train them to bring them to the same level as employees in urban BPOs. (Deka, 2015)

In one year, they found that a rural BPO would have a big cost advantage but there were three types of problems that needed to be surmounted:

Acceptance, Infrastructure, and Training:

Acceptance and Perception. Customers needed to be convinced about the concept of a rural BPO and its delivery capabilities. They decided to start with limited services and deliver, meeting and exceeding service level agreements to gradually gain acceptance. They would gradually expand their services.

Infrastructure. This was the biggest challenge, but it was very important to have infrastructure and data security in a rural setting that was as good as that at a major Indian city such as Delhi, Mumbai, or Bangalore.

Training. This was also very important and needed additional attention to train the rural educated youth in computer operations, office management, HR practices, data entry and Internet usage. (Ashwanath, nd; Deka, 2015; Kumar and Ganesh, 2012)

Saloni Malhotra and Prof. Jhunjhunwala and their team experimented with several business models but ultimately came up with a model that would set up micro-centers in villages near type II and type III towns, for the delivery of services. This would result in reduced costs by as much as 40%, reduced attrition of employees, and savings by not having to spend on corporate social responsibility. Each center would be set up with an initial investment of US$ 55,000 to US$ 160,000. Seed funding was provided by Saloni Malhotra and IIT Madras. In February 2007, IIT Madras, along with Villgro, set up the rural BPO, DesiCrew Solutions Pvt. Ltd as a commercial venture, with Saloni Malhotra as the CEO. It was incubated by the Rural Technology Business Incubator (RTBI) of IIT Madras and Villgro. (Kumar and Ganesh, 2012)

DesiCrew started its first center close to Bhavni (a town in the state of Tamil Nadu). The company had difficulty in getting its big client and accepted any work it could get. In 2008–2009, the company started making money. (Ashwanath, nd; Deka, 2015; Kumar and Ganesh, 2012)

DesiCrew launched DTOUCH 1.0 in 2010 within the company to train DesiCrew members in the skills required for BPO. The management designed the curriculum, built the content, and executed the training program. (Manivannan, 2018)

12.3.1.1.4 Circumscription
DesiCrew was established and started functioning but there were challenges mainly in continuous upgrading of the skills of employees.

12.3.1.2 Lap (Stage) 2 (2012–2017): Optimize Employee Training
12.3.1.2.1 Problem Definition
There was a need to scale up the business model of DesiCrew to meet the growing demands of customers. There was also a need to optimize the employee training content and methodology.

12.3.1.2.2 Suggestion
Seek and rely on external expertise for the needed training of employees.

12.3.1.2.3 Solution Development, Evaluation, and Implementation
Services provided were expanded. By now the services included: Digitization (scanning and data entry); Live chat responses; Mail room activities; New business set-up; Project management; Secondary research; Transcription; Translation; Beta testing of web products; Localization of web products;

Website monitoring; Customization. Rajiv Kuchhal invested in DesiCrew as an angel investor in 2008 and J.K. Manivannan joined as Chief Operating Officer in 2009. The company decided to let go of some smaller clients and retained a few key clients including a life insurance company and an Internet services company. (Kumar and Ganesh, 2012)

DTOUCH 2.0. was launched in 2012 for optimizing training content and training methodology. Skill development organizations were utilized to conduct training sessions, certifications, etc. DesiCrew raised INR (Indian Rupees) 7 crore (US$ 1.12 million) from ResponsAbility Ventures I and Ventureast Tenet Fund II soon after investment from the angel investor, Rajiv Kuchhal, in 2008, thus confirming that DesiCrew was following a valid approach. (Maivannan, 2018)

12.3.1.2.4 Circumscription

DesiCrew was doing well and had grown but there was a need to re-skill and upskill all employees to new technologies like artificial intelligence (AI) and machine learning to meet market demands. This was a need to offer services of higher complexity and quality. (Kumar and Ganesh, 2012)

12.3.1.3 Lap (Stage) 3 (2018-): Upgrade Employee Skills

12.3.1.3.1 Problem Definition

The market needed the performance of jobs that required new skills and knowledge of new technologies such as AI, machine learning, etc. The outsourcing industry was rapidly adopting these new technologies and DesiCrew could not afford to be left behind.

12.3.1.3.2 Suggestion

Train the employees in a more holistic approach that upgrades their knowledge, skills, and attitude.

12.3.1.3.3 Solution Development, Evaluation, and Implementation

The company launched DTOUCH 3.0, a new version of its training and learning program. It started transforming the entire DesiCrew group into a learning organization that would absorb emerging technologies and personality skills, thus fulfilling the objectives of this lap (stage). An online Learning Management System portal was launched with focus of imparting knowledge and skills, certification, and benchmarking. The goals were to have all the employees quickly certified in at least one Digital Skill and soon certified in at least three Digital Skills. (Manivannan, 2018)

12.3.2 Diffusion

DesiCrew has had significant social and economic impact on the local people it hires. They work near their homes in rural areas thus saving their expenses and increasing their social stature. This has the desirable effect of decreasing the migration of rural people to large cities in search of jobs. (Joshi and Rohrig, 2014)

DesiCrew was the first rural BPO company in India. Its success has resulted in the creation of many such companies (Majumder and Sharma, 2014); as of 2010, there were about 35 rural BPO centers in India with over 5,000 employees (Marathe, 2010).

12.4 INNOVATION RESULTS

DesiCrew provides back-office support to leading insurance companies, companies selling fast-moving consumer goods, IT companies, educational institutions, and telecom service providers as well as multinational corporations and startup companies. (Ashwanath, nd)

The company has made an impact in the rural areas it operates in. It has made significant contributions to the income and lifestyle of its employees—ability to support their families for education and better standard of living. The employees can save as much as "90% of their salaries." (Ashwanath, nd; Deka, 2015)

DesiCrew completed one billion transactions during the first ten years of its existence. The company provides secure locations with IP protection and the advantage of reliable and stable workforce. (DesiCrew website, 2022).

12.5 APPLICABLE KNOWLEDGE & KNOWLEDGE CONTRIBUTION

Models/Metamodels

Unmet Social Need (Hetherington, 2008; see Chapter 1)

Business Process Outsourcing has created many employment opportunities in urban India. There is an unmet social need for letting Business Process

Outsourcing create job opportunities in rural India. Meeting this need will create jobs among educated people in rural India and reduce the need for them to migrate to urban areas.

High Asset Use (Joshi and Rohrig, 2014); see Chapter 2)

The niche area that DesiCrew focuses on is the replication of Business Process Outsourcing (BPO) from urban centers to rural and semi-urban centers in India aided by the Internet, serving global clients. To be successful, DesiCrew has created the needed physical and human infrastructure and attempts to fully utilize it. The physical infrastructure it has created is a network of fully owned micro-centers across rural and semi-urban areas fully equipped with the needed computing power and the Internet. Creating and fully utilizing the needed human infrastructure in the rural and semi-urban areas has been the critical factor for the success of DesiCrew. It has done this by careful local recruitment of educated and trainable youth through village panchayat and employee referral and through extensive training and continuous on-the-job training of the employees. It has also tied with educational institutions for recruitment and to provide internship opportunities. (Joshi and Rohrig, 2014)

Making Innovation Financially Sustainable

It is easy for DesiCrew to become financially sustainable once it has made its services available at high quality and acceptable to its potential clients. This is because of the relatively low cost of its operations and having a very low attrition rate of its employees.

Creating Positive Social Impact

DesciCrew can make a positive social impact in the community. Employees can save 90% of income (as against 10% in urban areas) and this makes a big difference in the social stature of its employees and their families. (Ashwanath, nd; Deka, 2015)

Creative Matching (Hetherington, 2008; see Chapter 1)

DesiCrew involves an out-of-the-box idea but utilizes the model of existing IT-enabled urban business process outsourcing centers. It creates small decentralized BPOs employing rural educated people drawn from local areas. DesiCrew has created a network of such BPO centers in South India.

Distributed Operations Model (Sinha, 2009)

DesiCrew has utilized a distributed operations model to run and manage its rural micro BPO centers. The Chennai office acts as interface between the client and rural micro centers. A network of micro centers is created in rural

DesiCrew (business process outsourcing company for rural employment) Overall Business Model				
Mission Design and establish DesiCrew, a for-profit social enterprise, that provides business process outsourcing employment opportunities to people living in rural areas of India utilizing the Internet.				
Key Partners • Skill development organizations	**Key Activities** • Maintenance of adequate physical, IT, and communication infrastructure • Employee training • Delivery of contracted services **Key Resources** • Funding o Initial funding: Saloni Malhotra o Seed Funding: IIT Madras and Saloni Malhotra o Venture Funds • Local pool of educated people.	**Value Proposition** • BPO services in rural areas • Employment to rural people	**Customer/ Beneficiary Relationships** • Fulfilment of BPO services of clinte companies • Training and employment of local people **Channels** • DesiCrew portal • Employment agencies	**Customer/ Beneficiary Segments** • Multinational corporations • Local educated but unemployed or under-employed people
Cost Structures • Fixed Cost: Creation of needed infrastructure and web portal • Running Cost: Staff salaries, software			**Revenue Streams** • Compensation for contracted BPO services	
Impact • Impressive record of performance • Contribution to rural gainful employment • Rural population social stature enhancement				

FIGURE 12.1
DesiCrew Overall Business Model summarized in Social Enterprise Business Model Template shown in Figure 1.2.

and semi-urban locations, in territories with a population between 10,000 and 100,000, each center professionally run with a 25-seat facility working in two shifts. The workforce in the micro centers is built up by training educated but unemployed or underemployed people.

Social Enterprise Business Model Template (see Chapter 1, Section 1.2.2)

The model, shown in Figure 12.1, summarizes the overall business model of DesiCrew in accordance with the template provided by Figure 1.2 of Chapter 1. The eleven components of the business model are briefly described below.

Mission – Goals

DesiCrew provides a solution for the very important problem of unemployment of educated youth in rural India by establishing an internet-based company that provides business process outsourcing rural employment opportunities.

Key Partners – Needed for the Social Enterprise to Work

Skill development organizations constitute a key partner for DesiCrew to work. This is because, the biggest challenge of this company to work in a rural setting is to have its employees have the needed knowledge and skills and have them certified in the appropriate skills. The skills of the employees also needed to be regularly upgraded.

Key Activities – Performed for the Business to Function

There were three key activities – maintenance of adequate physical, IT and communication infrastructure after its creation, employee training, and delivery of contracted services. An online Learning Management System portal was launched with focus of imparting knowledge and skills, certification, and benchmarking. The goals were to have all the employees quickly certified in at least one digital skill and soon certified in at least three digital skills. A continuous upgrading of the skills of employees was planned.

The delivery of contracted BPO services is an important key activity of DesiCrew. Over one billion BPO transactions have been completed during the first ten years of its existence. The company provides secure locations with IP protection and the advantage of reliable and stable workforce.

Key Resources – Needed to Make the Business Model Work

Each center was set up with an initial investment of US$ 55,000 to US$ 160,000. Seed funding was provided by Saloni Malhotra and IIT Madras. Venture funds were also used. Local pools of educated and unemployed or underemployed people were identified.

Customer/Beneficiary Segments – Served by the Social Enterprise

The customer or beneficiary segments are the clients served by DesiCrew and the people employed by the company. The clients of DesiCrew include insurance companies, companies selling fast-moving consumer goods, IT companies, educational institutions, and telecom service providers, multinational corporations, and startup companies. The employees of DesiCrew are the local educated people who are trained and employed by the company.

Value Proposition – Products and/or Services that Create Value to Customers/ Beneficiaries

The services provided by the company are to provide business process outsourcing (BPO) from rural areas and to provide employment to people in those areas. The BPO services include providing back-office support to leading insurance companies, companies selling fast-moving consumer goods, IT companies, educational institutions, and telecom service providers, multinational corporations, and startup companies. These BPO centers provide employment to educated rural people in rural areas.

Customer/Beneficiary Relationships – with Customer/Beneficiary Segments

The relationships DesiCrew has with its client companies is that of fulfillment of their BPO services. Its relationship with the local educated but unemployed or underemployed people is that of training and employing them.

Channels – to Interface with Customer/Beneficiary Segments

The channels used are the DesiCrew portal and the employment agencies to find local available talent.

Cost Structures – Costs Incurred to Operate the Social Enterprise

The fixed cost consisted of creating the needed infrastrucure and web portal for a network of micro centers located in rural and semi-urban locations and building workforce by training educated but unemployed or underemployed people. The running cost included obtaining software and providing staff salaries.

Revenue Streams – Cash Generated from Each Customer/Beneficiary Segment

The revenue streams of the company are the funds received from its clients for the contracted services.

Impact

Over one billion BPO transactions have been completed during the first ten years of DesiCrew's existence. The company provides secure locations with IP protection and the advantage of reliable and stable workforce. It has made significant contributions to the employment of local (rural and semi-rural) educated unemployed people. The income and lifestyle of DesiCrew's employees have made them support their families for education and better standard of living. The employees can save as much as 90% of their salaries.

REFERENCES

Ashwanath, G. (nd). "Dream Big, Follow your Passion, and Enjoy the Process," CrazyEngineers. www.crazyengineers.com/founders_circuit/ashwanth-g-desicrew (last accessed on December 14, 2023).

Deka, J. (2015). "Desicrew's Saloni Malhotra Story," April 21, 2015. Social Entrepreneurship. https://socialentrepreneurshiprevisited.wordpress.com/2015/04/21/desicrews-saloni-malhotras-story/ (last visited on December 14, 2023).

DesiCrew (nd). www.desicrew.com (last accessed on January 17, 2022).

Eby, K. (2017). "Everything You Need To Know About Business Process Outsourcing," January 17, 2017. Smartsheet. www.smartsheet.com/everything-you-need-know-about-business-process-outsourcing (last accessed on December 14, 2023).

Hetherington, D. (2008). "Case Studies in Social Innovation: A Background Paper," Per Capita, October 2008. https://apo.org.au/sites/default/files/resource-files/2009-01/apo-nid3954.pdf (last accessed on December 12, 2023).

Joshi, S. and Rohrig, E. (2014). "Moving Innovation Forward; Case Studies: 10 Sustainable and Inclusive Business Models," GIZ India, New Delhi. www.giz.de/en/downloads/giz2014-en-moving-innovation-forward-india.pdf (last accessed on December 12, 2023).

Jhunjhunwala, A. (2010). "Case Study: Connecting Rural India with Broadband Wireless." www.itu.int/ITU-D/study_groups/SGP_2006-2010/events/Case_Library_old/asia_pacific/ITU%20India%20Case%20Study%2028%2006%2007.pdf (last accessed on December 14, 2023).

Kumar, K. and Ganesh, U. (2012). "DesiCrew Solutions Private Ltd," Villgro Innovations Foundation Case Study Series, July 2012. https://pdfslide.net/documents/villgro-innovations-foundation-case-study-series-draftvillgro-innovations.html (last accessed on December 14, 2023).

Majumder, S. and Sharma, R.P. (2014). "Indian ITES industry going rural: The road ahead," *Journal of Business & Economic Policy*, 1, p. 2, December 2014. http://jbepnet.com/journals/Vol_1_No_2_December_2014/8.pdf (last accessed on December 14, 2023).

Malhotra, S., Rathi, P., Gonsalves, T.A., Jhunjhunwala, A., and Giri, T. (2007). "Untapped Resources! Amazing Potential! TeNeT's Rural BPO Initiative." In A. Venkatesh,T. Gonsalves, A. Monk, K. Buckner, (Eds.), *IFIP International Federation for Information Processing* (pp. 21–33), Volume 241, Home Informatics and Telematics: ICT for the Next Billion. Boston: Springer. www.researchgate.net/publication/45814833_Untapped_Resources_Amazing_Potential_TeNeTs_Rural_BPO_Initiative (last accessed on December 14, 2023).

Manivannan, J.K. (2018). "DesiCrew- Transforming our Crew for Human Excellence (D-TOUCH)." In B. Chakrabarti, (Ed.), *Tata Social Entrepreneurship Challenge. E-Newsletter: Winners of the Tata Social Enterprise Challenge 2017–18*, April 2018. www.tatasechallenge.org/resource/national-agripreneurs-summit-2/#9162 (last accessed on December 14, 2023).

Marathe, M. (2010) "A Case Study of Rural BPOs in India." www.researchgate.net/profile/ Mahesh_Marathe/publication/324209031_A_Case_Study_on_Rural_BPOs_in_In dia/links/5ac4bf64458515564eafbc03/A-Case-Study-on-Rural-BPOs-in-India (last accessed on December 14, 2023).

Outsource2India (2022). "The BPO Industry in India," Flatworld Solutions. www.outsourc e2india.com/india/bpo-industry-india.asp (last accessed on December 14, 2023).

Ravi, R. R. and Raju, D.V. (2013, August). "Rural business process outsourcing in India – Opportunities and challenges," *International Journal of Business and Management Invention*, 2:8, 40–49. www.ijbmi.org/papers/Vol(2)8/Version-1/F0281040049.pdf (last accessed on December 14, 2023).

Rediff News (2007). "DesiCrew: A Girl's Pioneering Vision for Rural BPOs," November 29, 2007. http://specials.rediff.com/money/2007/nov/29sld1.htm (last accessed on December 14, 2023).

Saloni Malhotra (2021). en.bharatpedia.org/wiki/Saloni_Malhotra

Time Doctor (nd). "Business Process Outsourcing." https://biz30.timedoctor.com/business-process-outsourcing-industry/ (last accessed on December 14, 2023).

13

Infosys Global Education Center, India: Organization-Specific Career-Long Learning

13.1 OVERVIEW

Inaugurated in 2005, Infosys Global Education Center (GEC) is the corporate education center of Infosys for training and mentoring its professionals from all around the world. It is the largest corporate training facility in the world. Located in the 337-acre Infosys Mysore, India, campus, the total capacity of the center is to educate 13,500 professionals. (Infosys—GEC, 2023)

Infosys GEC provides Internship programs for its new employees, existing employees, and students. It also prepares leaders within the organization to take charge. The Infosys Global Education Center has a Foundation Program that enables fresh graduates to become corporate professionals. (Infosys—GEC, 2023)

The IT industry in India is a major contributor to its economy and employment. As of the financial year 2020, this industry generated an annual revenue of UD$ 180 billion including US$ 150 billion from exports and provided direct employment for 4.35 million people (4.5 million people by FY 2021). Infosys is a significant part of this industry. (Sun, 2021)

Infosys is a multinational information technology and consulting corporation with over 292,000 employees and revenue of US$ 15.64 billion with customers in over 50 countries. It was founded in 1981 as a seven-man startup with an initial capital of US$ 250. It is operating in the highly competitive IT sector in which technology is constantly changing. Without continuous training and retraining of its employees the company could not have grown and functioned so successfully. (Infosys, 2022—Overview)

DOI: 10.1201/9781003479086-17

Soon after the company was founded Infosys realized the need for training its new hires. Given the quick churn of technology in the IT sector and the need to provide new services to attract new contracts, Infosys put training and support of continuous employee-relevant learning at the core of its mission. To sustain itself there was a need to create a continuous learning environment that keeps its employees up to speed in the latest technologies and related areas, best practices, and associated behavioral training so that they can function most efficiently and contribute to the mission of the company. To achieve this, in 2005, it created its own corporate university—Global Education Center (GEC) in Mysore, India. GEC located in the 337-acre campus with over 350 instructors and more than 200 classrooms can train 13,500 employees at a given time on various technologies and knowledge areas. Global Education Center (GEC) of Infosys and its work on organization-specific career-long learning is the focus of this chapter. (AITSL, 2013; Infosys—E&R Journey, 2011; Infosys—GEC, 2022)

We treat GEC as a for-profit social enterprise of Infosys since it is providing a model for organization-specific, career-long learning of employees of information technology companies. Even though GEC by itself does not bring any revenue it is considered as for-profit social enterprise since it contributes to the capabilities and profit of Infosys.

The rest of the chapter describes in detail design of the for-profit social innovation (and the corresponding social enterprise), Infosys Global Education Center (Organization-Specific Career-Long Learning).

13.2 CONTEXT

Infosys had realized the importance of education and training of employees since its inception, to create a learning organization. For this purpose, a formal education department in the company, Education & Research department, was created in 1991. As the company grew, it made the department a core competency of the company to design and deliver courses that were "comprehensive, inter-connected and relevant", by educators within the company who were associated with real-life projects. The department determines what competencies the company needs and delivers the content for those needs through training and other means. The need to create a Global Education Center, a "centralized and strategic infrastructure," arose with the growth of the company. (Infosys—E&R Journey, 2011; Mallon, 2010)

13.3 INNOVATION DEVELOPMENT JOURNEY

13.3.1 Lap(s) / Stage(s)

13.3.1.1 Lap (Stage) (2002-): Develop Global Education Center

13.3.1.1.1 Problem Definition

The problem was to design an organization-specific career-long learning system. Since the company was a startup company with meagre resources, such a system would need to be designed to evolve and grow with the growth of the company. It was expected that the employees hired would have a reasonably good engineering/computer science education, but efforts needed to be made that all the employees had the needed training to be uniformly useful to the projects of Infosys and that they would grow their knowledge over time. This training needed to be multidimensional to cover needed skills, knowledge about the best domain-specific practices, and associated behavioral knowledge. (AITSL, 2013)

13.3.1.1.2 Suggestion

The solution would need to be one that evolves and grows over time. The necessary organizational infrastructure as well as the physical infrastructure would need to be created.

13.3.1.1.3 Solution Development, Evaluation, and Implementation

All the training and learning at Infosys is handled by the Education & Research department/group (E&R), created in 1991. It is led by its head who is also a vice president of the company. E&R is responsible for determining at any time the overall competencies and behavioral skills required by the company as well as deciding on the content of courses required for addressing the needed (evolving) competencies and delivering those courses as well as providing other services. The overall learning at Infosys is governed by the Competency Council headed by one of the Infosys board members. The council includes the head of E&R and some of the heads of the company's business groups. E&R consults with the Competency Council before starting a new program. (Mallon, 2010)

It was decided that learning at Infosys must be multi-dimensional, which includes knowledge about best domain-specific best practices and behavioral skills while fulfilling the following two broad goals (AITSL, 2013; Mallon, 2010):

a. Provide the core knowledge (changing over time) that all the employees must have and build deep (changing) specializations among the employees to handle special projects.
b. Build learning agility among the employees to quickly adapt to changing technology and changing mission of the company.

Fulfilling the first goal needed creation and delivery of courses that would additionally provide the foundation for achieving the second goal. The second goal is very important but required special effort and an infrastructure for informal learning. Part of this infrastructure deals with how general and specialized explicit and tacit knowledge at Infosys is handled and delivered.

To fulfill the *first goal*, it did not make sense to mimic the training provided in existing colleges and universities. Instead, the training and learning would need to be multidimensional to include the specifics of a new technology, the knowledge, and best practices of a domain, as well as the needed behavioral training. The training would include both face-to-face learning and e-learning. The training of a new employee or the retraining of an existing employee would also be directed by the employee manager based on appraisals. Training would be combined with work on the assigned group projects. Carefully orchestrated assessment would be coupled with the professional training and experiential learning, with the goal of the employee obtaining a new certification in a knowledge area that could lead to promotion or change in the career path. (Mallon, 2010)

The core body of knowledge would be taught to freshers through its Foundation Program. The Foundation (residential) Program was started at Mysore in 2002 with just fifty trainees, one instructor, and one classroom. The Foundation Program grew with the growth of Infosys. It has been taught in the Infosys Global Education Center (GEC) that was inaugurated in 2005; the center was in the 270-acre Infosys, Mysore campus and could accommodate 4,500 trainees at any given time. Infosys GEC was expanded in 2009 to train a total of 13,500 trainees at any time and size of the campus was expanded to 337 acres. By 2012, 100,000 freshers had successfully completed the Foundation Program conducted at the Global Education Center and over 238,000 professionals have been trained in the center since 2005. (Business Standard, 2013; Infosys—E&R Journey, 2011; Infosys—GEC Inauguration, 2005; Infosys—GEC II, 2009; Infosys—GEC, 2022; Infosys Training, 2012)

The Foundation Program is a 23-week training program to aid the new employees it hires from engineering colleges and institutions make transition from an educational environment to the Infosys corporate world. It provides generic training as well as stream-specific training in various areas and training in soft skills and leadership. The streams include new technology streams such as big data, Internet of Things, and blockchain in addition to traditional streams of Mainframe, Open Systems, Java, and Microsoft. The training program is delivered in courses in which the trainees participate in classroom sessions for half a day and spend the rest of the day in hands-on project work, group work, and e-learning. The courses have assignments that are graded, and each trainee is assessed for progress and learnability; they are provided coaching on their skills based on observations from the training staff. Upon completion of training, they are tested and must pass with a good score to continue at Infosys. After completion of the Foundation Program, the employees move on to their assigned business units that provide specialized training. (Infosys—GEC, 2022; Infosys Training, 2012; Mallon, 2010; UKEssays, 2015)

Evolving Knowledge Needs of Infosys. Infosys was started by seven people in 1981 as a startup company. Its revenue in the first decade was unimpressive but it started picking up after the first decade. In 1990s Infosys realized that the major global companies were not taking it seriously and needed to change its structure to scale up to getting bigger revenues while "maintaining the quality, agility, and effectiveness of a small company." It needed to become "agile and flexible in responding to new market trends." In 1998, it realized that its organizational structure was not facilitating this change. It therefore changed its structure using Global Delivery Model (GDM) as its underlying business model. The GDM is based on the principle of distributed project management, where a large project is divided into two types of tasks: one type of tasks, needing frequent interaction with customers, are developed and delivered at the client site; the other type of tasks having little customer interaction are developed and delivered from remote cost-competitive development centers in India and other countries. (Infosys—Global Delivery Model, 2004; Mehta, et al., 2007; Trimble, 2008)

The success of using the Global Delivery Model needed fulfillment of the *second learning goal* for employees of Infosys—learning agility to quickly adapt to changing technology and changing mission of the company. There was need for the employees to quickly get up to date on new technologies and the ability to handle new challenges. There was also a need for knowledge flows across numerous Infosys global development centers. Both needs pointed to the development and utilization of the company's knowledge assets for formal as well as informal learning. (Infosys—GDM, 2004; Mehta, et al., 2007; Trimble, 2008)

Knowledge Management and Knowledge Flows at Infosys. The need of infrastructure for knowledge flows and knowledge management within the organization was realized earlier by Nandan Nilekani, the new CEO, in 1999. A formal knowledge management program had therefore been launched. In addition to capturing and facilitating the flow of implicit company knowledge, the knowledge management program aimed to manage explicit knowledge such as "project documents, client reports, reusable software code, and previous architectural diagrams." A five-level Knowledge Management Maturity model (on the lines of the SEI Capability Maturity Model for software) was conceptualized to aid the knowledge management implementation. Overall, all this work resulted in the creation of Wikis; Blogs; Discussion Forums; K-mails (for employees to reach experts within the company), e-learning avenues, Knowledge Management Portal (K Shop); Process Asset Database (PAD), an online system that captures knowledge on project deliverables such as project plans, design documents; People Knowledge Map (PKM), directory of experts in various fields within the company; WebEx (for live meetings); Bulletin Boards for special interests; Tech Series seminars; InfyTV that broadcasts learning programs; online assessment tools; and Lex, an open-source mobile platform for teaching courses on the current skills that the employees need. (Chari and Gill, 2015; Gale, 2019; Garud, et al., 2005; Infosys—Wingspan/LEX, 2022; Mallon, 2010; Mehta, et al., 2007; Srinidhi and Priya, 2019)

Knowledge Management Portal, called K Shop, was developed as a central live resource for capturing and sharing explicit and implicit knowledge that the company has gained over the years through its work on client projects. K Shop had early beginnings when it was called Body of Knowledge (BoK). An important element of knowledge in K Shop is the knowledge contributed to it by the employees. The employees are encouraged and rewarded for their contributions. The usefulness of employee contributions is tracked over time and the top contributors are regularly presented awards. The knowledge within K Shop is organized using a taxonomy that includes the following at the topmost level: Technology, Methodology, Application Domain, Project Management, Culture, and Soft Skills. (Batool, 2017; Chari and Gill, 2015; Mallon, 2010; Mehta, et al., 2007)

The validity of the approach used by Infosys Global Education Center in providing organization-specific and career-long learning to the Infosys employees is confirmed by the success of the company and the external accolades Infosys GEC has received over the years.

13.3.2 Diffusion

Awards

Infosys has won numerous awards over the years, including the following awards related to the organization-specific career-long learning nature of this innovation (Infosys—Overview, 2022):

- Golden Peacock National Training Award for IT sector, 2006 (Varma and Ravi, 2017)
- NASSCOM Digital Skills Award, 2017
- CorpU's 'Learning Excellence and Innovation' Award, 2013
- Best Learning and Development Award, 2012
- Global Most Admired Knowledge Enterprises (MAKE) Award in 2007, 2005, 2004, and 2003 and entered the Global MAKE Hall of Fame

Overseas Expansion of Training

- Opening of a Design and Innovation Hub in Providence, Rhode Island, USA (Selingo, 2018)
- Five-year deal with Purdue University, Indiana, USA, for providing joint research and training for Infosys employees working in USA (Seltzer, 2017)
- Technology and Innovation Hubs (Infosys—Overview, 2022)
  i. Raleigh, North Carolina, USA
  ii. Hartford, Connecticut, USA
  iii. Indianapolis, Indiana, USA
  iv. Phoenix, Arizona, USA
  v. Richardson, Texas, USA

13.4 INNOVATION RESULTS

Infosys has become a global model for organization-specific career-long training (AITSL, 2013; Ark, 2019; O'Donnell, 2019; Pink, 2017)

Infosys Global Education Center has delivered over 45 "new-age technology courses" and trained 238,000 professionals since 2005 (Infosys—GEC, 2022).

13.5 APPLICABLE KNOWLEDGE & KNOWLEDGE CONTRIBUTION

Models/Metamodels

Unmet Social Need (Hetherington, 2008; see Chapter 1)

Despite good educational background, IT companies face the problem of employees often lacking the right disposition to operate in the workplace and to represent company ethos and values. Any company in the IT sector faces constant change in technology; each new technology represents a new learning requirement for employees. Infosys provides carefully crafted on-board training and supports continuous, relevant learning and development paths throughout an employee's career.

Global Education Center Continuous Improvement

Global Education Center keeps the training courses in tune with new technologies and learning requirements in the horizon. This is an example of Continuous Quality Improvement. (American Society for Quality, 2023)

Incorporating Multidimensionality

Infosys employs the central principle that new skills are multidimensional. Training is designed to cover all dimensions—specifics of a new technology, the necessary knowledge and practices of a domain, and associated behavior training. The training is coupled with a carefully orchestrated assessment. (AITSL, 2013; Mallon, 2010)

Social Enterprise Business Model Template (see Chapter 1, Section 1.2.2)

The model, shown in Figure 13.1, summarizes the overall business model of Infosys GEC in accordance with the template provided by Figure 1.2 of Chapter 1. The eleven components of the business model are briefly described below.

Mission – Goals

The mission of the Infosys Global Education Center is to design and develop an in-house corporate university—Global Education Center (GEC)—to provide organization-specific career-long learning to Infosys employees. It provides an orientation to new employees and continuous learning of current relevant and future IT knowledge as well as reskilling to its employees.

Infosys Global Education Center (Organization-Specific Career-Long Learning) Overall Business Model				
Mission Design and develop, Infosys Global Education Center, a for-profit social enterprise, for providing organization-specific career-long learning to the employees of Infosys.				

Key Partners	Key Activities	Value Proposition	Customer/ Beneficiary Relationships	Customer/ Beneficiary Segments
• Project managers and staff • Marketing managers and staff • Business managers and staff • Training managers and staff	• Creation and upgradation of organizational, physical, and technology infrastructure • Creation and maintenance of K Shop • Delivery of multidimensional face-to-face learning and e-learning • Identification of future knowledge and skill sets	• Infosys-specific career-long learning system (K Shop) • Ongoing training provided to new and existing employees.	• Face-to-face learning • e-Learning	• Employees of Infosys
	Key Resources • Funding from Infosys • Learning campus with appropriate physical and technology infrastructure • Qualified teaching staff		**Channels** • Classrooms • Online learning portal	

Cost Structures	Revenue Streams
• Fixed Cost: Creation of Infosys GEC, technology infrastructure, and learning web portal • Running Cost: Staff salaries, software, Infosys GEC maintenance and upgradation	• Funding from Infosys

Impact
• Productivity of Infosys employees • Attracting new contracts • Growth of Infosys

FIGURE 13.1

Infosys Global Education Center (GEC) Overall Business Model summarized in Social Enterprise Business Model Template shown in Figure 1.2.

Key Partners – Needed for the Social Enterprise to Work

The key partners of GEC are the different types of managers (and staff) – Project managers who identify the current knowledge and skill sets essential for Infosys employees; marketing managers who identify the future knowledge and skill sets essential for Infosys to stay competitive; business managers who create and upgrade the organizational knowledge; and training managers who deliver multidimensional face-to-face learning and e-learning.

Key Activities – Performed for the Business to Function

The following key activities are performed by GEC of Infosys to function:

  i. Creation and upgradation of the organizational, technology and physical infrastructure.

ii. Identification of the current knowledge and skill sets essential for Infosys employees—creation and ongoing maintenance of the K Shop of Infosys.

iii.Delivery of the multidimensional face-to-face learning and e-learning of Infosys employees.

iv. Identification of the future knowledge and skill sets essential for Infosys to stay competitive.

Key Resources – Needed to make the Business Model Work

The key resources needed by Infosys GEC to function are: Ongoing funding from Infosys; physical and technology infrastructure for the Global Education Center; and hiring of qualified training staff.

Customer/Beneficiary Segments – Served by the Social Enterprise

The customer/beneficiary segments served by GEC are the new and existing employees of Infosys.

Value Proposition – Products and/or Services that Create Value to Customers/ Beneficiaries

The products/services that create value to Infosys employees are an up-to-date Infosys-specific learning system for new and existing worldwide employees to bring them up to speed (using K Shop) and their ongoing training to upgrade their knowledge and skills to stay competitive.

Customer/Beneficiary Relationships – with Customer/Beneficiary Segments

The relationships GEC has with Infosys employees are the face-to-face multidimensional training it provides to the new and existing employees and the asynchronous e-learning it provides to them through its K Shop.

Channels – to Interface with Customer/Beneficiary Segments

The channels GEC uses to interface with the Infosys employees are the classrooms/training rooms and the online training it provides through it Learning Portal using its K Shop.

Cost Structures – Costs Incurred to Operate the Social Enterprise

The fixed costs of the Infosys GEC are the cost of creating its physical infrastructure, its technology infrastructure, and its learning web portal that includes the K Shop. The running cost of Infosys GEC comprises of its staff salaries, cost of its software, and the cost of the regular mainten-ance and upgrade of its physical, technology and learning web portal.

Revenue Streams – Cash Generated from Each Customer/Beneficiary Segment
Infosys GEC does not directly generate any cash. However, it contributes to the success and expansion of Infosys. Infosys funds GEC from its earnings.

Impact
The impact of GEC can be measured through the significant contribution it has made to the productivity of Infosys employees, Infosys success in acquiring new businesses, and the overall growth of Infosys.

REFERENCES

AITSL. (2013). "Organization-Specific, Career-Long Learning: Infosys," in *Six Case Studies of Innovation in Professional Learning and Performance and Development*, Australian Institute for Teaching and School Leadership (AITSL), October 2013. www.aitsl.edu.au/docs/default-source/default-document-library/case_studies_detailed.pdf?sfvrsn=e8c1ec3c_0 (last accessed on December 14, 2023).

American Society for Quality. (2023). "Continuous Improvement." https://asq.org/quality-resources/continuous-improvement (last accessed on December 14, 2023).

Ark, T.A. (2019). "How a Global Tech Giant Is Becoming a Learning Leader." *Forbes*, January 24, 2019. www.forbes.com/sites/tomvanderark/2019/01/24/how-a-global-tech-giant-is-becoming-a-learning-leader/#7e5c5d347623 (last accessed on December 14, 2023).

Batool, M. (2017). https://cupdf.com/document/case-study-infosys-58a07d9dbdfe9.html (last accessed on December 14, 2023).

Business Standard. (2013). "Infosys Announces Expansion of Mysore Campus," BS Reporter, January 20, 2013. www.business-standard.com/article/companies/infosys-announces-expansion-of-mysore-campus-109091500151_1.html (last accessed on December 14, 2023).

Chari, K. and Gill, G. (2015). "Infosys: Meeting the Knowledge Management Challenge," *Journal of Information Technology Education: Discussion Cases*, 4, p. 2, February 15, 2015. www.jite.org/documents/DCVol04/v04-02-Infosys.pdf (last accessed on December 14, 2023).

Gale, S.F. (2019). "The Success of Lex," April 16, 2019. www.chieflearningofficer.com/2019/04/16/the-success-of-lex/ (last accessed on December 14, 2023).

Garud, R., Sambamurthy, V., and Kumaraswamy, A. (2005). "Harnessing Knowledge Resources for Increasing Returns: Scalable Structuration at Infosys Technologies." In E. Hess and R. Kazanjian (Eds.), *The Search for Organic Growth* (pp. 211–243). Cambridge University Press. www.researchgate.net/publication/228648507_Harnessing_Knowledge_Resources_for_Increasing_Returns_Scalable_Structuration_at_Infosys_Technologies (last accessed on December 14, 2023).

Hetherington, D. (2008). "Case Studies in Social Innovation: A Background paper," Per Capita, October 2008. https://apo.org.au/sites/default/files/resource-files/2009-01/apo-nid3954.pdf (last accessed on Bhim (2020)). "Infosys Training for Freshers." https://infosysmysore.in/infosys-training/ (last accessed on December 14, 2023).

Infosys—E&R Journey. (2011). S. Gopalakrishnan: "The Education and Research Journey." www.infosys.com/content/dam/infosys-web/en/investors/reports-filings/annual-rep ort/annual/Documents/AR-2011/Theme-Pages/education_research.html (last accessed on December 14, 2023).

Infosys—GDM. (2004). "Global Delivery Model," April 15, 2004. www.infosys.com/newsr oom/press-releases/2004/global-delivery-model-evaluation.html (last accessed on December 14, 2023).

Infosys—GEC. (2023). "Global Education Center – Training at Infosys Global Education Center." www.infosys.com/careers/graduates/global-education-center.html (last accessed on December 14, 2023).

Infosys—GEC II. (2009). "Global Education Center II." www.infosys.com/newsroom/press-releases/2009/global-education-center-ii.html (last accessed on December 14, 2023).

Infosys—GEC Inauguration. (2005). "Global Education Center." www.infosys.com/newsr oom/press-releases/2005/pm-visit-mysore-infosys.html (last accessed on December 14, 2023).

Infosys—Overview. (2022). "Overview." www.infosys.com/about/Pages/index.aspx (last accessed on December 14, 2023).

Infosys Training. (2012). "Infosys celebrates a decade of training at its Mysore campus," www.infosys.com/newsroom/press-releases/2012/foundation-programme-mysore.html (last accessed on December 14, 2023).

Infosys—Wingspan/LEX. (2022). https://lex.infosysapps.com/en/public/about (last accessed on December 14, 2023).

Mallon, D. (2010). "Organizational Learning Agility: The Learning Organization at Infosys is the Engine Powering its Business Success." Case Study, Bersin & Associates, August 2010. https://documents.pub/document/adp-case-study-this-case-study-a-global-it-consulting-outsourcing-and-business.html (last accessed on December 14, 2023).

Mehta, N., Oswald, S., and Mehta, A. (2007). "Infosys Technologies: Improving organizational knowledge flows," *Journal of Information Technology*, 22, pp. 456–464. https://libres. uncg.edu/ir/uncg/f/N_Mehta_Infosys_2007.pdf (last accessed on December 14, 2023).

O'Donnell, R. (2019). "How Infosys Trains Employees to Keep Up with the Market," *HRDrive*, April 9, 2019. www.hrdive.com/news/how-infosys-trains-employees-to-keep-up-with-the-market/552183/ (last accessed on December 14, 2023).

Pink, A. (2017) "Lifelong Learning Is an Economic Imperative." *The Economist*. https://blog. anderspink.com/2017/01/lifelong-learning-is-an-economic-imperative-findings-from-the-economists-special-report/ (last accessed on December 14, 2023).

Selingo, J. (2018). "The Third Education Revolution," *The Atlantic Daily*, March 22, 2018. www. theatlantic.com/education/archive/2018/03/the-third-education-revolution/556091/ (last accessed on December 14, 2023).

Seltzer, R. (2017). "Purdue Tackles Job Training," *Inside-Higher-Ed*, News release on Purdue University contracting with Infosys for job training, August 18, 2017. www.insidehighe red.com/news/2017/08/18/purdue-play-key-role-infosys-us-hiring-and-training-push (last accessed on December 14, 2023).

Srinidhi, P. and Priya, B.K. (2019). "Implementation of knowledge management in Infosys," *Emperor International Journal of Finance and Management Research*, V (2), February 2019. www.eijfmr.com/2019/feb_2019/feb-2019-12.pdf (last accessed on December 14, 2023).

Sun, S. (2023). "IT Industry in India – Statistics & Facts," December 11, 2023. Statista.com. www.statista.com/topics/2256/it-industry-in-india/#dossierKeyfigures (last accessed on December 14, 2023).

Trimble, C. (2008). "Infosys: Maintaining an Edge," Case, Tuck School of Business at Dartmouth, 2008. https://mba.tuck.dartmouth.edu/pages/faculty/chris.trimble/osi/downloads/DisciplinedInnovation/20026-InfosysMaintaingAnEdge.pdf (last accessed on December 14, 2023).

UKEssays (2015). "Training and Development in Infosys Management Essay." www.ukessays.com/essays/management/training-and-development-in-infosys-management-essay.php (last accessed on December 14, 2023).

Varma, G.R. and Ravi, J. (2017, May). "Training and Development in MNC: A Case Study on Infosys," *International Journal & Magazine of Engineering, Technology, Management and Research*. 4, p. 5. www.ijmetmr.com/olmay2017/GedelaRakeshVarma-JaladiRavi-68.pdf (last accessed on December 14, 2023).

14

The Big Issue, United Kingdom: Income-Earning Model for Homeless People

14.1 OVERVIEW

Street newspapers or magazines are sold by homeless or poor people and are produced mainly to provide support to these segments of the population. Their origin dates to the late nineteenth century but the modern street newspaper began with the 1989 publication of *Street News* in New York City and the *Street Sheen* in San Francisco. *Street News* was an inspiration for the founding of *The Big Issue*. (Admin, 2018; Hetherington, 2008)

The Big Issue (TBI) is the world's best-known street magazine (newspaper) founded in 1991 in London (U.K.) by John Bird and Gordon Roddick as a not-for-profit social enterprise and is now published in four continents—Europe, Australia, Asia, and Africa, and in North and South America as sister publications; it was launched in Melbourne (Australia) in 1996. It helps homeless people or those at risk of homelessness to earn income. (Burns, 2016)

The Big Issue addresses homelessness by providing an income-earning model for individuals and builds their self-esteem. It operates a simple business model in which homeless people buy the paper at a discounted price—40 to 50% off the cover price, and then sell it at its retail cost, keeping the difference as profit. The purpose of the innovation is financial inclusion of homeless people though self-help and to build their self-esteem. (Hetherington, 2008)

Originally begun in the UK, The Big Issue has spread to Ireland, Australia, Japan, South Korea, Taiwan, South Africa, Malawi, Kenya, and Namibia. It has also expanded from traditional street newspaper fare to include fiction issues and has gone digital by selling an access card (for reading online rather than from a hardcopy edition) and has addressed cashless trends by providing

DOI: 10.1201/9781003479086-18

vendors with card readers. (Gerrard, 2017; Hetherington, 2008; The Big Issue, nd)

The rest of the chapter describes in detail design of the not-for-profit social innovation (and the corresponding social enterprise), The Big Issue (Income-Earning Model for Homeless People).

14.2 CONTEXT

John Bird and Gordon Roddick, social entrepreneurs, were aware of increasing homelessness in London. They were inspired by *Street News*, a newspaper (magazine) sold by homeless people in New York city. Thus, it was not based on an original idea. But the entrepreneurial drive of Bird and Roddick plus the favorable social perceptions towards homeless people in London were important factors in the launch of the newspaper and its success. (Hanks and Swinithinbank, 1997. Hetherington, 2008)

14.3 INNOVATION DEVELOPMENT JOURNEY

14.3.1 Lap(s) / Stage(s)

14.3.1.1 Lap (Stage) 1 (1991–2012): Develop Street Newspaper for London

14.3.1.1.1 Problem Definition

Provide a way for the homeless people of London to earn income.

14.3.1.1.2 Suggestion

Start by using the model provided by *Street News* of New York City to start a street newspaper in London to provide a means to earn income by homeless people.

14.3.1.1.3 Solution Development, Evaluation, and Implementation

A street magazine (newspaper) called *The Big Issue (TBI)* was mooted as a monthly publication. Homeless people would be made vendors of the magazine (newspaper). They would acquire copies of *The Big Issue* at wholesale cost and sell them at retail price, thus earning profit.

A social enterprise company called the Big Issue Company was set up for publication of The Big Issue. The Body Shop, a British cosmetic, skin care, and perfume company provided the initial capital of US$ 50,000. The magazine was sold for 80 pence, after buying it from *The Big Issue* at 35 pence. It was initially started as a monthly paper but on popular demand became fortnightly in 1992 and weekly in 1993. In 1995, The Big Issue Foundation was formed as a charity arm of The Big Issue Company with the aim of providing support to the magazine vendors on issues such as housing, health, and addiction. (Hanks and Swithinbank, 1997)

After the initial successful launch of the magazine with capital from the Body Shop, it gradually started getting financed from its sales and advertising revenue with surplus revenues given to The Big Issue Foundation. Initially the circulation of The Big Issue was 30,000 copies per month, which has grown to 300,000 per week. The Big Issue staff members also have grown from four to 90 in the London office. (Hanks and Swithinbank, 2017)

In addition to issues of homelessness, the magazine covers news and a broad range of topics including films, music, books, and current social issues. This way it remains interesting and engages the reader. Two thirds of the magazine readers are under the age of 44 and 60% are under the age of 34; fifty four percent of the readers are female. (Hanks and Swithinbank, 2017)

The potential vendors of The Big Issue need to register, and they need to provide proof for being homeless or nearly homeless. At the time of registration, the vendors sign a code of conduct and must complete a two-week training program. They are provided a badge, two free copies of the magazine, and a designated pitch where they must sell the magazine after buying copies of the paper from The Big Issue Company. The number of vendors who sell the magazine (including its regional issues) varies between 8,000 and 10,000. The income of the vendors varies depending upon the defined pitch where they sell the magazine, the number of hours they work per day, and their selling abilities. (Hanks and Swithinbank, 2017)

The Big Issue co-founded the Glasgow-based International Network of Street Papers (INSP) in 1994. INSP has helped in the growth of over 100 fellow street papers across 41 countries following a Street Paper Charter that spells out the principles of the international street paper movement. (Greenslade, 2012)

14.3.1.1.4 Circumscription

The business model of The Big Issue worked well and was adopted in other cities and countries. However, in-print newspaper publications were suffering increasing pressure from online options.

14.3.1.2 Lap (Stage) 2 (2012–2018): Provide Online Buying Option

14.3.1.2.1 Problem Definition

The number of online news sources had mushroomed by now. Thus, there was need to address the pressure to TBI from such sources. (Greenslade, 2012)

14.3.1.2.2 Suggestion

Provide an online option for TBI while continuing with the print editions.

14.3.1.2.3 Solution Development, Evaluation, and Implementation

The customers were enabled to opt for an online version. The vendors started selling a card with a code to access online version while continuing to sell the print edition of the paper, thus fulfilling the objectives of this lap (stage). (Greenslade, 2012)

14.3.1.2.4 Circumscription

The online option worked well – customer has option: pay for the print edition of the paper or buy the online access code for the paper. However, fewer customers were having cash.

14.3.1.3 Lap (Stage) 3 (2018-): Provide Non-cash Buying Option

14.3.1.3.1 Problem Definition

To retain viability, customers need to have non-cash option. (Siddique, 2018)

14.3.1.3.2 Suggestion

Let customers use credit or debit card for payment.

14.3.1.3.3 Solution Development, Evaluation, and Implementation

Card reader capability was provided to vendors. Simple, mobile card reader that is easily operated by vendor were provided, thus fulfilling the objectives of this lap (stage). (Siddique, 2018)

14.3.1.3.4 Circumscription

Next challenges may include widening content of publication, expanding from news to include fiction or other topical issues; or considering a rebranding of the TBI as "Helping Homeless Help Themselves" so that the newspaper cares as much as about providing quality content; or considering how to expand vendors' demographics (the majority of whom are men).

14.3.2 Diffusion

The Big Issue has proven to be a successful self-sustaining social enterprise. It started in the UK and over the years, it has expanded its coverage to many countries in four continents. In the very first twenty-five years, it has spread throughout the world with many sister publications and more than 100 street newspapers across 41 countries in cities such as Athens, Greece; Mexico City, Mexico; Seattle, Washington; St Petersburg, Russia; Bergen, Norway; Buenos Aires, Argentina. All these publications are linked through the Glasgow-based International Network of Street Papers, co-founded by The Big Issue. (Burns, 2016)

The Big Issue Foundation charity was formed by The Big Issue in 1995. The Foundation gets its funds from the surplus funds of the magazine as well as from donations of trusts, corporations, and pubic. It provides important tasks of providing housing assistance to vendors of the magazine, helping vendors to become effective sales teams, aiding in training them in basic skills, and counseling them in their alcohol or drug use. (Hanks and Swinithinbank, 2017)

In 2002, The Big Issue launched its social investment arm that was initially called Social Brokers but eventually became Big Issue Invest, whose mission is "to dismantle poverty by creating opportunity, through self-help, social trading and business solutions." Big Issue Invest provides loans through avenues of Early Stage Investing and Social Impact Loans as well as invests in established mission-led businesses. (The Big Issue Invest Impact Report, 2018)

The Big Issue has earned the following major awards:

- (October 2004): UN Habitat Scroll of Honor Award
- (October 2008): Ernst and Young Social Entrepreneur of the Year Award

14.4 INNOVATION RESULTS

The Big Issue has become a successful social not-for-profit enterprise. In the first twenty-five years of its existence it has spread throughout the world. It has provided its vendors a chance to work and earn some income. This increases their self-esteem and dignity. However, most vendors earn very limited income. While being vendors of The Big Issue, provides them social exposure, the public and visible nature of the work makes it stressful. Thus, based on a study in Australia, a market-based business initiative like TBI cannot be a substitute for government intervention in addressing structural inequalities in the society. (Burns, 2016; Gerrard, 2017; Hibbert, et al., 2002; Lin, 2017; Lobb, 2021; Schmidhauser, 2013)

With the accession of several central and east European countries to European Union starting in 2004, there was an increase in migration to UK from these countries. Becoming vendors of TBI provided a legal way to earn in UK for these people since TBI vendors are classified as self-employed. (Hills, 2013)

14.5 APPLICABLE KNOWLEDGE & KNOWLEDGE CONTRIBUTION

Models/Metamodels

Unmet Social Need (Hetherington, 2008; see Chapter 1)

This is what qualifies an innovation to become a social innovation and instantiates the Unmet Social Need metamodel discussed in Chapter 1. The basic social need addressed by this innovation is the dual problem of homeless people not getting employment due to employer mistrust and their inability to sustain employment due to lack of adequate skills and self-confidence. The Big Issue solved both problems by providing homeless people employment through self-help, which gradually improved their self-confidence and esteem.

Creative Matching (Hetherington, 2008; see Chapter 1)

It was observed that there was a latent demand for street newspapers, which could provide opportunity to provide work for homeless people.

This observation was combined with the idea of making the homeless self-employed vendors of the Big Issue instead of employing them, with the addition of making them sign a code of conduct that regulated their behavior. (Hetherington, 2008)

Iterative Development (Hetherington, 2008; see Chapter 1)

The newspaper had to experiment with what would be the right frequency of its publication. It started as a monthly publication, experimented with the fortnightly format, and finally settled for the weekly frequency, which proved to be successful. (Hetherington, 2008)

Adaptive Organizational Forms (Hetherington, 2008; see Chapter 1)

The Big Issue struggled with adapting to different phases of its growth. While John Bird was a very good startup champion and established the newspaper, he was not as capable of running the publication of a newspaper. The success of the newspaper provided opportunities for its international expansion through an international franchise, that was created and needed to be managed, which needed new skills. The international franchise helped the newspaper expand to Australia, Japan, and South Korea. The sustainability of the newspaper was another issue that needed to be carefully managed. It was a good decision to establish the newspaper as a not-for-profit social innovation. Over time, The Big Issue company started generating profits, which have been channeled through a foundation called the Big Issue Foundation. The foundation also supports various services for the homeless. (Hetherington, 2008)

Technology Empowerment (Joshi and Rohrig, 2014; see Chapter 1)

As time progressed, The Big Issue needed to provide options to buy online versions and the option to purchase using debit or credit cards. Such options were provided to maintain the customer base.

Social Enterprise Business Model Template (see Chapter 1, Section 1.2.2)

The model, shown in Figure 14.1, summarizes the overall business model of TBI in accordance with the template provided by Figure 1.2 of Chapter 1. The eleven components of the business model are briefly described below.

Mission – Goals

The mission of The Big Issue (TBI), a not-for-profit enterprise, is to develop a street newspaper in London that can serve as an income-earning

The Big Issue (Income Earning Model for Homeless People) Overall Business Model				
Mission: Develop the not-for-profit social enterprise, The Big Issue (TBI), a street newspaper publishing vehicle for providing an income-earning model for homeless people.				
Key Partners	Key Activities	Value Proposition	Customer/ Beneficiary Relationships	Customer/ Beneficiary Segments
• Body Shop, UK (Anita Roddick, Founder)	• Daily creation of content of TBI and its publication • Training of TBI vendors • Wholesale selling of TBI. **Key Resources** • Continuous funding from sales and advertising • TBI managerial, editorial, and other staff • Newspaper vendors— homeless people (or those at risk of homelessness)	• Homeless people earn a living. • Profit earned from selling TBI street newspaper.	• Selling street newspaper at wholesale price to homeless people (or those at risk of homelessness) **Channels** • TBI street newspaper in print and digital edition	• Homeless people or those at risk of homelessness
Cost Structures • Fixed Cost: Creation of organizational and physical infrastructure • Running Cost: Staff salaries, software, cost of publishing TBI newspaper		Revenue Streams • Sale of TBI and advertising revenues		
Impact • Earning and Empowerment of homeless people (or those at risk of homelessness) and building of their self-esteem				

FIGURE 14.1

The Big Issue (TBI) Overall Business Model summarized in Social Enterprise Business Model Template shown in Figure 1.2.

model for homeless people to earn a living by selling a local London Street newspaper.

Key Partners – Needed for the Social Enterprise to Work

The founding partner of TBI is Body Shop, a British skin care company founded by Anita Roddick (wife of Gordon Roddick). Body Shop provided the initial capital of US$ 50,000 for founding of the not-for-profit social enterprise company by John Bird and Gordon Roddick.

Key Activities – Performed for the Business to Function

The key activities performed to run The Big Issue (TBI) are: Daily content creation and its publication of TBI; wholesale selling of TBI; and training of TBI vendors.

Key Resources – Needed to make the Business Model Work

The key resources needed for the functioning of TBI after it was founded has been its continuous funding from its sales revenue and advertising revenue; its managerial, editorial, and other staff; and its vendors—homeless or potentially homeless people.

Customer/Beneficiary Segments – Served by the Social Enterprise

The customer/beneficiary segments of TBI are homeless and potentially homeless people, and the public who purchase the street newspaper.

Value Proposition – Products and/or Services that Create Value to Customers/ Beneficiaries

The Value Proposition of TBI is the respectable earnings by homeless people. Additionally, it is the profit earned from selling TBI street newspaper, which helps in sustaining and propagating the newspaper.

Customer/Beneficiary Relationships – with Customer/Beneficiary Segments

The customer/beneficiary relationships of TBI are the selling of the street newspaper at wholesale price to homeless or potentially people so that they can sell at a higher retail price and earn income and making available a street newspaper to public.

Channels – to Interface with Customer/Beneficiary Segments

The Big Issue newspaper interfaces with its vendors and readers in print and digital formats.

Cost Structures – Costs Incurred to Operate the Social Enterprise

The costs incurred to operate the business have two components: the fixed cost and the running cost. The fixed cost is in the creation of the organizational and physical infrastructure. The running cost includes staff salaries, cost of software, and the cost of publishing the TBI newspaper.

Revenue Streams – Cash Generated from Each Customer Segment

The revenue streams of TBI are the revenue from the wholesale sale of the street newspaper to its vendors (the homeless people) and the advertising revenues.

Impact

The street newspaper has produced a major impact regarding the homeless (and nearly homeless poor) people. It has created a new model for providing regular income to such people that also builds their image, self-respect, and self-esteem. It has thus empowered homeless people.

REFERENCES

Admin. (2018). "Building a Movement to End Homelessness," May 24, 2018. National Coalition for the Homeless. https://nationalhomeless.org/tbt-street-newspapers/ (last accessed on March 3, 2022).

Burns, A. (2016). "From London to the World: How the Big Issue Went Global," 27 October 2016, The Big Issue News. www.bigissue.com/news/london-world-big-issue-went-global/ (last accessed on December 14, 2023).

Gerrard, J. (2017). "This Is What the Lives of Big Issue Sellers Tell Us About Working and Being Homeless," *The Conversation*, September 21, 2017. http://theconversation.com/this-is-what-the-lives-of-big-issue-sellers-tell-us-about-working-and-being-homeless-83965 (last accessed on December 14, 2023).

Greenslade, R. (2012). "Big Issue magazine Goes Digital," *The Guardian*, October 25, 2012. www.theguardian.com/media/greenslade/2012/oct/25/the-big-issue-digital-media (last accessed on December 14, 2023).

Hanks, S., and Swithinbank, T. (1997, April). "The Big Issue and other street papers: a response to homelessness,". *Environment and Urbanization*, 9: 1, SAGE. https://journals.sagepub.com/doi/pdf/10.1177/095624789700900112 (last accessed on December 14, 2023).

Hetherington, D. (2008). "Case Studies in Social Innovation: A Background Paper," Per Capita, October 2008. https://apo.org.au/sites/default/files/resource-files/2009-01/apo-nid3954.pdf (last accessed on December 14, 2023).

Hibbert, S.A., Hogg, G., and Quinn, T. (2002). "Consumer response to social entrepreneurship: The case of the Big Issue in Scotland," *International Journal of Nonprofit and Voluntary Marketing*, 7 (3), pp. 288–301. www.academia.edu/16465430/Consumer_response_to_social_entrepreneurship_the_case_of_the_Big_Issue_in_Scotland (last accessed on December 14, 2023).

Hills, S. (2013). "A Third of Big Issue Vendors Are Now from East Europe, Magazine Founder Reveals," December 22, 2013. *Daily Mail*. www.dailymail.co.uk/news/article-2527822/A-Big-Issue-vendors-eastern-European-countries-magazines-founder-reveals.html (last accessed on March 14, 2022).

Joshi, S. and Rohrig, E. (2014). "Moving Innovation Forward; Case Studies: 10 Sustainable and Inclusive Business Models," GIZ India, New Delhi. www.giz.de/en/downloads/giz2014-en-moving-innovation-forward-india.pdf (last accessed on December 12, 2023).

Lin, S. (2017). "Inspiration Exploring for Entrepreneurship through Case Analysis on the Development of the Big Issue," *Universal Journal of Industrial and Business Management*, 5 (2), pp. 23–27. www.hrpub.org/download/20170830/UJIBM1-11610017.pdf (last accessed on December 14, 2023).

Lobb, A. (2021). "The Big Issue at 30: How Has Homelessness Changed since the First Issue," September 21, 2021. *The Big Issue News*. www.bigissue.com/news/the-big-issue-at-30-how-has-homelessness-changed-since-our-first-edition/ (last accessed on December 14, 2023).

Schmidhauser, T. (2013). "The Big Issue Magazine Brand Audit Report 2013," May 24, 2013. www.slideshare.net/TabataSch/the-big-issue-magazine-final-report (last accessed on December 14, 2023).

Siddique, H. (2018). "Big Issue to Trial Card Readers after Steep Decline in Carrying Cash," *The Guardian*, December 2, 2018. www.theguardian.com/society/2018/dec/03/big-issue-to-trial-card-readers-after-steep-decline-in-carrying-cash (last accessed December 14, 2023).

The Big Issue. (nd). "About Us." www.bigissue.com/about-the-big-issue-group/ (last accessed on December 14, 2023).

15

WorkVentures, Australia: Sustaining Independent Employment

15.1 OVERVIEW

WorkVentures (WorkVentures, 2020) is an Australian not-for-profit social enterprise (WorkVentures Ltd., 2023). It was established in 1979 by Steve Lawrence as a small Christian community entity, called Peninsula Exchange, dedicated to delivering social services to the disadvantaged. Its name was changed to WorkVentures in 1992. (Hetherington, 2008; Social Enterprise Alliance, nd)

Over more than four decades, WorkVentures has been involved in many different activities while not losing focus on its core mission of delivering innovative social services to the disadvantaged. WorkVentures seeks to provide social services without depending on government funded programming, doing this by identifying job skills training where sustaining employment opportunities exist, such as training in computing skills and then providing data-entry services for a community. WorkVentures has provided conventional employment services, business incubation services, as well as community services such as markets, gardens, or legal services. The current chapter focuses on its work for imparting skills to marginalized people to enable them sustained independent employment. (Herbst, 2017; Hetherington, 2008)

The rest of the chapter describes in detail design of the not-for-profit social innovation (and the corresponding social enterprise), WorkVentures (Sustaining Independent Employment).

DOI: 10.1201/9781003479086-19

15.2 CONTEXT

WorkVentures was incorporated in 1984 as Peninsula Community Services Ltd.; it was renamed as WorkVentures in 1992. The rest of the chapter focuses on the realization of WorkVentures in 1984 that its mission is best served by focusing on employment services and aiding in imparting technology skills to create and sustain independent employment. (Herbst, 2017; Hetherington, 2008)

15.3 INNOVATION DEVELOPMENT JOURNEY

15.3.1 Lap(s) / Stage(s)

15.3.1.1 Lap (Stage) (1979-): Establish WorkVentures.

15.3.1.1.1 Problem Definition

The problem addressed was how to assist marginalized persons to acquire and use skills to make them capable of independent employment and to get employment.

15.3.1.1.2 Suggestion

Information technology was an emerging hot area of employment. So, it would make sense to introduce the disadvantaged people to the information technology market.

Solution Development, Evaluation, and Implementation (Campbell, et al., 2020; Thompson, 2008; WorkVentures, 2019; WorkVentures, 2020; WorkVentures Ltd., 2023)

The solution strategy adopted was to be flexible, opportunistic, and collaborative in creating assistance and training programs in the electronics and information technology area.

Collecting and salvaging off-cast personal computers was an attractive area because of the large number of personal computers that were being sold and purchased. Salvaging defective computers and making them reusable would provide an area that could be used for providing productive skills to the disadvantaged. Such refurbished computers could also be used for distribution to the disadvantaged in collaboration with an organization. The training of the disadvantaged people in basic electronics and information technology skills would also make them available for data entry, software installation, technical repair services, and training in software suites.

The above solution approach was implemented in creating successful programs that would evolve in collaboration with the Australian government, corporations, and other like-minded organizations. The following summarizes the major initiatives and milestones reached.

WorkVentures started various skills training programs:

- 1986: It began partnership with Microsoft Australia. It started the *Sydney Information Technology Center* (*Sydney ITeC*) in Surry Hills, Sydney, Australia for job creation through labor market training in computing, electronics, employment placement, and small business development.
- 1988: WorkVentures started Business Incubator as a new business facility at Surrey Hills, Sydney, Australia; it started *ITeC Electronics Repair* (*Sydney ITeC Electronics Repair*) business as a startup in this incubation facility.

WorkVentures formalized its traineeship program:

- 1997: It started *WorkVentures Group Training*, an employment services program in partnership with host employers, that connects people with traineeships and employment opportunities. The selected people are placed with host employers, provided apprenticeship for one to three years, resulting in employment and award of a certificate.
- 2002: WorkVentures started a partnership with the Westpac Group; it established *ConnectIT Low-Cost PC Program* in collaboration with Westpac and Microsoft to supply refurbished computers loaded with software donated by Microsoft, to low-income families, schools, and not-for-profit organizations who could not otherwise afford them. Such computers were also sold at affordable prices.
- 2007: It started *iGetIT* program to provide computer hardware training for indigenous and disadvantaged youth. The program was piloted in areas of inner-city Sydney, regional NSW, and northern Queensland of Australia.
- 2008: WorkVentures began to work in remote communities; it started supplying computers and technical support to the Hope Vale Technology and Knowledge Centre on the Cape York Peninsula of Australia.

- 2010: It started working on i.settle.with.IT program funded by Microsoft targeted to migrant and refugee communities for improvement in software skills and employment opportunities.
- *2015:* WorkVentures founded *KickStart Academy*, a job services program. The academy provides skills for meaningful jobs and career paths to young, disadvantaged people and migrants.

Initiated partnership with IBM:

- 2018: WorkVentures started providing IT agile desk services to Westpac in collaboration with IBM.

15.3.1.1.3 Circumscription

The technical training, employment services programs, and the supply of computers to disadvantaged people has worked well and needs to be continued. There is an ongoing need to maintain existing partnerships and to establish new ones.

15.3.2 Diffusion

WorkVentures has played a major role in Australia in helping reduce the number of young people who are unemployed and in supporting social inclusion through digital technology. (WorkVentures, 2023)

In 2002, WorkVentures, along with three other organizations (AMP Foundation, Benevolent Society, and The Smith Family), established a non-for-profit organization called Social Ventures Australia that works with partners to overcome disadvantage. (Social Ventures Australia, nd).

In 2005, WorkVentures and Microsoft Australia won the Australian Prime Minister's Award in Community Business Partnership, Longevity category.

15.4 INNOVATION RESULTS

Over the years, WorkVentures has assisted many people in getting trained in useful skills that increase their employment opportunities. It has also helped in reducing the digital divide by providing access to computers and the Internet as well as imparting skills for their use. By numbers, WorkVentures has imparted work skills training to nearly 25,000 people and supplied nearly 80,000 computers and related technology and training to young people who otherwise could not access or afford them. (WorkVentures, 2020)

15.5 APPLICABLE KNOWLEDGE & KNOWLEDGE CONTRIBUTION

Models/Metamodels

Unmet Social Need (Hetherington, 2008; see Chapter 1)

The prime objective of WorkVentures has been to help the disadvantaged people of Australia given its resources and the external environment. The principle it adopted was to provide them with skills so that they become capable of independent employment. The use of this principle is what has made WorkVentures successful in helping the disadvantaged. (Hetherington, 2008)

Creative Matching (Hetherington, 2008; see Chapter 1)

Over time, the organization chose different profitable and fruitful activities that followed this strategy. In 1984, it started the Compuskill facility that provided computer training while at the same time the participants would provide book-keeping and desktop publishing services. It also started delving into building partnerships with the private sector. In 1986, it tied up with Microsoft, which made significant contributions to WorkVentures' first Information Technology Center (ITeC) in Surry Hills, Sydney, Australia. The access to external private sector funds enabled WorkVentures to make investments in new social enterprises. (Hetherington, 2008)

Iterative Development (Hetherington, 2008; see Chapter 1)

Iterative development has been extensively used in WorkVentures. Steve Lawrence did not shy from taking risks in trying new business options that could possibly help the disadvantaged. Some of these initiatives failed but WorkVentures used the failures as learning opportunities and bounced back with new initiatives. Examples of such failures are a music IT center in 1988–89 and a joint venture to contract IT services to large organizations in 1994. Use of iterative development has been a useful approach of WorkVentures to become a financially sound social venture. (Hetherington, 2008)

Adaptive Organizational Forms (Hetherington, 2008; see Chapter 1)

WorVentures has gone through many organizational changes through its evolution. It started in 1979 as Peninsula Exchange, a parish group, that offered local community services. It separated from the parish group in 1984 to become a not-for-profit company, Peninsula Community Services. In 1992 it transformed itself again to become WorkVentures that focused on growth and diversification. Steve Lawrence led all these transformations until his retirement in 2007. He, however, continued to be associated with the organization as 'Founder and Social Entrepreneur' to provide his creative ideas. (Hetherington, 2008)

Social Enterprise Business Model Template (see Chapter 1, Section 1.2.2)

The model, shown in Figure 15.1, summarizes the overall business model of WorkVentures in accordance with the template provided by

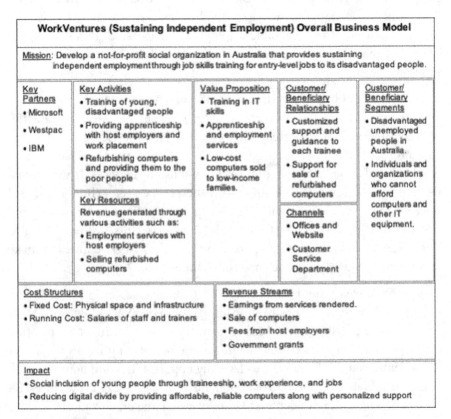

FIGURE 15.1

WorkVentures Overall Business Model summarized in Social Enterprise Business Model Template shown in Figure 1.2.

Figure 1.2 of Chapter 1. The eleven components of the business model are briefly described below.

Mission – Goals

The mission of WorkVentures is to create a not-for-profit social organization to provide sustaining independent employment through job skills training for entry-level jobs to its marginalized people so that they can be gainfully employed. The training of the disadvantaged people in basic electronics and information technology skills would also make them available for data entry, software installation, technical repair services, and training in software suites.

Key Partners – Needed for the Social Enterprise to Work

Microsoft, Westpac, and IBM have been the key partners of WorkVentures in fulfilling its mission.

Key Activities – Performed for the Business to Function

The key activities of WorkVentures have been varied but all of them have been in consonance with its mission of providing or to enabling it to provide job skills training for entry-level jobs to the disadvantaged poor people. In 1986 it started provided training young, disadvantaged people in computing, electronics, and other areas and soon thereafter in electronics repair. In 1997 it started an employment services program in partnership with host employers that connects people with apprenticeship and work placement. In 2002 It also started supplying refurbished computers loaded with donated software, to low-income families.

Key Resources – Needed to make the Business Model Work

WorkVentures is founded as a not-for-profit social organization but has attempted to not be dependent on government funding. It has therefore pursued activities that generated revenue to keep it self-sustaining while at the same time, built capabilities of the disadvantaged people. In carrying out this strategy it has benefited by collaborations with Microsoft Corporation, IBM, and Westpac Group while earning from such activities as proving employment services with host employers and selling of refurbished computers.

Customer/Beneficiary Segments – Served by the Social Enterprise

The company serves disadvantaged unemployed people in Australia and Individuals and organizations who cannot afford computers and other IT equipment.

Value Proposition – Products and/or Services that Create Value to Customers/ Beneficiaries

WorkVentures provides training in IT skills and apprenticeship as well as employment services to unemployed young people. It also provides cheap refurbished computers loaded with software to low-income families.

Customer/Beneficiary Relationships – with Customer/Beneficiary Segments

WorkVentures provides customized support and guidance to its trainees, support for the sale of cheap refurbished computers through the Call Center of ConnectIT, and Business Incubation service at Surrey Hills, Sydney, Australia.

Channels – to Interface with Customer/Beneficiary Segments

The channels WorkVentures uses to interface with its customers and beneficiaries are the offices and customer service departments in various locations and a website.

Cost Structures – Costs Incurred to Operate the Social Enterprise

The fixed cost involved are the cost of the physical space and infrastructure. The running cost incurred is the money spent on salaries to staff and trainers.

Revenue Streams – Cash Generated from Each Customer/Beneficiary Segment

The revenue streams include fees for services rendered to companies, the revenue from sale of computers, fees collected from host employers, and government grants.

Impact

WorkVentures is a successful not-for-profit social organization that has provided employment and social inclusion to young, disadvantaged people through traineeship, work experience, and jobs. It has also helped in reducing digital divide by providing affordable, reliable computers along with personalized support.

REFERENCES

Campbell, P., Barraket, J., Suchowerska, R., McNeill, J., and Moussa, B. (2020). "WorkVentures Case Study," February 2020. https://researchbank.swinburne.edu.au/file/8b2b6f17-5ab9-4e9e-b2e5-43811b79a5ee/1/2020-campbell-workventures_case_study.pdf (last accessed December 14, 2023).

Herbst, J.M. (2017). "How Australian social enterprises use strategic marketing and social marketing to drive accountability and change for sustainable development," Doctoral Dissertation, 2017. https://eprints.qut.edu.au/103631/1/Judith%20Herbst%20Thesis.pdf (last accessed December 14, 2023).

Hetherington, D. (2008). "Case Studies in Social Innovation – A Background Paper," June 2008. https://apo.org.au/sites/default/files/resource-files/2009-01/apo-nid3954.pdf (last accessed on December 14, 2023).

Social Enterprise Alliance. (nd). "A Business Planning Guide for Social Enterprises: Putting the pieces together," Social Ventures Australia, May 27, 2020 https://socialventures.com.au/assets/Business_Planning_Guide_for_Social_Enterprise.pdf (last accessed December 14, 2023).

Social Ventures Australia. (nd). www.google.com/url?sa=t&rct=j&q=&esrc=s&source=web&cd=&ved=2ahUKEwjMrYSStLf3AhXQmuAKHbYPD90QFnoECAgQAQ&url=https%3A%2F%2Fwww.socialventures.com.au%2F&usg=AOvVaw1wj9yBdN9AHb-0jK64IjeU (last accessed on December 14, 2023).

Thompson, D. (2008). "Forces at Work—How 10 not-for-profits tackled unemployment and more in their communities; Case Study 5 on WorkVentues," Jobs Australia. www.pc.gov.au/inquiries/completed/not-for-profit/submissions/sub104-attachment.pdf (last accessed on December 14, 2023).

Work Ventures. (2019). "Social Impact Report". https://workventures.com.au/wp-content/uploads/2020/04/Social-Impact-Report-2019.pdf (last accessed December 14, 2023).

WorkVentures. (2020). https://workventures.com.au (last accessed on December 14, 2023).

WorkVentures Ltd. (2023). www.acnc.gov.au/charity/charities/f748023d-38af-e811-a963-000d3ad24077/profile (last accessed December 14, 2023).

Part V

Transforming Farming

"If agriculture goes wrong, nothing else will have a chance to go right."

M. S. Swaminathan

"The ultimate goal of farming is not the growing of crops, but the cultivation and perfection of human beings."

Masanobu Fukoka

"The discovery of agriculture was the first step toward a civilized life."

Arthur Keith

Chapter 16: SEKEM, Egypt – Holistic Farming Initiative
Chapter 17: Cotton Stripper, India – Mechanizing Cotton Stripping
Chapter 18: M-Farm, Kenya – Monitoring Real-Time Crop Market Prices

This part has 'Transforming Farming' as its theme. It contains three design cases from three different countries: Egypt, India, and Kenya. These cases transform farming in different ways. Here are the abstracts for the three social innovation design cases:

DOI: 10.1201/9781003479086-20

16

SEKEM, Egypt: Holistic Farming Initiative

16.1 OVERVIEW

The SEKEM (meaning vitality in Ancient Egyptian language) organization was founded in 1979 by the Egyptian pharmacologist and social entrepreneur Dr. Ibrahim Abouleish to bring about sustainable human development in Egypt. The goals of SEKEM are to "restore and maintain the vitality of the soil and food as the biodiversity of nature" through sustainable organic agriculture and to support Egypt's social and cultural development. (Abouleish, 2013; Abouleish, 2019)

The SEKEM initiative is a successful demonstration of how a desert can be converted into an oasis within a few years. Dr. Ibrahim Abouleish and his wife Gudrun bought 70 hectares (about 173 acres) of desert land in 1977, nearly 40 miles northeast of Cairo and a quarter of a mile from the banks of the Nile, with the aim of farming. Armed with Dr. Abouleish's background in pharmacology and vision of generating fertility using biodynamic principles and practices—composting, cover cropping, crop rotation, and integration of livestock in farming—and the use of organic farming, coupled with perseverance and hard work, the SEKEM initiative started growing enough medicinal plants and food ingredients to start exporting them. Over the years, the SEKEM initiative has evolved into a private company that produces food, cotton, and herbal medicine, and distributes them in Egypt, Europe, and North America. It has grown to include over 2,000 farmers and partner organizations. (Abouleish and Abouleish, 2008; Global Alliance for the Future of Food, 2021)

SEKEM has grounded its operations in available scientific knowledge and conduct of local field research when needed. In 1991, SEKEM was not satisfied with the practice of aerial spraying of pesticides on cotton fields and conducted field research to find a non-pesticide effective and sustainable way for pest control. To achieve its goals, SEKEM has taken many initiatives and

DOI: 10.1201/9781003479086-21

even spread its experiences and acquired knowledge to several countries—India, Palestine, Senegal, Turkey, and South Africa. SEKEM's work and vision is to utilize its advances in agriculture to encompass broader goals of social and economic development of Egypt. The rest of the chapter will, however, focus on its work in agriculture. (Abouleish, 2013; Abouleish, 2019; Global Alliance for the Future of Food, 2021)

The rest of the chapter describes in detail design of the for-profit social innovation (and the corresponding social enterprise), SEKEM (Holistic Farming Initiative).

16.2 CONTEXT

The idea of establishing SEKEM has its origin in a 1975 cultural visit of Dr. Abouleish to visit Egypt from Austria where he had stayed for 19 years. He was touched by the deplorable economic and social situation in the country of his origin and decided to establish SEKEM in 1979 to start a cultural renewal project in Egypt based on promoting biodynamic agriculture to reduce poverty and to improve the livelihoods of farmers in Egypt; biodynamic agriculture is closely related to organic farming and treats soil fertility, plant growth, and livestock care as interrelated tasks. (Abouleish and Abouleish, 2008; Joshi and Rohrig, 2014)

16.3 INNOVATION DEVELOPMENT JOURNEY

16.3.1 Lap(s) / Stage(s)

16.3.1.1 Lap (Stage) 1 (1977–1982): Establish SEKEM to promote Biodynamic and Organic Agriculture

16.3.1.1.1 Problem Definition

Promote biodynamic and organic agriculture in Egyptian desert.

16.3.1.1.2 Suggestion

a. Use compost to turn desert land into living healthy soil, use resilient crops and natural predators to reduce use of chemical fertilizers and pesticides.

b. Make all business decisions based on the vision of sustainable human development.
c. Use biodynamic agricultural methods to revitalize desert land and to develop agricultural business.

16.3.1.1.3 Solution Development, Evaluation, and Implementation

It was a long and treacherous journey undertaken by Ibrahim Abouleish to realize his dream of having a thriving garden in the middle of a desert that follows biodynamic and organic principles of farming. (Abouleish and Abouleish, 2008; Hatem, 2007; Mader, et al., 2011; SEKEM, 2018)

The following are highlights of the work done by Dr. Abouleish for establishing SEKEM:

a. 70 hectares (nearly 175 acres) of land in desert land bordering the farm-land of the Nile Valley were purchased in 1977. SEKEM was founded in 1979.
b. A thick border of trees was planted to encircle the land.
c. A forest was planted on part of the land.
d. 120,000 casuarina (Australian pine), eucalyptus and Persian lilac seedlings were planted using biodynamic principles.
e. Production of a medicinal compound, ammoidin (extract of Lace flower—Ammi majus) was started.
f. Manufacturing herbal teas and a company to market fresh biodynamic produce in Europe was started.

SEKEM sent the first shipment of medicinal herbs and food ingredients to USA in 1981, thus confirming the successful establishment of SEKEM.

16.3.1.1.4 Circumscription

SEKEM had a good start with focus on export driven production of medicinal plants. The initial work needed to be leveraged to make SEKEM a globally competitive business organization.

16.3.1.2 Lap (Stage) 2 (1983-): Expand SEKEM into other areas.

16.3.1.2.1 Problem Definition

Expand SEKEM into business areas of pharmaceuticals derived from plants (phyto-pharmaceuticals), food cultivated biodynamically, and textiles made from organic cotton.

16.3.1.2.2 Suggestion

Use a humanistic approach to business development based on trust, mutual support, and collective work.

16.3.1.2.3 Solution Development, Implementation, and Evaluation

SEKEM launched several successful trading companies to produce and process foods, herbal teas, and beauty products (Isis Organic), medicinal herbs and medicines (ATOS Pharma), and organic cotton products (NatureTex), thus fulfilling the objectives of this lap (stage). (Abouleish, 2019; Hatem, 2007; Mader et al., 2011; Papageorgio, 2013; SEKEM, 2018):

a. 1983, Isis Organic: Isis Organic first launched herbal remedies under the brand, Sekem Herbs. It continued with producing and packing organically certified herbal teas, dairy products, oils, spices, and other products for consumers in Egypt and abroad.

b. 1986, Atos Pharma: It was launched as a joint venture with the German Development Bank and Dr. Schaitte AG to research and develop medicines from natural sources.

c. 1988, Libra: It was responsible for supplying the raw materials that the SEKEM companies processed and used. In 1994, it started to grow cotton biodynamically over 1,000 acres under an intense cooperation arrangement with scientists and small-scale farmers.

d. 1994, Naturetex: This company was launched to produce cotton fabrics without using harmful chemicals. It involved collaboration with scientists and Egyptian companies.

e. 1996, Hator: It packs fresh biodynamic fruits and vegetables grown by Libra as per customer specifications.

f. 1997, ISIS Organic: It manufactures and packs healthy foods and beverages from biodynamic raw materials grown by Libra.

g. 2005, LOTUS. LOTUS company was founded to process organic biodynamic herbs and spices.

16.3.2 Diffusion

In addition to promoting biodynamic farming and providing livelihood to many small and medium scale farmers, SEKEM has created a wide social impact by making community investments in multiple areas such as education and healthcare—medical center, school based on Waldorf pedagogy, community school for disadvantaged groups, vocational training center, Egyptian Biodynamic Association, Heliopolis University for Sustainable Development, Sekem Development Foundation. (Abouleish, 2013; Global Alliance for the Future of Food, 2021; Gordon, et al., 2015; Hatem, 2008; Joshi and Rohrig, 2014; Mader, et al., 2011; Papageorgiou, 2013; Seelos and Mair, 2005; SEKEM, 2018)

Awards and Recognitions (SEKEM, 2018):

a. 2003: The Schwab Foundation for Social Entrepreneurship recognized Ibrahim and Helmy Abouleish as Outstanding Social Entrepreneurs.

b. SEKEM received numerous awards such as: Alternative Nobel Prize or Right Livelihood Award (2003); Business for Peace Award by Oslo Business for Peace Foundation (2012); One World Family Award, Stuttgart, Germany (2013); Golden Award of the Technical University of Graz, Austria (2015); Land for Life Award from United Nation Convention to Combat Desertification (2015); Highest Honorary Medal from the German governorate of Baden-Wuerttemberg (2015); Luxembourg Peace Prize (2018)

16.4 INNOVATION RESULTS

SEKEM is a successful story of turning a piece of desert land in Egypt into a thriving farm that grows organic produce such as medicinal plants, food, and cotton. It has helped in turning Egypt into a top producer of organic produce. Over the first thirty years of its establishment, it generated revenue of 200 million Egyptian pounds. Its revenue has been growing fast; it grew from US$ 10 million in 2000 to US$ 19 million in 2005. Following the vision of Dr. Ibrahim Abouleish, SEKEM has spurred the establishment of successful business ventures, schools, and medical centers spread all over Egypt. (Abouleish and Abouleish, 2008; Hatem, 2007)

The main contribution of SEKEM is the demonstration of using organic methods in agriculture and the viability of new holistic approaches to development in Egypt. SEKEM has demonstrated alternatives to the use of pesticides for cotton and other crops. This led to Egyptian government banning the use of spraying pesticides on cotton crops in 1993. (Abouleish and Abouleish, 2008)

16.5 APPLICABLE KNOWLEDGE & KNOWLEDGE CONTRIBUTION

Models/Metamodels

Unmet Social Need (Hetherington, 2008; see Chapter 1)

SEKEM fulfills the unfilled social need of restoring and maintaining the vitality of soil in the in the Egyptian desert and demonstrates how a desert can be converted into an oasis within a few years of using holistic farming.

High Asset Use (Joshi and Rohrig, 2014; see Chapter 2)

The niche area of SEKEM is biodynamic farming in Egypt. This was something new for Egypt. So SEKEM needed to develop and adapt the concept for Egyptian conditions and then to standardize it. SEKEM went through a long process of fully developing the concept for Egypt and eventually standardizing it. In 1994 it created Egyptian Biodynamic Association (EBDA), a non-government organization (NGO) for conducting biodynamic research and providing extension services. The standard process it developed for transforming a piece of desert land into fertile land takes three years. In the first year, the land is prepared for biodynamic cultivation. In the second year, plantation of crops takes place in accordance with biodynamic principles in consultation with EBDA. In the third year the EBDA consultants help the farmers in their farm management and documentation to get certified as an organic farm according to international standards. As of 2014, 200 farms with total area of 3,361 hectares (about 8,300 acres) are in EBDA; 16% of this land is under SEKEM. Nearly 75% of the farmers in EBDA sell their products to SEKEM. (Joshi and Rohrig, 2014)

Process Reengineering (Joshi and Rohrig, 2014; see Chapter 1)

Biodynamic farming had originated from Europe. Using it and adapting it to the extreme soil and weather conditions of Egypt was a complex task. The cultivation method was studied in detail and divided into small steps to find how the process can be readjusted and reengineered to the conditions of Egypt. One of the areas identified for such process reengineering was cotton farming. Cotton farming is an important cash crop of Egypt that was highly affected by harmful pests that worked in a gradual manner. SEKEM developed a biodynamic concept for organic cultivation of cotton based on the use of chemical substances produced by insects called pheromones, which controlled cotton pests. This reduced the use of pesticides by 90%. (Joshi and Rohrig, 2014)

Promoting Positive Social Impact

SEKEM has promoted biodynamic (holistic) farming and thereby provided livelihood to many small and medium scale farmers. In addition, it has created a wide social impact by investing in many community projects in education and healthcare.

Exploration and Experimentation (Malouf, 2018)

Dr. Abouleish discovered that the cotton fields were sprayed with chemical pesticides that were causing the presence of traces of pesticides in the medicinal plants that SEKEM was growing. Entomologists were consulted to find organic alternatives. It was found that there is an organic way to stop the insects in cotton fields from multiplying. These methods were tested in some selected cotton fields and found to be effective and resulting in 10% higher yield of raw cotton. The results were confirmed by testing over large cotton fields for three years. This led to the ban of using chemical pesticides for cotton farming in Egypt. This is an example of carrying out exploration and experimentation by SEKEM.

Abouleish's Decision Making Model (Mader, et al., 2011)

Abouleish developed and used a decision-making model that was based on four interconnected principles:

a. *Ideals*—Business is a deeply human activity based on trust, mutual support, and collective work to achieve a higher goal.
b. *Experiences*—Human approach to business based on experiences is desirable and feasible.
c. *Facts*—Let facts drive value and business success.
d. *Future*—Securing the future is reflected in the ideal of sustainable development in Egypt.

Humanistic Approach to Business (Mader, et al., 2011)

The approach is based on the following principles:

a. Development of biodynamic agricultural methods suitable for Egypt's climate, agricultural crops planted in Egypt.
b. Development and production of consumer goods meeting real needs of consumers in environmentally responsible manner.
c. Human-oriented marketing of products.
d. Personal development of employees and providing them to express their opinions and ideas.

e. Creation of social conditions of cooperation between employees.

f. Support and cooperation with organizations that participate in social and cultural development of Egypt.

g. Spreading the SEKEM idea throughout Egypt and enable them to apply it to develop Egypt's future generations.

Social Enterprise Business Model Template (see Chapter 1, Section 1.2.2)

The model, shown in Figure 16.1, summarizes the overall business model of SEKEM in accordance with the template provided by Figure 1.2 of Chapter 1. The eleven components of the business model are briefly described below.

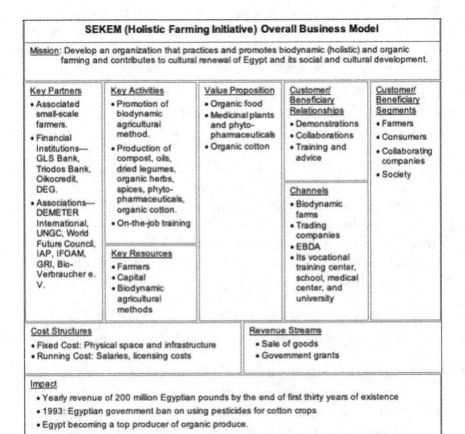

FIGURE 16.1

SEKEM Overall Business Model summarized in Social Enterprise Business Model Template shown in Figure 1.2.

Mission – Goals

The mission of SEKEM is the development of a multifaceted social and business organization that uses sustainable organic agriculture and biodynamic (holistic) principles to grow medicinal herbs, cotton, food and create community investments like education, healthcare and vocational training contributing to Egypt's social and cultural development.

Key Partners – Needed for the Social Enterprise to Work

SEKEM's strength is based on the development of longstanding partnerships. Its key partners include large number of small-scale farmers; financial Institutions—The GLS Bank, European Triodos Bank, Oikocredit (cooperative that finances small to medium-sized enterprises), DEG (finances private-sector investments in developing countries); Associations—DEMETER International (promotes biodynamic agriculture), UNGC (United Nations Global Compact), World Future Council, IAP (International Association of Partnership in Ecology and Trade), IFOAM (International Federation of Organic Agriculture Movement), GRI (Global Reporting Initiative), Bio-Verbraucher e.V. (German not-for-profit Association that creates links between organic producers, traders, and consumers).

Key Activities – Performed for the Business to Function

The key activities of SEKEM are development and promotion of biodynamic agricultural method; production of compost, oils, dried legumes, organic herbs, spices, phyto-pharmaceuticals, and organic cotton; vocational training.

Key Resources – Needed to make the Business Model Work

The key resources of SEKEM are small scale farmers, capital from banks, and knowledge of biodynamic agriculture methods.

Customer/Beneficiary Segments – Served by the Social Enterprise

The customer/beneficiary segments served by SEKEM are the collaborating small-scale farmers, consumers of its organic produce, its collaborating companies, and the Egyptian society.

Channels – to Interface with Customer/Beneficiary Segments

SEKEM interfaces with its customers and beneficiaries through its biodynamic farms; its trading companies (Hator and Libra for produce and processed foods), ISIS Organic for herbal teas and beauty products,

ATOS Pharma for medicinal herbs and medicines, and NatureTex for organic cotton); EBDA (Egyptian Bio-Dynamic Farmers Association); Heliopolis University (university for sustainable development); medical center; a school based on the principles of Waldorf pedagogy (promoting holistic education); and vocational training center.

Value Proposition – Products and/or Services that Create Value to Customers/Beneficiaries
The products and services that create value to SEKEM's customers and beneficiaries are: Organic food, Medicinal plants, and phyto-pharmaceuticals (extracts of medicinal plants), Organic cotton, and community development in education and vocational training.

Customer/Beneficiary Relationships – with Customer/Beneficiary Segments
SEKEM's relationships with its customers and beneficiaries are as a helpful hand-holding guide to small-scale farmers for adopting organic farming, as a collaborator, and as a resource for vocational training and advice.

Cost Structures – Costs Incurred to Operate the Social Enterprise
After incurring the fixed cost of creating its physical space and infrastructure, the running Cost of SEKEM include salaries, licensing costs, and interest on loans.

Revenue Streams – Cash Generated from Each Customer/Beneficiary Segment
The cash generated from SEKEM's customers and beneficiaries are the revenue from sale of goods and the funds received from government grants and bank loans.

Impact
SEKEM has been a successful social and business enterprise. It started from scratch to bring a yearly revenue of 200 million Egyptian pounds by the end of first thirty years of existence. It made a major contribution to organic cotton farming and the production of organic produce in Egypt. Through its field research it found a non-pesticide way to control harmful pests with the help of using a variety of insects, which resulted in Egyptian government's ban on using pesticides for cotton crops in 1993. SEKEM has thus contributed to Egypt becoming a

top supplier of organic cotton and other types of produce. It has also created institutions that have contributed to the social and cultural revival of Egypt.

REFERENCES

Abouleish, H. (2013). "Greening the Desert SEKEM – Egypt. www.planet-diversity.org/filead min/files/planet_diversity/Programme/Plenary_Session/13_05/Abouleish_13_5_S ekem_ppt_en.pdf (last accessed on December 14, 2023).

Abouleish, H. (2019). "SEKEM Report – 2018," SEKEM Holding for Investments Company S.A.E., June 15, 2019. www.sekem.com/wp-content/uploads/2019/06/SEKEM-Report-2018-EN.pdf (last accessed on December 14, 2023).

Abouleish, I. and Abouleish, H. (2008). "Garden in the Desert—Sekem Makes Comprehensive Sustainable Development a Reality in Egypt." *Innovations: Technology, Governance, Globalization* 3:3: 21–48. www.mitpressjournals.org/doi/pdf/10.1162/itgg.2008.3.3.21 (last accessed on December 14, 2023).

Global Alliance for the Future of Food (2021). "SEKEM: From the Egyptian Desert Rises New Life." https://futureoffood.org/insights/sekem/ (last accessed on December 14, 2023).

Gordon, A., Saber, S., Ludemann, R., and Roefs, M. (2015). "SEKEM Impact Evaluation Study," Centre for Development Innovation, June 2015. www.sekem.com/wp-content/uploads/ 2016/12/SEKEM-report-full-digital-copy_Oikocredit.pdf (last accessed December 14, 2023).

Hatem. (2007). "SEKEM: A Holistic Egyptian Initiative," Case Study. United Nations Development Programme. http://devel.sekem.com/assets/undp-2007-sekem—a-holis tic-egyptian-initative.pdf (last accessed on May 9, 2022).

Hetherington, D. (2008). "Case Studies in Social Innovation: A Background Paper," Per Capita, October 2008. https://apo.org.au/sites/default/files/resource-files/2009-01/apo-nid3 954.pdf (last accessed on December 14, 2023).

Joshi, S. and Rohrig, E. (2014). "Moving Innovation Forward; Case Studies: 10 Sustainable and Inclusive Business Models," GIZ India, New Delhi. www.giz.de/en/downloads/ giz2014-en-moving-innovation-forward-india.pdf (last accessed on December 12, 2023).

Mader, Steiner, G., Zimmermann, M., and Spitzeck, H. (2011). "SEKEM – Humanistic Management in the Egyptian Desert." in E. V Kimabowitz, M. Pirson, et al. (Eds.), *Humanistic Management in Practice* (pp. 204–214). New York, NY: Palgrave Macmillan. www.researchgate.net/profile/Clemens_Mader/publication/235923468_SEK EM_-_Humanistic_Management_in_the_Egyptian_Desert/links/550fd04d0cf212874 16c2b44/SEKEM-Humanistic-Management-in-the-Egyptian-Desert.pdf (last accessed on December 14, 2023).

Malouf, D. (2018). "Exploration over Experimentation." https://davemalouf.medium.com/expl oration-over-experimentation-cdc590863a62 (last accessed on December 14, 2023).

Papageorgiou, K. (2013). "Healing Nature, Transforming Culture: A Story of Social Innovation in Egypt." www.transitsocialinnovation.eu/content/original/Book%20 covers/Local%20PDFs/115%20SF%20Paper%20Papageorgiou%20Healing%20nat ure%20transforming%20culture%20Egypt%202013.pdf (last accessed on December 14, 2023).

Seelos, C. and Mair, J. (2005). "Sustainable Development: How Social Entrepreneurs make it Happen," Working Paper (WP No. 611), IESE Business School, University of Navarra, October 2005. www.google.com/url?sa=t&rct=j&q=&esrc=s&source=web&cd= &cad=rja&uact=8&ved=2ahUKEwjJxLW2u9fpAhUFHs0KHWu2DSwQFjAJegQIC RAB&url=https%3A%2F%2Fwww.researchgate.net%2Fpublication%2F4817369_ Sustainable_Development_How_Social_Entrepreneurs_Make_it_Happen&usg= AOvVaw27LQSCjAjVwjwjcaBS1QA5 (last accessed on December 14, 2023).

SEKEM. (2018). "Sustainable Development since 1977." www.sekem.com/en/index/ (last accessed on December 14, 2023).

17

Cotton Stripper, India: Mechanizing Cotton Stripping

17.1 OVERVIEW

Cotton is a soft fiber that grows in a rounded capsule (protective case) called a boll or pod in tropical and subtropical regions of the world. India is the largest producer of cotton producing 6.19 million metric tons in 2022 (World Population Review, 2022). For dryland indigenous variety of cotton (Kalyan) grown in many parts of India, it is difficult to harvest the cotton lint directly from the field; instead, the bolls are harvested from the field and the lint is normally separated from the cotton bolls, which is a laborious and time-consuming process. The Chetak stripper innovation mechanizes this process. (Gupta, et al., 2019; Indian Science, Technology & Innovation. 2018)

Cotton Stripper marketed as 'Chetak' is a grass-roots innovation (Sarkar and Pansera, 2017) by Mansukhbhai Patel that has revolutionized the cotton industry in India. Chetak mechanically removes lint from the cotton shell in a quick and efficient manner and prepares it for ginning (separation of cotton fibers from cotton seeds). It reduced the cost of stripping cotton in India by 95%. The innovation was awarded an Indian as well as a US patent. (Chandra, 2011; GIAN, 2003; Yadav and Goyal, 2015)

The rest of the chapter describes in detail design of the not-for-profit social innovation (and the corresponding social enterprise), Cotton Stripper (Mechanizing Cotton Stripping).

DOI: 10.1201/9781003479086-22

17.2 CONTEXT

The indigenous variety of cotton (V797 Kalyan) grown in the state of Gujarat, India bears pods that cannot be opened easily. The pods must be picked and manually cracked open to extract the boll. This work is tedious and cumbersome and is mostly performed by women and children. (National Innovation Foundation-India, nd)

Mansukhbhai Patel was from a small village near Viramgam in the state of Gujarat, India. While growing up he watched his father's work in the cultivation of the Kalyan, the rain-fed variety of cotton, and had worked on manually separating shells from cotton. He was fully aware of the tediousness, huge costs, and the delays involved in realizing returns from the cotton crop. He studied till 9th grade and dropped out due to poverty and the need to help his family. Right from his childhood, he had great interest in mechanical and electrical appliances, and enjoyed tinkering with them. He gained skills and knowledge of machinery while working as a helper in a tube manufacturing company and running errands for maintenance fitters and electricians. Eventually he secured the job of a deputy electrical engineer in Asarva Mills Limited, Ahmedabad. With his first-hand knowledge of the drudgery in removing cotton from unopened and semi-opened pods as well as his knowledge of electrical and mechanical machinery, he realized the possibility of developing a machine (stripper) for removing cotton from unopened and semi-opened pods. There did not exist any machine for doing this initial work while there existed machinery for the later stages of ginning (separating cotton seed and trash from the cotton fiber) and pressing cotton fiber into bales. (Shah, 2016)

17.3 INNOVATION DEVELOPMENT JOURNEY

17.3.1 Lap(s) / Stage(s)

17.3.1.1 Lap (Stage) 1 (1991–1994): Initial Development of Cotton Stripper

17.3.1.1.1 Problem Definition

The problem for the innovation was how to mechanically strip the indigenous variety of cotton in Gujarat (rainfed cotton—Kalyan – V:797; G-13, etc.) from shells. This problem needed to be solved.

17.3.1.1.2 Suggestion

Based on the experience of Mansukhbhai Patel in opening the closed and semi-closed bolls and his knowledge of and experience with mechanical and electrical machinery, Mr. Patel was certain that this process can be mechanized. But the actual process needed to be invented and implemented.

17.3.1.1.3 Solution Development, Evaluation, and Implementation

Mansukhbhai Patel had been thinking about the problem of mechanization of cotton stripping for a long time and in 1991 he contrived the actual process that could be used in the mechanization. He discussed his mechanization idea with his colleagues at the factory he was working at and with relatives, who encouraged him to proceed with implementing the idea. He met Kantibhai Patel, a factory manager of a related company, who promised INR 150,000 to become the first investor for initiating the development of the proposed machine (stripper). With this money, he rented a shed and got hold of some basic machinery to start developing the proposed machine. He started working on developing a prototype for the proposed machine in the evenings after his daytime work at the factory. (Gupta, et al., 2019; Shah, 2016)

After iterating through many models and aided by voluntary work from his factory colleagues and workers, he developed the first prototype of the cotton stripper in 1994 and demonstrated it in his village. He himself was not satisfied with the performance of the machine, but was flooded with orders; he sold 50 machines based on this prototype. The machines he sold did not perform well and did not satisfy his customers, and the machines were returned. He refunded the money he had received from the customers. He soon identified a trivial technical problem in the machine that was making it malfunction. In addition to fixing the technical problem, he wanted to make further improvements in the machine to make it perfect.

17.3.1.1.4 Circumscription

The initial version (prototype) of the cotton stripper was developed but it needed major improvements in its design.

17.3.1.2 Lap (Stage) 2 (1995–2000): Final Development and Commercialization

17.3.1.2.1 Problem Definition

How to improve the design and implementation of the prototype developed by Mansukhbhai Patel in 1994.

17.3.1.2.2 Suggestion

Utilize the knowledge gained in the development of the prototype and its field performance and make improvements. Seek external guidance and advice for improvements in the design and implementation of the machine. (GIAN, 2003; Gupta, et al., 2019; Patel, 2002; Shah, 2016; Vikaspedia, 2022)

17.3.1.2.3 Solution Development, Evaluation, and Implementation

Mansukhbhai Patel was enthused by the confidence shown by his customers and intensified his efforts in fixing the glitches in his 1994 prototype and making improvements in its design over the next three years. Meanwhile, in 1995, Hitendra Rawal was looking for innovators while studying at a rural Gandhian institution. He heard about the interesting case of Mansukhbhai's innovation; he had sold the machine based on the innovation to customers who were later refunded their money because of malfunctioning of his machine. Hitendra Rawal found the whereabouts of Mansukhbhai Patel and met him. He sent his meeting notes to SRISTI (Society for Research and Initiatives for Sustainable Technologies and Institutions), a Gujarat (India) based developmental voluntary organization set up in 1993. This led to the innovation being noticed by GIAN (Gujarat Grassroots Innovations Augmentation Network), an offshoot of SRISTI, set up in 1997.

GIAN realized that the innovation of Mansukhbhai Patel had a large potential for commercialization and providing social benefits. To realize the potential, it assessed the status of the prototype and what types of assistance needed to be provided. It found that the design of the stripper machine needed improvements to optimize its performance for which assistance from technical and design institutions would be needed. It also found that the innovator would need financial assistance and administrative aid. GIAN obtained technical assistance from IIT Bombay and design assistance from National Institute of Design (NID), Ahmedabad, India. It invited Professor Kishor Munshi of the Industrial Design Centre at IIT Bombay to review the design of the stripper machine prototype and to provide suggestions for improvements. From National Institute of Design, Alexander Bosnjak, a design student on exchange from Germany took up the stripper machine as a final year project. GIAN helped Mansukhbhai secure 580,000 Indian Rupees (INR) under the Technopreneur Promotion Program (TePP) Scheme of the Department of Science and Industrial Research (DSIR), Government of India.

With the active involvement of GIAN and technical and design assistance from IIT Bombay and NID Ahmedabad, four improvement iterations were made over the 1994 concept model until a final commercial prototype was developed in 2000. A market research and feasibility study was carried out for the machine with the help of Nirma Institute of Management Studies and GIAN. The study indicated positive demand for the machine. Chetak Agro Industries, a partnership firm, was created to manufacture the machine. FOSS (Friends of SRISTI in Singapore) provide venture assistance of INR 250,000 in October 2000. A patent application was filed in India (2001) with the help of National Research Development Corporation. GIAN filed the USA patent application in 2002. The US patent was granted in 2003 and the Indian patent was awarded in 2006.

The innovation was recognized: 1st Award by National Innovation Foundation Award in Feb. 2002; Best Technology Award for the year 2003 by National Research Development Corporation, Government of India in 2004. Mansukhbhai Patel was honored by SRISTI (Society for Research and Initiatives for Sustainable Technologies and Institutions) by including him in its Governing body.

17.3.2 Diffusion

The invented machine, Chetak, received market feedback and media coverage from its display at many technology fairs and exhibitions such as the Indian Science Congress. It was also demonstrated in different parts of Gujarat, India. The demonstrations were effective in convincing the consumers about the usefulness and efficiency of the machine. (Gupta, et al., 2019)

Impact: The innovation has made a positive change in the lives of cotton farmers in India by avoiding their drudgery in cotton stripping. It drastically reduced the cost of cotton stripping, reducing it from Indian rupee (INR) 1/kg to INR 1/20 kg. It also reduced the time of processing cotton; the machine resulted in processing 400 kg of cotton per hour. The machine, however, has limitations to its future use as the farmers have switched from cultivating the Kalyan variety to Bt cotton variety (a genetically modified pest resistant variety) whose bolls split open spontaneously upon maturity; Mansukhbhai has already diversified his business and is doing well commercially. (Chandra, 2011; Gupta, et al., 2019; Prabu, 2012).

17.4 INNOVATION RESULTS

The result of the innovation is the development of the cotton stripper and the commercial exploitation of the innovation. The innovation has been granted

US and Indian patents. The eleven components of the business model are briefly described below.

17.5 APPLICABLE KNOWLEDGE & KNOWLEDGE CONTRIBUTION

Models/Metamodels

Unmet Social Need (Hetherington, 2008; see Chapter 1)

The pods borne by the indigenous variety of cotton (V797 Kalyan) grown in the state of Gujarat, India, cannot be opened easily. The tedious work of cracking the pods used to be done manually by women and children. There was a big social need to do this work mechanically and this need was unfulfilled until Manusukhbhai Patel developed a machine (stripper) for doing this work.

Iterative Development (Hetherington, 2008; see Chapter 1)

The work of developing a stripper that would be acceptable to customers required several iterations. After iterating through many models, the first prototype was developed in 1994. The protype needed further improvements in its design and implementation. The additional iterations were made after getting design and technical assistance from National Institute of Design, Ahmedabad and IIT Bombay. The final prototype was developed in 2000 and applications filed for US and Indian patents, which have been granted.

Innovation Development Model

The model shown in Figure 17.1 is based on the work led by Manusukhbhai Patel. He was the innovator of the machine. He developed the initial prototype based on his experiences and ideas. The final prototype was developed with the help of suggestions from design, business, and technical institutions as well as venture funding from government and financial institutions. The invention was granted US and Indian patents, and led to the commercial stripper, Chetak, and the setting up Chetak Agro Industries. (Gupta, et al., 2019; Shah, 2016).

Social Enterprise Business Model Template (see Chapter 1, Section 1.2.2)

The model, shown in Figure 17.2, summarizes the overall business model of Cotton Stripper in accordance with the template provided by Figure 1.2 of Chapter 1. The eleven components of the business model are briefly dscribed below.

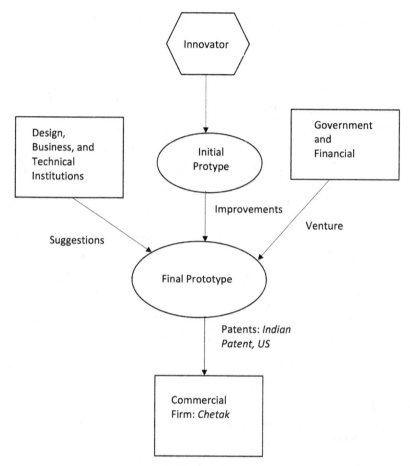

FIGURE 17.1
Cotton Stripper Development Model.

Mission – Goals

Design and development of a machine for mechanizing cotton stripping that mechanically separates cotton seeds and trash from unopened and semi-opened pods and removes cotton fibers and presses cotton fibers into bales in a quick and efficient manner at a lower cost than the cost for the manual process.

Key Partners – Needed for the Social Enterprise to Work

The key partners of the innovation are SRISTI (Society for Research and Initiatives for Sustainable Technologies and Institutions); Gujarat Grassroots Innovations Augmentation Network (GIAN); National Institute of Design (NID), Ahmedabad; Department of Science and

Cotton Stripper (Mechanizing Cotton Stripping) Overall Business Model				
Mission Design and develop a machine for mechanization of the cotton stripping process—removal of lint from the cotton shell—to reduce the cost and effort for stripping cotton.				
Key Partners • GIAN • SRISTI • IIT Bombay • NID Ahmedabad • DSIR	**Key Activities** • Design and development of Chetak stripping machine protype • Iterative improvement of the prototype • Patent applications • Commercial production **Key Resources** • Inventor ingenuity • Technical and design assistance • Investments	**Value Proposition** • Providing a machine to Kalyan variety cotton farmers for stripping cotton bolls • After sale warranty and service of the Chetak machine	**Customer/ Beneficiary Relationships** • Patent publication • Sale of the Chetak machine • Warranties and after sale service **Channels** • Patent offices • Displays at technology fairs and exhibitions. • Demonstrations	**Customer/ Beneficiary Segments** • Kalyan cotton farmers • Cotton ginning industry • Society at large
Cost Structures • Fixed Cost: Physical space and infrastructure • Running Cost: Salaries, utility bills		**Revenue Streams** • Royalty income • Sale of the Chetak stripper machines.		
Impact • Drastically reduced the cost of stripping cotton bolls. • Reduced the cost of processing Kalyan variety of cotton.				

FIGURE 17.2
Cotton Stripper Overall Business Model summarized in Social Enterprise Business Model Template shown in Figure 1.2.

Industrial Research (DSIR), Government of India; and Indian Institute of Technology, Bombay.

Key Activities – Performed for the Business to Function
The key activities done for the development of the innovation are design and development of the prototype cotton stripping machine, iterative improvement of the design to get the final commercial prototype using external guidance and advice, filing of patent applications, and commercial production of Chetak stripper machine.

Key Resources – Needed to make the Business Model Work
The key resources for the development of the innovation are ingenuity and persistence of the inventor, Mansukhbhai Patel, technical and design assistance from IIT Bombay and National Institute of Design (NID)

Ahmedabad, grants from Government of India, and angel as well as venture investments.

Customer/Beneficiary Segments – Served by the Social Enterprise
The customer and beneficiary segments of the Chetak cotton stripper are the Kalyan cotton farmers, Cotton ginning industry in India, and the society at large.

Value Proposition – Products and/or Services that Create Value to Customers/ Beneficiaries
The value proposition of the innovation is mechanization of the cotton stripping process for Kalyan variety cotton, building of a machine for stripping cotton bolls faster and at a much-reduced cost, and providing after sale warranty service for the Chetak cotton stripper resulting from the innovation.

Customer/Beneficiary Relationships – with Customer/Beneficiary Segments
The customer and beneficiary relationships of the innovation are the publication of the patent resulting from the innovation, and sale of the Chetak machine resulting from the innovation as well as its after-sale and warranty service.

Channels – to Interface with Customer/Beneficiary Segments
The channels used to interface with the customer and beneficiary segments are the patent offices in India and outside India, displays at technology fairs and exhibitions, demonstrations, and the Chetak Agro Industries website.

Cost Structures – Costs Incurred to Operate the Social Enterprise
The fixed cost includes the costs involved in developing the innovation and the manufacturing and sale of the Chetak machine, and the cost of physical space, machines and infrastructure. The running cost includes salaries and utility bills.

Revenue Streams – Cash Generated from each Customer/Beneficiary Segment
The revenue streams generated from the innovation are any royalty income from the Chetak stripper patent and the income from the sale of the Chetak stripper machines.

Impact
The innovation has made major measurable impact. It has made a positive change in the lives of Indian cotton farmers by avoiding their

drudgery for stripping cotton bolls, drastically reduced the cost of stripping cotton bolls, and reduced the cost of processing Kalyan variety of cotton—reducing it from Indian rupee (IR) one/kg to IR1/20 kg. It has also reduced the time taken for processing cotton; the resulting machine (Chetak) processes 400 kg of cotton per hour.

REFERENCES

Chandra, K. (2011). "Amazing story of a stripping machine that revolutionized cotton industry," *The Weekend Leader*, 2 (29), 22 July 2011. www.theweekendleader.com/Innovation/597/barefoot-inventor.html (last accessed on December 14, 2023).

GIAN. (2003). "NRDC Award Winning Technology: A Case Study on Cotton Stripping Machine." Grassroots Innovation Augmentation Network (GIAN), Gujarat, India.

Gupta, A., Shinde, C., Dey, A. Patel, R. Patel, C., Kumar, V., and Patel, M. (2019). "Honey Bee Network in Africa: Co-creating a Grassroots Innovation Ecosystem in Africa – Appendix 1: The Cotton Stripper," 28–31, ZEF Working Paper Series, ISSN 1864-6638, Center for Development Research, University of Bonn, February 27, 2019. https://papers.ssrn.com/sol3/papers.cfm?abstract_id=3332251 (last accessed on December 14, 2023).

Hetherington, D. (2008). "Case Studies in Social Innovation: A Background paper," Per Capita, October 2008. https://apo.org.au/sites/default/files/resource-files/2009-01/apo-nid3954.pdf (Last accessed on December 14, 2023).

Indian Science, Technology & Innovation (2018). "Cotton Stripper," October 31, 2018. www.indiascienceandtechnology.gov.in/hi/innovations/grassroot-innovations/cotton-stripper (last accessed on December 14, 2023).

National Innovation Foundation-India (nd). "Cotton Stripper," 2002 National Award. http://nif.org.in/innovation/cotton_stripper_machine/199 (last accessed on December 14, 2023).

Patel, M. (2002). "US Patent – US20020092133A1 – Apparatus and methods for stripping cotton." https://patents.google.com/patent/US20020092133A1/en (last accessed on December 14, 2023).

Prabu, M.J. (2012). "Mechanised Cotton Stripper Makes Work More Easy," *The Hindu*, April 5/July 13, 2012. www.thehindu.com/sci-tech/agriculture/mechanised-cotton-stripper-makes-work-more-easy/article3281894.ece (last accessed on December 14, 2023).

Sarkar, S. and Pansera, M. (2017). "Sustainability-driven innovation at the bottom: Insights from Grassroots Ecopreneurs," *Technological Forecasting & Social Change*," 114, January 2017, pp. 327–338. www.sciencedirect.com/science/article/abs/pii/S0040162516302487 (last accessed on December 14, 2023)

Shah, D. (2016). Chapter 5: "Initiatives by Government and NGOs for Sustainable Inclusive Growth – Case No. 5.2: Innovative Machine for Cotton Farmers," 130–141, in *Sustainable Inclusive Growth: A Framework for the Process of Capability Building in Gujarat*, Doctoral Dissertation, Sardar Patel University. Department of Business Studies, Gujarat, India, 2016. https://shodhganga.inflibnet.ac.in/bitstream/10603/148693/14/14_chapter%205.pdf (last accessed on December 14, 2023).

Vikaspedia. (2022). "Cotton Stripper," Indian Patent No. 198755, January 8, 2001; US Patents No. US20020092133A1, July 18, 2002, No. US6,543,091 B2, April 8, 2003. https://vik aspedia.in/agriculture/best-practices/innovations-agricultural-equipments/cotton-stripper (last visited on December 14, 2023).

World Population Review (2022). "Cotton Production by Country 2022." https://worldpopul ationreview.com/country-rankings/cotton-production-by-country (last accessed on December 14, 2023).

Yadav, V. and Goyal, P. (2015). "User innovation and entrepreneurship: case studies from rural India," *Journal of Innovation and Entrepreneurship*, December 22, 2015, 4, p. 5. https:// link.springer.com/article/10.1186/s13731-015-0018-4 (last accessed on December 14, 2023).

18

M-Farm, Kenya: Monitoring Real-Time Crop Market Prices

18.1 OVERVIEW

M-Farm is an ICT (Information and Communication Technology) tool that enables Kenyan farmers to monitor real-time market prices, connect with wholesale buyers and farm suppliers. The mobile-based tool is supported by ICT management systems and offline networks to enable small farmers to work together to offer their products jointly to regional or international markets. It is an SMS and web-based application that can be accessed free but requires a transaction fee for every deal done using the app. It also helps farmers to plan what to harvest in terms of profitability. M-Farm is a product of M-Farm Limited, a "Kenyan software solution and agribusiness company," co-founded in 2010 (operations starting in 2011) by all-female team of Linda Kwamboka, Jamila Omwenga Abass, Susan Eve Oguya. M-Farm was initially started at iHub and later secured an office at m:Lab followed by moving to a subsidized physical space in the building housing iHub and m:Lab. (ASHOKA, 2014; Baumüller, 2015; Ekiru, 2011; Emeana, et al., 2020; Engineering for Change, 2018/2024; M-Farm, 2022; M-Farm, Limited, Kenya, 2022)

The rest of the chapter describes in detail design of the for-profit social innovation (and the corresponding social enterprise), M-Farm (Monitoring Real-Time Crop Market Prices).

DOI: 10.1201/9781003479086-23

18.2 CONTEXT

In the first decade of this century, smallholder farmers in Kenya, like in other developing countries, did not have up-to-date market information on wholesale prices of their crops. They were dependent on this information from the middlemen who would buy their produce and as a result they would not get good price. The information and communication technology had the ability to solve this problem but there was need for the right entrepreneurs to produce the needed application.

Jamila Abbas graduated in software engineering at Strathmore University in Kenya. Susan Oguya graduated in computer science from the same university. Both wanted to become entrepreneurs and utilize their knowledge to contribute back to the society. They connected with each other at iHub, a technology company where technologists, investors, tech companies, and hackers came together to share ideas. They also became members of AkiraChix, an organization for women with an interest in information technology. In September 2010, they decided to do something using information and communication technology to help the Kenyan small farmers. They knew that mobile phones and SMS messaging were widely used. So, Jamila Abbas, Susan Eve Oguya, and Linda Kwamboka (a student at Strathmore University) developed a website and a simple SMS-messaging based app for farmers to get the market prices for their crops, and founded a company called M-Farm based on this app in 2010. (Career Point Kenya, 2014/2021; M-Farm, 2022; Nation News, 2011/2020; Solon, 2013; Startuplist Africa, 2022)

Jamila Abbas, Susan Eve Oguya, and Linda Omwenga Kwamboka heard about IPO48, a software development competition organized by HumanIPO based in Estonia to be held at Strathmore University, Kenya, in November 2011. The idea of the competition was to develop a computer application, which can be turned into a marketable business within 48 hours. The winner of the competition would get a prize of KSh 1 million (approximately US$ 10,000). (Nation News, 2011/2020)

18.3 INNOVATION DEVELOPMENT JOURNEY

18.3.1 Lap(s) / Stage(s)

18.3.1.1 Lap (Stage) (2010-): Develop M-Farm

18.3.1.1.1 Problem Definition

How to improve smallholder farmers in Kenya by letting them access better markets to increase their revenue. (Abbas, 2016)

18.3.1.1.2 Suggestion

Deliver information on pricing directly to farmers (without the middleman).

18.3.1.1.3 Solution Development, Evaluation, and Implementation

Jamila Abass, Susan Eve Oguya, Linda Kwamboka, had developed a simple text-messaging app to provide up-to-date whole-sale price information to farmers and a website that provides weather, soil, and other agricultural information. They had launched an agri-business company, M-Farm in 2010. They set about further developing the app and the website with some additional Strathmore University students with the idea of competing for IPO48 competition with a business model (described below) using the app. M-Farm was based at the innovation space provided by iHub in Nairobi, Kenya. The team won the competition and secured seed funding of KSh 1 million (about US$ 10,000) in the competition that had 100 contestants divided into 17 teams. The M-Farm team was also promised KSh 3 million to help launch the company in the market. Using the prize money, M-Farm was incorporated in 2011 with Jamila Abbas as CEO; Susan Eve as COO, Linda Omwenga Kwamboka and Catherine Kiguru as Marketing Officers, and Lillian Niduati as Public Relations Officer. The IPO48 competition provided M-Farm publicity that attracted US$ 100,000, half in charity and half as a loan from the UK based charity, techfortrade, that promotes innovative approaches to alleviating poverty. M-Farm has also been supported by the World Bank's infoDev program. The company was run on a pilot basis for the first year and limited its use to only one region, Kinangop. (Baumüller, 2015; M-Farm, 2022; Myllynpaa, 2016; Nation News, 2011/2020; Tran, 2013).

The initial business plan of M-Farm provided three services to farmers (Baumüller, 2015):

Price Information for Produce: This service provides wholesale price information, Monday-Saturday, for 42 crops including legumes and cereals such as wheat and rice, for five major markets in Kenya: Nairobi, Mombasa, Kisumu, Eldoret, and Kitale. The farmers access this information from a database by sending an SMS short code from their mobile phones using Safaricom This information is also available from the M-Farm website through an app developed in collaboration with Samsung; the app is available in Android and Samsung's Bada based phones (Kachewanya, 2012). The price information is gathered by human data collectors who upload the data using their smart phones.

Selling Produce: M-Farm can let a farmer, or a group of farmers sell their produce directly. For this service, farmers must first subscribe to the (fee-based) service by sending a message to the short code providing their full name and location and another message providing the name of the produce, its weight and price.

Buying Inputs: M-Farm initially let a group of farmers buy farming input such as fertilizers and seeds, but this service had to be put on indefinite hold because farmers do not have enough capital to purchase the farm inputs.

The pilot rollout of M-Farm was successful and by the end of its first year of pilot operation, over 5,400 farmers were using its services. The use of its services was now expanded to other regions of Kenya. From this point onward, the operation of M-Farm was constantly reviewed, and evolved over time as summarized below (Baumüller, 2015).

While the M-Farm app and its functionality remained stable, the business plan had to undergo many iterations based on the difficulties faced in its implementation and the feedback from users. The price of produce service has become the main service of M-Farm. M-Farm has been made to function as a virtual cooperative where farmers in the same area can possibly connect with each other and together find buyers (Abass, 2016). In addition, changes have been made to ensure the reliability of the price information and the information dissemination channels have been expanded.

The reliability of price information has been ensured by having a second data collector for each market to cross-check the information and the data collectors have been provided with GPS-enabled phones to track the location from where they upload the information. The frequency of collecting price data has been adjusted based on the crop and the market.

In addition to providing crop price information through SMS messaging and the M-Farm website (that also includes price trends), M-Farm developed apps to sell the information to other parties such as media outlets, restaurants, traders, and NGOs.

The service for selling of produce for farmers near Nairobi has evolved to creating a phone-based open market facilitated by the M-Farm website and managed by M-Farm (using M-Pesa for receiving money from buyers and transferring to farmers) to help farmers get better price for their crops; farmers can also directly post information about their produce on the M-Farm website. The buyers can buy the crops directly from farmers, but they often prefer to buy it through M-Farm (paying a commission) to ensure quality since M-Farm staff first checks the quality of the produce before selling it. For farmers in other districts, the selling of crops in the open market is facilitated by aggregators (cooperatives) who send SMS to farmers informing them about what a buyer is interested to purchase.

Marketing of M-Farm to farmers

Marketing of M-Farm to small-scale farmers has been difficult and has required training and outreach programs. The aggregators (cooperatives) tied up with M-Farm have raised awareness of the M-Farm services in the districts of Kenya. They have provided training and facilitated group selling. (Baumüller, 2015)

Revenue sources

M-Farm's initial funding came from social investors through the IPO48 competition; social investors continue to be an important source of revenue. Safaricom Foundation provided seed funding of US$ 235,000 in 2013. In addition, M-Farm has been funded in two rounds of venture funding: the latest one in 2015 by Novastar Ventures. The main source of on-going funding is the commissions M-Farm earns from produce buyers making purchases using M-Farm and the income it generates from price information using SMS. The other sources of revenue include the sale of price information to media houses and the subscription fees paid by farmers for ability to sell crops though M-Farm. (Baumüller, 2015; FSD Kenya, 2015; Startuplist Africa, 2022)

Since 2015, M-Farm faced funding difficulties and has been relaunched by Linda Kwamboka in 2019, basing its headquarters at Strathmore University while continuing with the goal of letting farmers easily access the M-Farm mobile app to digitally connect farmers to buyers in urban markets. Since the relaunch of M-Farm, Linda enlisted six field agents to recruit farmers to the M-Farm network. This has helped the company to expand its network to 40,000 farmers by the end of 2019.

18.3.1.1.4 Circumscription

Farmers use the app to find current market pricing, though radio is still used. There is some evidence to suggest that farmers are changing planting behavior based on information. Still, it is mostly seller/buyer market, with not much aggregation of selling.

18.3.2 Diffusion

Impact

The first 686 farmers using the platform in 2012 saw a 100% increase in profits on average and by 2014 7,400 farmers were using M-Farm (ASHOKA, 2014). By 2015, 15,000 farmers were using M-Farm (Evans, 2015). This number grew to 40,000 by the end of 2019 (Bradford, 2022).

The impact of M-Farm on the Kinangop community in Kenya was studied in 2013. They found their crop yield increased, cost of fertilizer decreased (from KSh 4,000 to KSh 2,500) per bag through access to information on inputs, leading to savings and increase in the area they farm. They also reported a general improvement in their standard of living. (Mutiga and Thiga, 2014)

The impact of M-Farm can be much higher if farmers are provided appropriate transportation for produce, cold storage, and other crucial infrastructure such as access to capital. (Abass, 2016)

18.4 INNOVATION RESULTS

The results of this innovation are the establishment of an SMS-based and website-based information for providing farmers real-time wholesale prices of several crops in many regions of Kenya. The service also provides information on farm inputs and connects farmers with suppliers, provides weather information, and additional soil and other agricultural information.

18.5 APPLICABLE KNOWLEDGE & KNOWLEDGE CONTRIBUTION

Models/Metamodels

Unmet Social Need (Hetherington, 2008)

Smallholder farmers in Kenya did not have up-to-date information on the wholesale market prices of their crops. They would sell their produce to middlemen at prices offered by them and as a result they would not get good prices. There was a social need to solve this problem. M-Farm developed an ICT (information and communication technology) SMS and web-based app that was able to provide such information free of cost and connect the farmers to wholesale buyers.

Overcoming Business-to-Business Barrier

M-Farm got rid of middlemen between buyers and sellers. It visually displayed real-time data to aid market players to connect with each other and thus connected farmers, wholesale buyers, and agriculture input suppliers. It used both sophisticated ICT management systems and offline ground networks to build an entrepreneurial data-driven commercial farming infrastructure.

Iterative Development (Hetherington, 2008; see Chapter 1)

M-Farm's business plan had to undergo many iterations because of the difficulties it faced in its implementation and because of feedback from its users. The difficulties are mainly because of the rural poverty and lack of good transportation infrastructure. It faced funding difficulties by 2015 and had to be relaunched in 2019 by one of its co-founders, Linda Kwamboke. With its relaunch, it focused on enlisting field agents who cultivated relationships with farmers and farmers communities. This helped M-Farm to substantially increase the numbers of its farmers in its network.

Social Enterprise Business Model Template (see Chapter 1, Section 1.2.2)

The model, shown in Figure 18.1, summarizes the overall business model of M-Farm in accordance with the template provided by Figure 1.2 of Chapter 1. The eleven components of the business model are briefly described below.

Mission – Goals

The mission of M-Farm is the development of a mobile-based tool that enables Kenyan farmers to monitor market prices of agricultural products and connects them to wholesale buyers and farm suppliers.

M-Farm (Monitoring Real-Time Crop Market Prices): Overall Business Model				
Mission: Develop an ICT tool for monitoring real-time crop market prices, to provide up to date market prices of agricultural products to farmers and to connect them to wholesale buyers and farm suppliers.				
Key Partners • Kenyan farmers • iHub • m:Lab • Samsung	Key Activities • Software development and maintenance • Operation and management of M-Farm • Marketing of M-Farm to small-scale farmers through training and outreach. Key Resources • Competition Award money • Seed funding from Safaricom Foundation • Venture funding from Novastar Ventures	Value Proposition • Providing current crop market prices in different markets and/or regions through SMS inquiries and the (free downloadable) M-Farm website. • Collective crop selling and access to M-Farm contracted exporters to buy crops directly from farmers using M-Farm website.	Customer/ Beneficiary Relationships • Providing selling price information for produce. • Selling of farm produce Channels • SMS messaging • M-Farm website • Aggregators (cooperatives tied up with M-Farm)	Customer/ Beneficiary Segments • Farmers in Kenya • Media houses and other outlets that get current farm prices.
Cost Structures • Fixed Cost: M-Farm app development, physical space, and infrastructure • Running Cost: M-Farm App maintenance, salaries, and utility bills		Revenue Streams • Commissions from produce buyers • Income from providing price information through SMS messages. • Sale of price information to media houses.		
Impact • Positive economic, social, and cultural impact on the farming community				

FIGURE 18.1

M-Farm Overall Business Model summarized in Social Enterprise Business Model Template shown in Figure 1.2.

The overall goal of the tool is to enhance their income by enabling them to sell their produce at a good price and to allow them to buy their seeds and fertilizer directly from the suppliers.

Key Partners – Needed for the Social Enterprise to Work

The key partners of M-Farm, Kenya have been farmers in Kenya, the innovation space provided by iHub in Nairobi, Kenya and the office space provided by m:Lab, and Samsung which partnered in developing the M-Farm app.

Key Activities – Performed for the Business to Function

Key activities of M-Farm are software development and maintenance; operation and management of M-Farm; and marketing of M-Farm to small-scale farmers through training, outreach programs, and aggregators. The aggregators (cooperatives) tied up with M-Farm have raised awareness of the M-Farm services.

Key Resources – Needed to Make the Business Model Work

The key resources for the functioning of M-Farm are the competition award money (about US\$ 10,000) that also attracted US\$ 100,000 from techfortrade (half in charity and half as loan); seed funding of US\$ 235,000 from Safaricom Foundation; and venture funding (unknown amount) from Novastar Ventures.

Customer/Beneficiary Segments – Served by the Social Enterprise

The customer and farmer segments served by M-Farm, Kenya are the Kenyan farmers who get connected with buyers of their crops and the media houses and other outlets who get current farm prices.

Value Proposition – Products and/or Services that Create Value to Customers/ Beneficiaries

M-Farm provides current crop market prices in different markets and/ or regions through SMS inquiries and the free downloadable M-Farm website. The website allows collective crop selling and provides access to M-Farm contracted exporters to buy crops directly from farmers.

Customer/Beneficiary Relationships – with Customer/Beneficiary Segments

The relationships M-Farm has with its customers and beneficiaries are serving as a vehicle to provide current selling price information for produce to enable selling of farm produce.

Channels – to Interface with Customer/Beneficiary Segments

M-Farm uses SMS-messaging, its website, and the aggregators (cooperatives) tied up with M-Farm to interface with its customers and beneficiaries. The aggregators (cooperatives) raise awareness of the M-Farm services in the districts of Kenya and provide training and facilitated group selling.

Cost Structure – Costs Incurred to Operate the Social Enterprise

The cost incurred to run the business are its Fixed Cost: M-Farm App development cost, and cost of the physical space and infrastructure; Running Cost: M-Farm App maintenance cost, salaries, and utility bills.

Revenue Streams – Cash Generated from Each Customer/Beneficiary Segment

The ongoing cash generated from its customers and beneficiaries are the commissions from produce buyers making purchases using M-Farm, the income it generates from providing price information using SMS messages, and the sale of current price information to media houses and other outlets.

Impact

M-Farm has provided a significant positive economic, social, and cultural impact on the farming community. The farmers have seen significant increase in profit by selling crops without the middlemen. The cost of fertilizer has decreased. The farmers have been able to buy more land for farming. The first 686 farmers using the platform in 2012 saw a 100% increase in profits on average and by 2014 7,400 farmers were using M-Farm. By 2015, 15,000 farmers were using M-Farm. This number grew to 40,000 by the end of 2019.

REFERENCES

Abbas, J. (2016). "I Built a Mobile App to Help Africa's Farmers but Our Countries' Infrastructure Must Work Too," QUARTZAFRICA, January 27, 2016. https://qz.com/africa/603214/i-built-a-mobile-app-to-help-africas-farmers-but-our-countries-infrastructure-must-work-too/ (last accessed on December 14, 2023).

ASHOKA. (2014). "Social Entrepreneurs Changing Lives Through UCT," September 2014. https://issuu.com/ashokachangemakers/docs/social_innovation_mapping_report_ic/1?e=0/9376572 (last accessed on December 14, 2023).

Baumüller, H. (2015). "Agricultural Innovation and Service Delivery through Mobile Phones Analyses in Kenya," Doctoral Dissertation, June 15, 2015. www.researchgate.net/publication/299347924_Agricultural_Innovation_and_Service_Delivery_through_Mobile_Phones_Analyses_in_Kenya (last accessed on December 14, 2023).

Bradford, F. (2022). "Innovating Kenya's Trading System through Mobile Technology: A Case Study of M-Farm in Nairobi, Kenya," Master's Project, Cornell University, December 2022. https://ecommons.cornell.edu/bitstream/handle/1813/113237/Bradford_Fante_Project.pdf?sequence=1&isAllowed=y (Last accessed on December 14, 2023).

Career Point Kenya. (2014/2021). "Meet Forbes Powerful Kenyan Women Who Quit their Well-paying IT Jobs." www.careerpointkenya.co.ke/2014/12/meet-forbes-powerful-kenyan-women-who-quit-their-well-paying-it-jobs/ (last accessed on December 14, 2023).

Ekiru, R. (2011). "M-Farm: Boosting Kenya's Agricultural Sector, One SMS at a Time," Africa Business Insight, 28 September 2011. www.howwemadeitinafrica.com/m-farm-boosting-kenyas-agricultural-sector-one-sms-at-a-time/12620/ (last accessed on December 14, 2023).

Emeana, E.M., Trenchard, L., and Dehnen-Schmutz, K. (2020). "The Revolution of Mobile Phone-Enabled Services for Agricultural Development (m-Agri Services) in Africa: The Challenges for Sustainability," *Sustainability*, 12 (485), pp. 1–27. www.google.com/url?sa=t&rct=j&q=&esrc=s&source=web&cd=&ved=2ahUKEwi-o4T6kuTpAhWwd98KHVz_AZAQFjAJegQIBxAB&url=https%3A%2F%2Fwww.mdpi.com%2F2071-1050%2F12%2F2%2F485%2Fpdf&usg=AOvVaw1kEvxcDQPqbW5g1XSs11p- (last accessed on December 14, 2023).

Engineering for Change (2018/2024). "M-Farm." www.engineeringforchange.org/solutions/product/m-farm/

Evans, R. E. (2015). "How M-farm Is Helping Kenya's Agriculture Industry Thrive," October 12, 2015. https://sites.psu.edu/ist110pursel/2015/10/12/how-m-farm-is-helping-kenyas-agriculture-industry-thrive/ (last accessed on December 14, 2023).

FSD Kenya (2015/2022). "M-Farm," August 3, 2015, www.fsdkenya.org/themes/digital-finance/m-farm/ (last accessed on December 14, 2023).

Hetherington, D. (2008). "Case Studies in Social Innovation: A Background paper," Per Capita, October 2008. https://apo.org.au/sites/default/files/resource-files/2009-01/apo-nid3954.pdf (Last accessed on December 14, 2023).

Kachewanya, K. (2012). "Mfarm and Samsung Kenya to Launch M-Farm price application," June 4, 2012. www.kachwanya.com/2012/06/04/mfarm-and-samsung-to-launch-m-farm-price-application/ (last accessed on December 14, 2023).

M-Farm. (2022). www.crunchbase.com/organization/m-farm (last accessed on December 14, 2023).

M-Farm, Limited, Kenya. (nd). "M-Farm," Farm-D: Forum for Agricultural Risk Management and Development. www.farm-d.org/organization/mfarm-ltd-kenya/ (last accessed on December 14, 2023).

Mutiga, M. and Thiga, M. (2014). "How Apps Impact Farming Communities," 22 April 2014, *ICT Update Newsletter*, Issue 77, pp. 18-19. https://cgspace.cgiar.org/bitstream/handle/10568/75318/ICT077E_PDF.pdf?sequence=1&isAllowed=y (last accessed December 14, 2023).

Myllynpaa, V. (2016). "Mobile Applications, Solution for Sustainable Agriculture? – Study of mAgriculture Services in Kenya," Master's Thesis, Lappeenranta University of Technology, School of Energy Systems. http://itinerariosparaorganizaciones.com/images/infografias/desarrollo_juvenil/info9.pdf (last accessed on December 14, 2023).

Nation News. (2011/2020). "Girls Who Created Social Network for Farmers," January 7, 2011 (updated, July 3, 2020). https://nation.africa/kenya/news/girls-who-created-social-network-for-farmers--752000 (last accessed on December 14, 2023).

Solon, O. (2013). "Startup Gives Farmers Shot at Fair Prices, Market Access via Text Messages," June 23, 2013. *arsTechnica*. https://arstechnica.com/information-technology/2013/06/startup-uses-sms-to-give-farmers-shot-at-fair-prices-market-access/ (last accessed on December 14, 2023).

Startuplist Africa. (2022). "M-Farm." https://startuplist.africa/startup/m-farm (last accessed on December 14, 2023).

Tran, M. (2013). "Cassava on eBay? M-Farm SMS Helps Kenya's Farmers Get Better Prices," *The Guardian*, July 4, 2013. www.theguardian.com/global-development/2013/jul/04/m-farm-kenya-food-security (last accessed on December 14, 2023).

Part VI

Addressing Climate Change

"*The world must come together to confront climate change. When the well is dry, we know the worth of water.*"

Benjamin Franklin

"*Climate change is the single greatest threat to a sustainable future but, at the same time, addressing the climate change presents a golden opportunity to promote prosperity security and a brighter future for all.*"

Ban Ki-Moon

Chapter 19: Tetra Pak, Sweden – Reducing Climate Impact
Chapter 20: Elopak, Norway – Becoming Carbon-Neutral
Chapter 21: Johnson & Johnson, US – Reducing Carbon Emissions

This part of the book has 'Addressing Climate Change' as its theme. It contains three design cases from three different countries: Sweden, Norway, and the USA. All of them describe how three large companies: Tetra Pak, Elopak, and Johnson & Johnson based in the respective countries are addressing climate change. All three design cases have evaluation as integral parts of their solution

DOI: 10.1201/9781003479086-24

development and implementation phases since they use measurements to evaluate the results of their actions to reduce carbon emissions.

The following is a summary of what climate change means and what the world community is doing about it.

It is now generally believed that emission of greenhouse gases (carbon dioxide and other gases) by human activity is causing global warming that is resulting in climate change. In 1988, the United Nations Environment Program and the World Meteorological Organization established the Intergovernmental Panel on Climate Change (IPCC) with membership from 195 governments. IPCC has published several Assessment Reports, which have become authoritative source of scientific information on climate change. Since 1988 there have been several intergovernmental conferences on climate change leading to the international treaty, United Nations Framework Convention on Climate Change (UNFCCC), that has been ratified by 195 countries, which came into force in 1994. In 1997, UNFCCC adopted the Kyoto Protocol that came into force in 2005. The Kyoto Protocol operationalizes UNFCC by committing industrialized countries and countries in transition to reduce greenhouse gases (GHG) emissions in accordance with agreed individual targets. The protocol allowed the trading of emissions, leading to the concept of net carbon emissions, which is the balance between GHG emissions emitted to the atmosphere and removed from the atmosphere. (Riedy, 2016; United Nations Climate Change, 2020)

The three design cases in this part of the book, Tetra Pak, Elopak, and Johnson & Johnson, are major successful corporations. All of them are engaged in reducing GHG emissions and taking other actions for addressing climate change. It is this work that qualifies them to be engaged in for-profit social innovations; this work does not bring any revenue by itself, but it enhances the image and revenue of the companies. The following are the abstracts of the three social innovation design cases:

REFERENCES

Riedy, C. (2016). "Climate Change," chapter in book: Blackwell Encyclopedia of Sociology (Ritzer, G., Ed.), Blackwell. www.researchgate.net/publication/311301385_Climate_Change (last accessed on December 14, 2023).

United Nations Climate Change (2020). "What is the Kyoto Protocol?" United Nations Climate Change. United Nations Framework Convention on Climate Change, 2020. https://unfccc.int/kyoto_protocol (last accessed on December 14, 2023).

19

Tetra Pak, Sweden: Reducing Climate Impact

19.1 OVERVIEW

Tetra Pak is a worldwide producer of paper-based packaging for liquids as well as other products such as ice cream, cheese, vegetables, and pet foods (Robertson, 2002). The company, currently the largest food packaging company in the world by sales, was established by Rubin Rausing in Sweden in 1952. It is always in fierce competition with another such company, Elopak from Norway. (CISION PR Newswire, 2019; Laird, 2014; Tetra Pak, nd)

Tetra Pak espouses a corporate philosophy based on the tenet that "A package should save more than it costs." Such philosophy reflects Tetra Pak's ability to optimize the sustainable use of resources and its commitment to reducing the environmental impact of its operations as well as to enhancing the environmental performance of its products and solutions. (Tetra Pak, nd)

Tetra Pak's innovation approach to reducing its climate impact includes establishing key performance metrics for operational energy use, working with suppliers of its resources, and seeking to align its clients' commitments to energy efficiencies.

The rest of the chapter describes in detail design of the sustainability related for-profit social innovation (and the corresponding social enterprise), Tetra Pak (Reducing Climate Impact).

19.2 CONTEXT

United Nations Framework on Climate Change took effect in 1994. (United Nations Climate Change, nd). It was operationalized as the Kyoto Protocol in 2005. The Kyoto Protocol commits industrialized countries and economies in transition to limit and reduce greenhouse gases (GHG) emissions in accordance with agreed individual targets. (United Nations Climate Change, 2020).

The greenhouse gas emissions have been categorized as Scope 1, 2 and 3 emissions, by the Greenhouse Gas Protocol. Scope 1 emissions are "direct emissions" of an organization, emissions by the things it owns or controls. Scope 2 emissions are "indirect" emissions" created by the energy bought by the organization. Scope 3 emissions are also indirect emissions, but they are produced by its suppliers for producing the products that the organization uses or by its customers using its products. (Greenhouse Gas Protocol, 2023; World Economic Forum, 2022)

The innovation journey of Tetra Pak in reducing climate impact is about the company's efforts in reducing the three types of its emissions.

19.3 INNOVATION DEVELOPMENT JOURNEY

19.3.1 Lap(s) / Stage(s)

19.3.1.1 Lap (Stage) 1 (2005-): Reduce Direct Emissions (Scope 1 and 2 emissions)

19.3.1.1.1 Problem Definition

Addressing energy had been a Tetra Pak goal, but it was not aligned with climate change goals, and not well defined as a business objective. The lack of a well-defined business objective meant that energy issues were not easily communicated to management or employees and efforts in regard to reducing environmental impacts of energy use were not seen as a core value. Tetra Pak's energy goals of course began with addressing energy efficiency by improvements in energy use and better operations. However, inevitably they had to address the energy supply chain – ensuring that the energy that they used was green.

19.3.1.1.2 Suggestion

Enter partnership with a group for whom the environment is a core issue and work together on a focused energy goal. NGO-Business Partnerships can have high impact with complex issues such as climate change. Communication between an NGO and a business may be blurred to "speak the same language" (for instance, on carbon reduction), but this can allow a business to see "outside the box" in devising solutions. (Lindgren and Riedel, 2012)

Develop procurement policy to ensure that a supplier of green energy does produce from "green" sources and that, further, the premium price paid for the energy is indeed invested (by supplier) into more green energy production (e.g., not used to support non-green energy.)

19.3.1.1.3 Solution Development, Evaluation, and Implementation

Corporate Social Responsibility is noted as a significant factor that drives companies to adopt and achieve social goals, such as reducing environmental impact (Coelho, 2018). The establishment of company-wide policy clearly is desirable, but the establishment of standards frameworks such as Global Reporting Initiative, which uses International Organization for Standardization (ISO) metrics guidelines, or the 2015 United Nations Sustainable Development Goals (SDGs) (United Nations, nd) are important in driving action toward fulfilling those goals. Of the 17 UN SDGs, one can recognize the issue of environmental impact in at least 7 of them:

1. Clean Water and Sanitation
2. Affordable and Clean Energy
3. Sustainable Cities and Communities
4. Responsible Consumption and production
5. Climate Action
6. Life Below Water
7. Life on Land

Of course, the degree to which a company adopts values based on such frameworks and goals can vary. Tetra Pak has taken specific actions on its own to address its corporate social responsibility. The first such action can perhaps be its participation in partnerships as a key success factor. The UN's 17th SDG is "Partnerships for the Goals." Tetra Pak's membership in World Wildlife Fund's Climate Savers Program is an example of the strategic value, and opportunities, of such partnerships (Lindgren and Riedel, 2012).

With insights from new NGO-Business partnerships Tetra Pak reframed its core energy goal – not a goal focused on energy costs, but rather a goal focused on energy efficiency. An important aspect of this reframed goal was Tetra Pak's team structure, such that everyone in the company became engaged. Additionally, Tetra Pak has looked beyond itself and its supplier chain for achieving energy efficiency; it has also considered its clients and even the shaping of the next generation.

To achieve energy efficiency, Tetra Pak focused on entering partnership with World Wildlife Fund's Climate Savers Program and working with Science Based Targets Initiative. This resulted in procuring green energy, conducting energy audits, setting of science-based targets, and accurate demonstration of Tetra Pak's contribution to low carbon economy as discussed below.

Upon entering partnership with World Wildlife Fund's Climate Savers Program in late 2005, Tetra Pak established a target for achieving energy efficiency in conjunction with purchasing green energy – the premium cost of purchasing green energy to be offset by energy efficiency per product. Especially important was the fundamental refocusing of the business object-ives with respect to energy use policy. Rather than focusing on manager (and, in effect, employee) performance on "energy cost per unit," the focus became "energy efficiency per unit." (WWF, 2009)

Tetra Pak worked with WWF to establish policy directives to ensure pro-curement of energy from green sources. This would often require Tetra Pak working with suppliers to formulate new green energy practices in conjunc-tion with local governments. Part of Tetra Pak's method was conducting energy audits to determine, sources, consumption, and efficiency of its fac-tories' energy supplies. However, such audits were not standard, not always applied, and tended to focus on only strategic areas, such as cooling and ventilation.

Tetra Pak refocused its management teams' Key Performance Indicators (KPI) on the re-defined energy targets, energy efficiency (not cost). Management teams were structured as "Pillars," cross-functional teams of staff, engineers, supervisors, working together from different parts of the factory. This improved communication and help ensure that the new energy efficiency goals were clear to all. Local environmental pillars communicated with corporate level pillars on progress. Especially effective was that problems and solutions identified by local pillars were then shared across Tetra Pak, with data and metrics, encouraging best practices dis-semination world-wide.

In 2015, Tetra Pak also began adopting metrics and approaches promulgated by the Science Based Targets organization as an additional method to ensure that Tetra Pak's longer-term energy commitments would continue to improve. The Science Based Targets initiative champions science-based target setting as a powerful way of boosting companies' competitive advantage in the tran-sition to the low-carbon economy. It is a collaboration between Customer

Data Platform (CDP), World Resources Institute (WRI), the Worldwide Fund for Nature (WWF), and the United Nations Global Compact (UNGC). (Science Based Targets, 2017)

Tetra Pak's Brazilian factory units were more challenged when conducting energy audits as 85% of Brazil's energy was hydro-electric, so achieving additional energy efficiency was especially complicated. The Brazil unit worked with a machine supplier to implement a "full energy audit," going beyond the low-hanging fruit of cooling and ventilation systems. The resulting energy audit tool and methodology was shared (via Tetra Pak's management/corporate pillar teams), so that a comprehensive, standardized audit tool could be applied even to Tetra Pak's European sites, achieving yet additional energy efficiencies. By 2022, Tetra Pak achieved getting 80% of its energy from renewable sources. (CISION PR Newswire, 2022)

The Climate Group's publication "Green Power Market Development Group – Europe – Case Studies," highlights Tetra Pak's commitment to reducing energy consumption (The Climate Group, 2007). The case study highlights the strategy of Tetra Pak acquiring energy that meets the Eugene Standard. Eugene (European Green Electricity Network) is an independent green energy certification and accreditation system that seeks to ensure that the energy source is "green," that it is voluntary (e.g., not forced by a governmentally mandated regulation), and that it is generated by "new" facilities (generally ones that are focused on clean energy from the start – not older plants rebalancing their energy mix).

Further implementation of supply chain conformance to energy efficiency is evidenced by an agreement that Tetra Pak entered with WWF in 2006. (WWF, 2006). By the agreement, not just would Tetra Pak reduce its own energy footprint, but it committed to sourcing its forest products only from responsibly produced and managed forests. The agreement supported the Global Forest & Trade Network, a WWF and forest industry initiative, to eliminate illegal logging and improving forest management and creating a resource center as global source of forestry conservation. In 2009, Tetra Pak began extending its climate strategy with suppliers other than for energy, engaging with aluminum and polymer suppliers.

Partnership with WWF helped Tetra Pak in the process of identifying key success factors for its energy and environment impact initiative. The partnership helped Tetra Pak establish corporate energy efficiency goals with Key Performance Indicators related to energy efficiency as part of managers' performance evaluations. Implementing cross-functional task forces of employees facilitated sharing of insights on successful local solutions.

Problems and their solutions were identified by local pillars via coordinating management pillars and were shared across Tetra Pak (along with data and metrics) encouraging best practices dissemination world-wide.

The WWF partnership also led to Tetra Pak defining science-based targets for its energy strategy. The success of such partnerships is reflected further by Tetra Pak's work with Science Based Targets (SBT) Initiative formed in 2015 to help companies set energy targets based on science. Tetra Pak's Mario Abreau, VP for Environment said: "The collaboration with the SBT initiative has helped us accurately define our greenhouse gas emission targets and set a direction for the company in a scientific way. The new targets ensure we can openly and accurately demonstrate the contribution we are making to a low carbon economy among customers and other stakeholders." (Tetra Pak, 2017; Tetra Pak 2018 Sustainability Report, 2019; Tetra Pak 2022 Sustainability Report, nd)

Working with the Science Based Targets (SBT) initiative, Tetra Pak has committed to reduce its scope 1 and 2 emissions 42% by 2030, and 58% by 2040 from a 2015 base-year. (Science Based Targets, 2017). In doing so, Tetra Pak became the first company in the food packaging industry to have its climate impact reduction targets approved by the Science Based Targets (SBT) initiative. As of 2022, the greenhouse gas emissions (GHG) were down by 36%. (CISION PR Newswire, 2022; Tetra Pak-News Archive, 2017)

Focusing on energy sources of its suppliers, helps Tetra Pak stay truly clean, and not practicing "green washing" (a term applied to deceptive claims of clean energy use). The development of a full energy audit tool associated with Eugene – European Green Electricity Network) standard was necessary for its Brazilian units to achieve greater energy efficiencies. This tool was adopted by Tetra Pak's German unit, so that it could itself achieve greater energy efficiencies. (The Climate Group, 2007). Use of the Eugene (European Green Electricity Network) tool was discontinued in 2009, which highlights challenges in assuring clean energy sources from suppliers, with Tetra Pak now having to negotiate each energy source, and its "greenness" individually with each supplier.

Tetra Pak's extension of its energy efficiency commitment to all its resource suppliers (not just energy suppliers), helped it offset potential setbacks such as the discontinuation of Eugene certification and accreditation mechanisms, not to mention it helped raise the bar of the suppliers as to their own energy efficiencies.

19.3.1.1.4 Circumscription

There was need to pay attention to Scope 3 emissions as well in addition to Scope 1 and 2 emissions.

19.3.1.2 Lap (Stage) 2 (2011-): Reduce other Indirect Emissions (Scope 3 Emissions)

19.3.1.2.1 Problem Definition

If the goal is continual sustainable improvements in energy efficiencies, how does a business achieve additional improvements after it has "cleaned its own house," and even pushed energy efficiencies through its supplier chain? Indeed, as more businesses compete based on the reputation of clean energy and low environment impacts, how does a business differentiate itself?

19.3.1.2.2 Suggestion

Look the other way, not back at the supplier chain, but at the customer base and the demand side for the packaging that Tetra Pak produces.

19.3.1.2.3 Solution Development, Evaluation, and Implementation

As in lap (stage) 1, here too evaluation through use of metrics is central to making claims related to CO_2 emissions reduction and other similar claims. The following provides details on what Tetra Pak has done on reduction of Scope 3 (indirect) emissions.

Tetra Pak's focus on customers and retailers can lead to understanding the demand side of products (Coelho, 2018). Customers have perceptions of the value of what is being purchased and this can be important in understanding what drives demand. Retailer and customer views are critical to changing the buying habits – with consequences and opportunities for additional reduction of energy use (e.g., if you don't have to refrigerate, less energy is used by retailers and consumers).

Tetra Pak's "2018 Sustainability Report" states: "Linking our sustainability agenda with that of our customers is one of the biggest opportunities for us to drive change, so we proactively work with them to find out how we can best support them. Our customers want to make their operations as efficient as possible, which means reducing water and energy usage, carbon emissions, and food and packaging waste. We work on all these fronts to offer our customers the best possible solutions, with the smallest carbon footprint." (Tetra Pak 2018 Sustainability Report, 2019)

Among the actions that Tetra Pak has taken was joining the Circular Economy (CE100) a multi-stakeholder organization supporting a restorative, regenerative economy in 2016. An example of restorative/regenerative economy is the development of plastics from renewal feedstocks that can be recycled, and bio decayed. Tetra Pak supports the EU's Action Plan for Circular Economy and backs the EU Strategy on Plastics.

Tetra Pak began to roll out (in 2018 after 2017 pilot program) a Holistic Customer Experience program and has offered Expert Services to customers. For example, in a seven-week project Tetra Pak helped a North America juice producer achieve "20% reduction in CO_2 emissions, a 30 percent reduction in water use and a cost saving of half a million euros." (Tetra Pak 2018 Sustainability Report, 2019)

Additionally, as an indication of how Tetra Pak is reaching out even to future customers, World Wildlife Children's Book "Grow a Green Gene" was published in partnership with Tetra Pak. It directly addresses children on climate change issues and how they have individual standing and a collective impact. (Raghbeer & Baruah, 2011; WWF, 2011)

19.3.1.2.4 Circumscription

Tetra Pak is incorporating its customer/retail base as part of its sustainability planning, seeking communication of value proposition of its practices to support its initiatives of environmental sustainability.

19.3.2 Diffusion

The diffusion of Tetra Pak's approach to climate and environmental stewardship can be characterized by the innovation steps it has taken.

First, Tetra Pak recognized the value of establishing partnerships, even ones that were counterintuitive: between an NGO like WWF and a business like itself, with perhaps counter poised core objectives. This partnership helped Tetra Pak see beyond the boundaries of its own, self-imposed energy goals and adopt a re-framing of its energy goals, from one focused on cost to one of efficiency. This enabled Tetra Pak to communicate its business objectives clearly to its own management and staff, which became critical to ensure success of its emissions goals. The adoption of science-based metrics and targets also became a powerful way to measure progress toward its goals, and to demonstrate clearly to stakeholders the impacts of its actions.

Second, the diffusion can be seen as well in how, as Tetra Pak pushed its energy goals to greater improvements, it influenced its suppliers, first suppliers of energy, but then suppliers of other resources as well used by Tetra

Pak production. This led to Tetra Pak's development of a full audit energy tool, which was shared among its world-wide units. This inclusion of its worldwide suppliers led inevitably to the involvement of governments and local legislation and policies, expanding the sphere of awareness.

Third, one should keep in mind that business is a competitive endeavor. As Tetra Pak, touted its own environment friendly strategic goals, others saw the value proposition of adopting similar strategic goals, of attaining similar certifications. The Public Relations value of participating in organizations such as WWF, SBT, and others, each with their own public relations campaigns, has important value.

Fourth, Tetra Pak recognized its customers and retailers as part of their success and hence part of the overall energy goals. Perhaps one could view the Tetra Pak experience as one of strategic partnerships, linked together in an innovative eco-system of mutually aligned goals.

19.4 INNOVATION RESULTS

An innovation journey with new NGO-Business partnerships such as World Wildlife Fund certainly enabled Tetra Pak to remain competitive by applying a social innovation strategy (IMD, 2009). Tetra Pak, however, still has ongoing pressure on established businesses from low-cost competitors (Andreason and Wind, 2014), so use of social innovation strategies will not be the only means of achieving success.

Tetra Pak reduced its Scope 1 and 2 emissions by 54.3% between 2016 and 2021 (CSRWire, 2023). In 2022, Tetra Pak reduced GHG emissions by 39%, with using 84% of its energy supply from renewable sources. It reduced its GHG emissions by 70% from 2010 to 2020. Its target is to reach net zero emissions by 2030. (Tetra Pak, 2023)

19.5 APPLICABLE KNOWLEDGE & KNOWLEDGE CONTRIBUTION

Models/Metamodels

Unmet Social Need (Hetherington, 2008; see Chapter 1)
Climate change is an imminent threat to the wellbeing of people all over the world. Emission of greenhouse gases has been recognized as a contributor

to climate change. United Nations Framework on Climate Change was operationalized as Kyoto Protocol in 2005. The protocol commits industrialized countries and countries in transition to limit greenhouse emissions in accordance with agreed targets. Being the current largest food packaging company in the world, Tetra Pak needed to take proactive steps to mitigate climate impact.

External Partnerships

Tetra Pak's participation in partnerships has been a key success factor in reducing its climate impact. Partnership with World Wildlife Fund's Climate Savers Program helped Tetra Pak to refocus its energy use policy to energy efficiency per unit. Its partnership with Science Based Targets Organization helped it to adopt metrics to improve its long-term energy commitments in its transition to low-carbon footprint. (WWF, 2009)

Social Enterprise Business Model Template (see Chapter 1, Section 1.2.2)

The model, shown in Figure 19-1, summarizes the overall business model of Tetra Pak in accordance with the template provided by Figure 1-2 of Chapter 1. The 11 components of the business model are briefly described below.

Mission – Goals

The sustainability related mission of Tetra Pak is to reduce its climate impact using a well-designed strategy that monitors and demonstrates its progress in achieving this mission.

Key Partners – Needed for the Social Enterprise to Work

Tetra Pak established partnerships with several non-government organizations to achieve its sustainability goals: 1) World Wildlife Fund. This partnership helped it to establish goals for energy efficiency along with purchasing green energy. and link management team's key performance indicators with energy efficiency targets. 2) Science Based Targets Initiative. The partnership helped it to use metrics to accurately monitor its greenhouse gas emissions and to demonstrate progress in reducing its impact on climate change.

Key Activities – Performed for the Social Enterprise to Function

Tetra Pak performed multiple key activities related to sustainability. These included establishing and using targets for energy efficiency (instead of energy cost). It linked management teams' Key Performance Indicators with achieving energy efficiency targets and used them for measuring performance. It also started using metrics for measuring its progress on meeting its climate impact reduction targets approved by the Science Based Targets Initiative.

Tetra Pak (Reducing Climate Impact) Overall Business Model

Mission
Reduce the climate impact of Tetra Pak to fulfill its sustainability related goal.

Key Partners	Key Activities	Value Proposition	Customer/Beneficiary Relationships	Customer/Beneficiary Segments
• WWF (Worldwide Wildlife Fund) • SBT (Science Based Targets Initiative)	• Establishment and use of targets for energy efficiency and purchase of green energy. • Linking of management team's KPIs with energy efficiency targets for performance evaluation. • Adoption and use of metrics to monitor GNG emissions.	• Reduction of climate impact in Tetra Pak's manufacturing processes. • Reduction of climate impact by the types of packages it manufactures and sells to its customers.	• Maintenance of good relationships with suppliers, customers, end-consumers, the government, United Nations, and society. Channels • Online Portal • Meetings • Presentations at national and international forums	• Dairy and food industry • End consumer of Dairy and Food Industry • Society at large • United Nations and climate impact NGOs
	Key Resources • Resources provided by Tetra Pak company.			

Cost Structures
• Energy efficiency cost
• Additional cost of using renewable energy
• Sustainability related staff salaries

Revenue Streams
• Additional revenue generated by sustainability related positive perception of the company.

Impact
• Reduced Scope 1 and 2 emissions by 54.3% between 2021 and 2022.
• Reduced GHG emissions by 39%, using 84% energy supplies from renewal sources in 2022.
• Reduced GHG emissions by 70% between 2020 and 2020.

FIGURE 19.1
Tetra Pak Overall Business Model summarized in Social Enterprise Business Model Template shown in Figure 1.2.

Key Resources – Needed to make the Business Model to Work
All the key resources used by Tetra Pak to its climate related goals have been provided by the company.

Customer/Beneficiary Segments – Served by the Social Enterprise
The customer/beneficiary segments of Tetra Pak for climate impact reduction are 1) The dairy and food industry who use Tetra Pak packages for their products and the end-consumers of their products as well as its suppliers. 2) The government, United Nations, and society. They are positively influenced by Tetra Pak's production of packages that do not contribute or minimally contribute to climate change.

Value Proposition – Products and/or Services that create Value to Customers/Beneficiaries

Tetra Pak creates value to its customers/beneficiaries by reducing climate impact in the manufacturing processes used by it and by the types of Tetra Pak packages it manufactures and sells to its customers and are used by the end-consumers.

Customer/Beneficiary Relationships – with Customer/Beneficiary Segments
Tetra Pak keeps maintains good relationship with its suppliers, customers, end-consumers, the government, United Nations, and society to create an environment for business sustainability.

Channels – to Interface with Customer/Beneficiary Segments
The channels used by Tera Pak to interface with its customers and beneficiaries are its online portal, meetings, and presentations at national and international forums.

Cost Structures – Costs incurred to Operate the Social Enterprise
The costs incurred by Tetra Pak in carrying out its sustainability efforts are the cost of improving its energy efficiency, additional costs incurred in using energy supply from renewable sources, and the costs of salary of staff devoted to addressing its work on sustainability.

Revenue Streams – Cash Generated from each Customer/Beneficiary Segment
The sustainability related revenue streams of Tetra Pak are the additional revenues realized by generating positive perception of the company as a company that is reducing climate impact.

Impact
Tetra Pak has created public relations value through its participation in organizations such as World Wildlife Fund, Science Based Targets, and others. It reduced its Scope 1 and 2 emissions by 54.3% between 2020 and 2021. In 2022, it reduced its greenhouse gas emissions by 39% with the use of 84% of energy supplies from renewable sources. It reduced its greenhouse gas emissions by 70% between 2010 and 2020 and aims to reach the target of net zero emissions by 2030.

REFERENCES

Andreason, E., and Wind, G. (2014). "How To Respond to Low-cost Competition – A Case Study," Master Thesis, Lund University. 2014. www.pm.lth.se/fileadmin/pm/Exjobb/Filer_fram_till_foerra_aaret/Exjobb_2015/Andreasson___Wind/How_to_respond_to_low_cost_competition_Gustav_Wind_Erik_Andreason.pdf (last accessed December 14, 2023)

CISION PR Newswire. (2019). "Liquid Packaging Carton Market Growth Analysis to 2028," Radiant Insights, Inc., December 9, 2019. www.prnewswire.com/news-releases/liq uid-packaging-carton-market-growth-analysis-to-2028--key-players-tetra-laval-elo pak-stora-enso--greatview-radiant-insights-inc-300971193.html (last accessed on December 14, 2023).

CISION PR Newswire (2022). "Tetra Pak Highlights New Milestones in 2022 Sustainability Report," 23 August 2022. www.prnewswire.com/news-releases/tetra-pak-highlig hts-new-milestones-in-2022-sustainability-report-301611116.html (last accessed on December 14, 2023).

Coelho, P.M.M. (2018). "A Tetra Pak Case Study. Improving Sustainability Strategy in the Supply Chain," MSc Thesis, Utrecht University. September 2018. www.academia.edu/ 42531041/A_Tetra_Pak_case_study (last accessed on December 14, 2023).

CSRWire. (2023). "Tetra Pak Recognized as European Climate Leader 2023," *Financial Times.* www.csrwire.com/press_releases/773756-tetra-pak-recognised-european-climate-lea der-2023-financial-times# (last accessed on December 14, 2023).

Greenhouse Gas Protocol. (2023). https://ghgprotocol.org/about-us (last accessed on December 14, 2023).

Hetherington, D. (2008). "Case Studies in Social Innovation: A Background paper," Per Capita, October 2008. https://apo.org.au/sites/default/files/resource-files/2009-01/apo-nid3 954.pdf (Last accessed on December 12, 2023).

IMD. (2009) "Breaking down Alignment Barriers: Tetra Pak Pulls Together Allies to Reach Climate Goals," December 29, 2009, www.imd.org/case-study/breaking-down-alignm ent-barriers-tetra-pak-pulls-together-allies-to-reach-climate-goals/ (last accessed on April 6, 2024).

Laird, K. (2014). "Elopak Plays One-upmanship Game with Tetra Pak," December 15, 2014. www.plasticstoday.com/plastics-processing/elopak-plays-one-upmanship-game-with-tetra-pak (last accessed on July 12, 2023).

Lindgren, E., Riedel, A. (2012). "WWF's Approach to Businesses. Moving beyond Interactional Difficulties To Address Climate Change," Master Thesis. Copenhagen University. June 28, 2012. https://research-api.cbs.dk/ws/portalfiles/portal/58442128/emma_lindgren_ og_anne_riedel.pdf (last accessed December 14, 2023).

Raghbeer, A., and Baruah, V.P. (2011). "Grow a Green Gene, Children's Book," WWF-India (& Tetra Pak India), 56 pp. https://d2391rlyg4hwoh.cloudfront.net/downloads/grow_ a_green_gene_book.pdf (last accessed December 14, 2023).

Robertson, G.L. (2002). "The Paper Beverage Carton: Past and Future," *Food Technology Magazine*, July 2002, Volume 56, No. 7. www.ift.org/news-and-publications/food-tec hnology-magazine/issues/2002/july/features/the-paper-beverage-carton-past-and-fut ure (last accessed on December 14, 2023).

Science Based Targets. (2017). "Science Based Targets Case Study: Tetra Pak," 2017. https:// sciencebasedtargets.org/wp-content/uploads/2017/04/Case-study_TetraPak.pdf (last accessed December 14, 2023).

Tetra Pak. (2017). 2017 Sustainability Report. www.responsiblebusiness.com/wp-content/uplo ads/2017/10/2017-sustainability-report.pdf (last accessed on July 12, 2023).

Tetra Pak. (2023). www.tetrapak.com/about-tetra-pak (last accessed on December 14, 2023).

Tetra Pak-News Archive. (2017). "Tetra Pak Announces Science-based Targets for Climate Impact Reduction. First in Food Packaging Industry to Receive SBT Approval," February 2, 2017. www.tetrapak.com/about-tetra-pak/news-and-events/newsarchive/ science-based-targets-for-climate-impact-reduction (last accessed December 14, 2023).

Tetra Pak 2018 Sustainability Report. (2019). https://consumerlab.it/wp-content/uploads/ 2019/02/Tetrapak.pdf (last accessed December 14, 2023).

Tetra Pak 2022 Sustainability Report. (nd). www.tetrapak.com/content/dam/tetrapak/public web/us/en/sustainability/Tetra%20Pak%20USCA%202022%20Sustainability%20Rep ort%20GLOBAL%20COMBINED%20FINAL.pdf (last accessed December 14, 2023).

The Climate Group (2007). "Green Power Market Development Group — Europe Corporate Case Studies," June 2007.

United Nations. (nd). Sustainable Development Goals. https://sdgs.un.org/goals (last accessed on December 14, 2023).

United Nations Climate Change. (nd). "What Is the United Nations Framework Convention on Climate Change?". https://unfccc.int/process-and-meetings/what-is-the-united-nati ons-framework-convention-on-climate-change (last accessed on December 14, 2023).

United Nations Climate Change. (2020). "What Is the Kyoto Protocol?". United Nations Framework Convention on Climate Change, 2020. https://unfccc.int/kyoto_protocol (last accessed December 14, 2023).

World Economic Forum. (2022). "What Is the Difference between Scope 1, 2, and 3 Emissions, and What Are the Companies Doing To Cut All Three?" www.weforum.org/agenda/ 2022/09/scope-emissions-climate-greenhouse-business/ (last accessed on December 14, 2023).

WWF. (2006). "WWF and Tetra Pak Sign Deal to Work on Forestry and Climate Change Issues," February 13, 2006. wwf.panda.org/wwf_news/?61820/Tetra-Pak-and-WWF-sign-deal-to-work-on-forestry-and-climate-change-issues (last accessed December 14, 2023).

WWF. (2009). *Climate Savers Innovation Case Studies*, December 01, 2009. https://c402277. ssl.cf1.rackcdn.com/publications/380/files/original/Climate_Savers_Innovation_C ase_Studies.pdf?1345748036 (last accessed on December 14, 2023).

WWF (2011). "WWF-India, Tetra Pak Concludes National 'Young Climate Savers' Programme," September 6, 2011. www.wwfindia.org/?6180/Young-Cli (last accessed December 14, 2023).

20

Elopak, Norway: Becoming Carbon-Neutral

20.1 OVERVIEW

Climate change is a global problem that is crossing borders. Reducing emissions helps manufacturers to maintain a low carbon footprint. Energy efficiency and phasing in renewable energy both reduce greenhouse gas emissions. In addition, manufacturers must compensate for their residual emissions like those from the transport of raw materials and finished goods, as well as emissions from business travel. By compensating residual emissions and becoming carbon neutral, manufacturers are positively contributing to climate change mitigation. (Packaging Europe, 2022)

Elopak is Norwegian maker of paper-based producer of cartons for liquids, founded in 1957 as a European licensee of Pure-Pak; the gable-top Pure-Pak patent was awarded in 1915. Elopak is among the world's top three beverage carton manufacturing companies, the second such company from Scandinavia (the other such company being Tetra Pak from Sweden) and is always in fierce competition with Tetra Pak. (Laird, 2014; Elopak, nd)

Elopak adopted actions for reduction of carbon emissions early. Still, it committed to a more aggressive policy when it was clear that its early efforts were modest in regulation compliance and business as usual could not make enough impact. A new CEO in 2007 sought to adopt a more rigorous climate policy, gain commitment and internal buy-in, establish business targets and systematic reporting, and make its energy policy part of its competitive advantage through public relations. Elopak evolved its approach over time, extending its efforts so that what began as compliance with existing regulations, reached outside its production operations to achieve a carbon neutral position that included raw material sourcing and after-customer recycling markets.

DOI: 10.1201/9781003479086-26

The rest of the chapter describes in detail design of the sustainability related for-profit social innovation (and the corresponding social enterprise), Elopak (Becoming Carbon Neutral).

20.2 CONTEXT

Global issues like climate change, and its pressure for sustainable development impact how businesses operate in a world that sees unintended consequences from increasingly complex and interconnected factors. While development of products to benefit customers is part of a business bottom line, businesses must develop strategies to address climate friendly energy practices, which have costs, so that those products have a net positive effect. Among available strategies are partnerships with non-governmental organizations (NGO) and businesses to provide mutual benefit – an NGO in advancing its agenda (e.g., addressing climate impacts) and a business gaining expertise to improve its operations. (Boué and Kjaer, 2010)

20.3 INNOVATION DESIGN JOURNEY

20.3.1 Lap(s) / Stage(s)

20.3.1.1 Lap (Stage) 1 (1990s-2006): Follow Environmental Standards

20.3.1.1.1 Problem Definition

Climate and environment were clearly identified as worldwide issues in the last part of the 20th century (United Nations Climate Change, 2020). Elopak sought to identify its approach to environment issues.

20.3.1.1.2 Suggestion

Accepted strategies were to reduce energy use and to ensure product materials met recycling standards. Elopak should analyze its business with respect to such standards.

20.3.1.1.3 Solution Development, Evaluation, and Implementation

Recycling and compliance standards were embraced. Life cycle assessments were conducted to determine Elopak's carbon footprint with respect to its paper packaging. Such assessment determined that the carbon footprint of paper-based carton packages was significantly lower compared to other packaging (cans, bottles). Elopak pitched its products as more environment-friendly, seeking to promote its products as a better choice for customers who were looking to support recycling policies adopted by many countries. (WWF, 2009)

20.3.1.1.4 Circumscription

Focus on packaging was not part of a comprehensive plan. While Elopak had the marketing edge (more environment-friendly packaging than glass or cans alternatives), this position did not have a comprehensive business rationale overall.

20.3.1.2 Lap (Stage) 2 (2007–2013): Establish Climate Policy

20.3.1.2.1 Problem Definition

Elopak had addressed recycling compliance as a response toward climate change issues, yet this was not seen as a very proactive stance, nor did Elopak have any comprehensive approach to carbon emissions reduction. The problem addressed in this lap was to overcome these deficiencies.

20.3.1.2.2 Suggestion

Establish a comprehensive climate and energy plan that could be executed proactively.

20.3.1.2.3 Solution Development, Evaluation, and Implementation

Expertise in climate action was sought. A comprehensive data analysis was performed to establish business case for targeting opportunities. All executives and employees worldwide were engaged to support Elopak's climate policy.

Having addressed recycling and compliance as Elopak's responsibility toward climate change issues, a newly appointed CEO, Niels Petter Wright, in May 2007, sought to improve Elopak's approach to climate and energy. He engaged Deloitte to audit Elopak's carbon footprint and company-wide carbon impact. The audit revealed that while Elopak's paper-based packaging was better than glass or metal packaged products, there was little strategy in place as far as its operations in creating those paper-based products were concerned.

Elopak began partnership with World Wildlife Fund (WWF) Norway to develop an emissions reduction goal and a comprehensive climate change action policy. WWF Norway guided Elopak in its biodiversity and climate strategy that included identifying targets for carbon emission reduction, establishing performance goals, and achieving Forest Stewardship Council certification. (Boué and Kjaer, 2010; WWF, 2009)

In 2009, Elopak committed to reducing its absolute CO_2 emissions by 15% from 2008 to 2011. The new CEO engaged company management to ensure that buy-in on the corporate energy policy began at the top. When executives questioned the 15% emission reduction target recommended by WWF, the CEO "helped them understand the business logic behind it: reducing CO_2 emissions means reducing energy consumption and cutting costs; reducing CO_2 means aligning with some of our clients that are leading the way on the issue in their own industry. It is, as a matter of fact, good for business." (WWF 2009)

The thinking of Elopak was changed from one of the burdens of reducing CO_2 emissions, to the opportunity of reducing energy consumption, and therefore costs, and aligning its energy and carbon-reduction policy with its clients.

Elopak issued a "Green Challenge" in which it invited all employees to contribute suggestions for reducing energy emissions. Elopak shared specific data on targets and progress with all employees, at all levels of its companies. It provided performance incentives for energy-saving suggestions. Elopak also made its new energy policy known to its customers, both to show how Elopak was aligning with customer emission reductions (such as recycling) or to encourage customer to undertake such efforts. (WWF, 2009)

Elopak announced its "FutureProof 2020" sustainability policy in 2012, noting that "the strategy is provocatively ambitious in the goals it set". Elopak summarized its progress "by the end of 2011, across all of the subsidiaries that are 100 per cent owned by Elopak, we successfully achieved a reduction of CO_2 emissions of 17% per produced carton and an absolute emission reduction of 10% compared to 2008." (Elopak 2013 Environmental Status Report, 2013)

Elopak's Environmental Status report, 2013, describes a comprehensive approach to reducing carbon emissions, covering three different scopes: direct greenhouse gas emissions from its core operations, indirect emissions related to that generated by purchased energy, and indirect emissions from other business activities (such as travel). As such the report demonstrated that Elopak was addressing carbon emission from a complete lifecycle of its business. It is noted, as well, that Elopak is part of Carbon Disclosure Project so that it provides data reporting in a globally standard way, thus underlining the fact all claims of emission reduction are based on evaluations backed by measurements and data. (Elopak 2013 Environmental Status Report, 2013)

20.3.1.2.4 Circumscription

Elopak's partnership with WWF Norway resulted in a formal, comprehensive business strategy around carbon emissions reduction. Goals were established and progress was monitored. Yet, cutting carbon emissions does not happen in a static environment, so challenges are ongoing. Elopak's progress was interrupted in 2013 due to a build-up of production capacity to meet demand. (Elopak 2013 Environmental Status Report, 2013)

20.3.1.3 Lap (Stage) 3 (2014-): Achieve and Maintain Carbon Neutrality

20.3.1.3.1 Problem Definition

Elopak needed to work on achieving and maintaining carbon neutrality.

20.3.1.3.2 Suggestion

Reduce emissions and offset emissions deficit through external projects. Extend a full life-cycle approach by looking outside one's immediate fully owned companies to identify additional opportunities.

20.3.1.3.3 Solution Development, Evaluation, and Implementation

In its 2016 Environment, Elopak states "Time is something we don't have. So, in parallel to trudging through the green transitions, we must find projects worldwide that can cut emissions quickly; preferably right now." (Elopak 2016 Environmental Report, 2019)

Therefore, Elopak looked beyond its fully owned operations to its suppliers, to its customers, and even outside Elopak entirely. In 2016, Elopak Environmental reported that it had begun to source only renewable electricity for use in all fully owned factories and offices and that it achieved carbon neutrality, thereby offsetting residual emissions. (Elopak 2016 Environmental Report, 2019; Elopak Carbon Neutral Approach, nd)

Elopak outlined its three steps for achieving carbon neutrality: first, measure Elopak's own emissions; second, reduce those emissions; third, undertake to support other emission reductions through carbon offsetting. "In carbon offsetting, a party can finance a project elsewhere in the world such as a US methane capture project." (Elopak 2016 Environmental Report, 2019)

Elopak achieved carbon offsetting by supporting external projects (one in Uganda related to improved cook stoves; one in Indonesia to preserve rain forests) which had their own emission reduction potential – that could only be realized by external funding. Importantly, Elopak's 2016 report shows that the rise in 2013 emissions (due to its production operations' expansion) was reined in again such that Elopak had, by 2016, achieved 68% reduction in greenhouse gas emissions from the 2008 level. (Elopak 2016 Environmental Report, 2019)

With respect to its sourcing of raw materials, Elopak undertook to improve its packaging further, substituting organic materials such as renewable polyethylene, ensuring that materials originate from Forest Stewardship Certified forests.

With respect to customers, Elopak developed DEEP (Dynamic Elopak Environmental Performance tool) that helps customers understand the carbon footprint of various carton options that are available. Elopak also supports recycling of its cartons, firstly by ensuring that its cartons are 100% recyclable, and by Elopak's active membership in industry associations in Europe and America. (Elopak 2016 Environmental Report, 2019)

Recycling has become a focus of the European Union. As the effectiveness of recycling does depend on the origination of product materials, Elopak's energy policy promotes a full lifecycle of energy focus: source materials well, produce efficiently, and so enable/promote high recycling rates. (Ruttenborg, 2017)

20.3.1.3.4 Circumscription

Elopak's carbon neutrality success resulted from not just how Elopak itself was meeting its emission reduction goals, but how it could reach out to external entities which had aligned their carbon emission goals with that of Elopak. (Elopak 2019 Sustainability Report, 2020; Elopak 2021 Annual Report, 2022; Elopak 2022 Annual Report, 2023; Elopak 2022 Sustainability Highlights, 2023)

20.3.2 Diffusion

The diffusion of Elopak's carbon emissions climate strategy had three aspects – Elopak executives and employees; Elopak's connected supply and customer chains; external projects with like-minded carbon reduction goals.

Important to Elopak's core success was the diffusion of its energy policy throughout the company. The CEO championed the carbon reduction goals, the company executives understood and supported the agenda, and information (mission, goals, progress) was transmitted throughout the employee base. Perhaps a key part of this diffusion was that Elopak brought everyone into the picture – every employee understood how they might effect change, and there were incentives (individual, business benefit) to reward actions.

Instrumental to this diffusion was partnerships, such as with the World Wildlife Fund Norway, Forest Stewardship Council, Carbon Disclosure Project, or the industry organizations in which Elopak participated. Interestingly, diffusion while likely thought of as one "from" Elopak's efforts outward, one can also recognize the diffusion (infusion, effectively) of ideas, perspectives, and expertise from these partnerships "into" Elopak. Perhaps this is not so far from the mark, for certainly it reflects the idea of a full life cycle connection of Elopak's comprehensive energy policy.

Elopak's DEEP tool (Elopak 2016 Sustainability Report, 2019) can be seen as a diffusion mechanism, providing customers with a message and comparative information of various Elopak products and their carbon footprint.

Elopak's achievement of carbon neutrality was achieved also by its funding of non-Elopak carbon reduction projects—more efficient, healthier cook stoves in Uganda, rainforest preservation in Indonesia. Certainly, these projects not only raised awareness of the needs for and benefits from carbon reductions in these locations but served as an example to the world community.

Moreover, Elopak's diffusion of its own success with achieving carbon neutrality is strongly mediated by its participation in a worldwide effort, and Elopak's sharing of its own results via its own public relations as well as that of organizations with which it participated.

20.4 INNOVATION RESULTS

One can identify a number innovation results from Elopak's experience in achieving carbon neutrality:

There is the innovation of engaging with non-company, non-governmental organizations to achieve very specific company-oriented business objectives. Such partnerships would seem to be counter intuitive: an NGO whose mission is actively promoting, or seeking enforcement, of policies which are costly and burdensome on for-profit businesses. (Boué and Kjaer, 2010) Yet there occurs a reframing of perspectives that enables success. The NGO seeks to understand business perspectives and how to frame compliance as opportunity. The business curbs its instinct to bristle at criticism and instead learns of its responsibility in a wider (indeed, worldwide) context; the business adopts, for instance, Carbon Disclosure Project reporting standards as a step toward sharing results (and indeed, generating positive public relations). (Elopak, 2013)

Elopak's inclusion of all employees—CEO, executive managers, supervisors, line employees—can be seen as innovative in transparently communicating company carbon reduction policy, and so ensuring everyone worked toward the common goal.

By setting rather aggressive carbon reduction targets, Elopak incentivized itself to take bolder steps to achieve its goals. Elopak developed even more friendly organic and carbon neutral packaging. It committed to renewable energy sources as a core principle for running its operations (both production and offices). It developed its DEEP tool to help customers understand the comparative carbon footprint of Elopak product choices.

One might argue that Elopak's carbon offsetting activity was maybe not so innovative—since it was a strategy developed outside of Elopak per se, but one must admit that Elopak's adoption of carbon offsetting projects in Uganda and Indonesia was innovation from its business perspective. Neither project was linked to Elopak in a business way, yet Elopak saw the overall benefit for the world community.

20.5 APPLICABLE KNOWLEDGE & KNOWLEDGE CONTRIBUTION

Models/Metamodels

Unmet Social Need (Hetherington, 2008; see Chapter 1)
Elopak was generally taking actions for reduction of carbon emissions, but it was not enough for regulation (such as the UN Kyoto Protocol) compliance. There was therefore a social need for it to adopt a more rigorous climate policy, which would also make it gain competitive advantage.

External Partnerships
Elopak's partnership with World Wildlife Fund Norway helped it to identify targets for carbon emission reduction, establishing performance goals, and achieving Forest Stewardship Council certification. (WWF, 2009)

Innovative Management for Achieving Sustainability

Elopak committed to reducing its absolute CO_2 emissions by 15% from 2008 to 2011 based on recommendation by World Wildlife Fund. This was an ambitious goal and needed company-wide buy-in. The CEO started from the top and made the company executives understand the business logic behind the emissions reduction goal as creating an opportunity for reducing energy consumption and therefore costs. Elopak also issued a "Green Challenge" in which it invited its employees to contribute suggestions for reducing revenue streams by the sustainability energy emissions. (WWF, 2009)

Social Enterprise Business Model Template (see Chapter 1, Section 1.2.2) The model, shown in Figure 20.1, summarizes the overall business model of Elopak in accordance with the template provided by Figure 1.2 of Chapter 1. The eleven components of the business model are briefly described below.

Elopak (Becoming Carbon Neutral) Overall Business Model

Mission
Achieve carbon neutrality of Elopak for mitigating climate change to fulfil its sustainability related goal.

Key Partners	Key Activities	Value Proposition	Customer/Beneficiary Relationships	Customer/Beneficiary Segments
• World Wildlife Fund (WWF) • Carbon Disclosure Project • Elopak management, employees, customers, suppliers • External carbon offsetting projects	• Measurement and quantification of emissions. • Continuous reduction of emissions. • Compensation of residual emissions by supporting projects outside value chain. **Key Resources** • Funds provided by Elopak	• Carbon neutrality • Healthier cook stoves in Uganda • rainforest preservation in Indonesia.	• Measurable reduction in Elopak's GNG emissions. • Positive attitude of beneficiaries of carbon offsetting **Channels** • Elopak online portal • Meetings and presentations at national and international forums	• Environment and world climate. • End-consumers using Elopak packages. • People benefited by Elopak's carbon offsetting projects.

Cost Structures	Revenue Streams
• Cost incurred for reduction in energy consumption to reduce emissions. • Costs for external projects offsetting residual emissions.	• Savings from reduced energy usage. • Enhancement of revenues by the positive perception through sustainability work.

Impact
Elopak became carbon neutral in 2016 and has since compensated remaining emissions through carbon neutrality projects.

FIGURE 20.1
Elopak Overall Business Model summarized in Social Enterprise Business Model Template shown in Figure 1.2.

258 • *Addressing Climate Change*

Mission – Goals

The sustainability related environmental mission of Elopak is to achieve carbon neutrality, i.e., to achieve net zero greenhouse gas (GHG) emissions by reducing its emissions and offsetting any residual emissions by supporting projects outside its value chain, which have been proven to reduce GHG emissions.

Key Partners – Needed for the Social Enterprise to Work

The key partners of Elopak are:

a. World Wildlife Fund Norway for developing emissions reduction goal and strategy for achieving it.
b. Carbon Disclosure Project for helping Elopak report its emissions data in a globally standard manner.
c. Management and employees who participate in the company's work on reducing greenhouse gas emissions.
d. Suppliers of Elopak's green energy and its suppliers of renewable raw materials.
e. Elopak customers for using Dynamic Environmental Performance (DEEP) tool.
f. External projects that help Elopak offset its carbon footprint.

Key Activities – Performed for the Social Enterprise to Function

The key sustainability related activities of Elopak are:

a. Measurement and quantification of its emissions in partnership with Carbon Disclosure Project.
b. Establishment of performance goals in partnership with World Wildlife Fund.
c. Continuously reducing emissions.
d. Compensation of residual emissions by supporting external projects.

Key Resources – Needed to Make the Carbon Neutrality Business Model to Work

All the resources used by Elopak for its sustainability work are provided by the company.

Customer/Beneficiary Segments Served by the Social Enterprise

The customer/beneficiary segments of Elopak for its sustainability work are the environment and society all over the world that is affected by climate change, sustainability related non-government organizations and groups, the end-consumers who use Elopak packaging, and the people who get benefitted by its carbon-offsetting projects such as people in Indonesia benefited by Elopak's rainforest preservation projects and people in Uganda using healthier cook stoves.

Value Proposition – Products and/or Services that Create Value to Customers/ Beneficiaries

Elopak creates value to its beneficiaries by its sustainability work of becoming carbon-neutral and by its external carbon-offsetting projects such as rainforest preservation in Indonesia and Uganda people getting healthier cook stoves.

Customer/Beneficiary Relationships – with Customer/Beneficiary Segments

The relationships Elopak has with its customers/beneficiaries are:

a. The measurable reduction that Elopak has made in its greenhouse gas emissions.

b. More efficient, healthier cook stoves in Uganda and rainforest preservation in Indonesia. They raised awareness of the needs for and benefits from carbon reduction in these locations and served as examples to the world community for such efforts.

Channels – to Interface with Customer/Beneficiary Segments

The channels Elopak uses to interface with its customers/beneficiaries are the company online portal, meetings, and presentations at national and international forums.

Cost Structure – Costs Incurred to Operate the (Carbon Neutrality) Social Enterprise

The costs Elopak incurred are the costs for reducing carbon emissions and the costs for operating external carbon reduction projects to compensate for residual carbon emissions.

Revenue Streams – Cash Generated from each Customer/Beneficiary Segment

The revenue streams for the sustainability work of Elopak are the savings from reduced energy usage and the enhancement of Elopak's revenue because of the positive perception among the end consumers of its packages resulting from its work on carbon neutrality.

Impact

Elopak became carbon neutral in 2016 and has since compensated remaining emissions to maintain carbon neutrality. To get to net zero greenhouse emissions, Elopak has supported projects outside of its value chain through third-party verified carbon emission reduction credits.

REFERENCES

Boué, K. and Kjaer, K. (2010). "Creating Value through Strategic Partnerships between Business and NGOs – A Descriptive Case Study of Six Partnerships in Norway," Master Thesis, Copenhagen Business School, 2010. https://research-api.cbs.dk/ws/portalfiles/portal/58817387/kim_boue_og_kristine_kjaer.pdf (last accessed December 14, 2023).

Elopak. (nd). History. www.elopak.com/about/history/ (last accessed on December 14, 2023).

Elopak Carbon Neutral Approach. (nd). www.elopak.com/usa/packaging-by-nature/carbon-neutral-approach/ (last accessed on December 14, 2023).

Elopak 2013 Environmental Status Report. (2013). https://silo.tips/downloadFile/environmental-status-report-2013 (last accessed December 14, 2023).

Elopak 2016 Environmental Report. (2019). "Carbon Neutral." www.elopak.com/app/uploads/2019/12/EnvironmentalReport_2016_LR.pdf (last accessed on December 14, 2023).

Elopak 2019 Sustainability Report. (2020). www.elopak.com/app/uploads/2020/07/Sustainability-Report-2019.pdf (last accessed on December 14, 2023)

Elopak 2021 Annual Report. (2022). www.elopak.com/app/uploads/2022/03/Arsrapport_2021_FINAL_WEB-1.pdf (last accessed on December 14, 2023).

Elopak 2022 Annual Report. (2023). "Resilience in Changing Climates." www.elopak.com/app/uploads/2023/03/Annual-Report-2022.pdf (last accessed on December 14, 2023)

Elopak 2022 Sustainability Highlights. (2023). https://sustainabilityreport2022.elopak.com/wp-content/uploads/sites/5/2023/03/Sustainability-highlights-2022_highres_-1.pdf (last accessed on December 14, 2023).

Hetherington, D. (2008). "Case Studies in Social Innovation: A Background paper," Per Capita, October 2008. https://apo.org.au/sites/default/files/resource-files/2009-01/apo-nid3954.pdf (last accessed on December 12, 2023).

Laird, K. (2014). "Elopak Plays one-upmanship game with Tetra Pak," December 15, 2014. www.plasticstoday.com/plastics-processing/elopak-plays-one-upmanship-game-with-tetra-pak (last accessed on July 13, 2023).

Packaging Europe. (2022). "Finalist Interview: Elopak's Pure-Pak® eSense carton," 4 November 2022. https://packagingeurope.com/finalist-interview-elopaks-pure-pak-esense-carton/9046.article (last accessed on December 14, 2023).

Ruttenborg, V. (2017). "Life Cycle Assessment of Fresh Dairy Packaging at ELOPAK," Master Thesis, February 2017. https://ntnuopen.ntnu.no/ntnu-xmlui/bitstream/handle/11250/2442424/16219_FULLTEXT.pdf?sequence=1&isAllowed=y (last accessed December 14, 2023).

United Nations Climate Change. (2020). "What Is the Kyoto Protocol?". United Nations Framework Convention on Climate Change. https://unfccc.int/kyoto_protocol (last accessed December 14, 2023).

WWF. (2009). *Climate Savers Innovation Case Studies*, December 01, 2009. https://c402277.ssl.cf1.rackcdn.com/publications/380/files/original/Climate_Savers_Innovation_Case_Studies.pdf?1345748036 (last accessed December 14, 2023).

21

Johnson & Johnson, USA: Reducing Carbon Emissions

21.1 OVERVIEW

Johnson & Johnson (J&J) is an American multinational corporation founded in 1886. It produces medical devices, pharmaceutical and consumer package goods. It has a good environment record; it was ranked third in 2009 Green Ranking among US 500 companies. (Reuters Johnson & Johnson Profile, 2023)

Johnson & Johnson's approach to addressing climate change began with a worldwide policy to reduce carbon emissions through reducing its energy needs. The focus on reducing emissions was followed by a push beyond "business as usual" with Johnson & Johnson adopting a specific energy policy and setting measurable goals (Johnson & Johnson, 2004). This policy applied equally to all its individual units and needed significant commitment of financial capital for various projects to realize their target goals. Johnson & Johnson established financial support mechanisms to realize the energy goals.

The rest of the chapter describes in detail design of the sustainability related for-profit social innovation (and the corresponding social enterprise), Johnson & Johnson (Reducing Carbon Emissions).

21.2 CONTEXT

At the end of the 20th century, the world was clearly in agreement as to the effect of climate change. The United Nations had operationalized its Framework Convention on Climate Change with the adoption of the Kyoto Protocol in 1997 (United Nations Kyoto Protocol, 2020). The Kyoto Protocol entered a ratification phase that culminated in February 2005.

DOI: 10.1201/9781003479086-27

Countries (eventually 192 – all but 2) around the world were working toward meeting their obligations. Large, international corporations such as Johnson & Johnson were looked to for leadership in this effort. Non-Governmental Organizations established initiatives to provide guidance and structure for climate efforts.

21.3 INNOVATION DEVELOPMENT JOURNEY

21.3.1 Lap(s) / Stage(s)

21.3.1.1 Lap (Stage) 1 (2003-): Establish Company-Wide Policy on Energy

21.3.1.1.1 Problem Definition

Having recognized climate concerns during the 1990s and having taken steps to improve energy use through "using less," Johnson & Johnson recognized a need for a more comprehensive and strategic policy approach.

21.3.1.1.2 Suggestion

Establishment of formal policy guidelines for the Johnson & Johnson organization worldwide was viewed as a necessary step.

21.3.1.1.3 Solution Development, Evaluation, and Implementation

Engaging with standards groups or like-minded organizations addressing climate issues was part of Johnson & Johnson's strategy. Much like the worldwide Y2K effort at the close of the 20th century, those addressing world climate would benefit from working together, sharing ideas, establishing common frameworks, and measuring progress in standardized ways.

Johnson & Johnson embarked on its "Climate Friendly Energy Policy" in 2003 with its chairman, noting that continuing "business as usual" (e.g., focusing only on using less energy) was not sufficient and that Johnson & Johnson would address "implementing state-of-the-art technologies to improve energy efficiency and harness renewable resources such as solar and wind power." (Johnson & Johnson, 2003/2022; Johnson & Johnson, 2004; Johnson & Johnson, 2005)

Johnson & Johnson's 2004 Sustainability Report (Johnson & Johnson, 2004) was prepared based on the Global Reporting Initiative's (GRI) 2002

Sustainability Reporting Guidelines (Global Reporting Initiative, 2020). The mission of GRI is to promote international harmonization in the reporting of relevant and credible corporate economic, environmental, and social performance information to enhance responsible decision-making. GRI is a pioneer of sustainability reporting, assisting "businesses and governments worldwide understand and communicate their impact on critical sustainability issues such as climate change." (Global Reporting Initiative, 2023)

GRI metrics provided a sound basis for setting goal targets and measuring progress – a common framework that normalized Johnson & Johnson's performance in relation to that of other corporations. The use of GRI metrics makes the reported information credible.

Further, Johnson & Johnson worked with the World Wildlife Fund to found Climate Savers Business Initiative (Schueneman, 2017; World Wildlife Fund, 2007) with specific goal of worldwide CO_2 emissions reduction. (World Wildlife Fund, 2007)

The Carbon Disclosure Project's "3% Solution report" (Carbon Disclosure Project, 2013), which resulted from a 6-year effort by input and expertise of a wide array of climate, energy and corporate sustainability experts, is an example of insight gained from a community-wide effort. The report helped reframe climate and energy efforts from that of liability and cost to one of business opportunity. Paul Simpson, CEO of CDP (Carbon Disclosure Project), noted that as a cumulative result of 10 years of data collection, "In 2012 over 4,100 companies globally submitted vital environmental data to CDP, detailing over 6,000 actions taken to reduce emissions. The average payback period was less than 3 years." The pooling of data, actions, and company outcomes resulted in a rich resource for planning and executing climate strategies.

Johnson & Johnson became a member of Green Power Market Development Group-Europe. As part of their re-focused energy policy to invest in renewable energy, Johnson & Johnson, implemented geothermal and wood chip boiler projects in Europe. (Climate Group, 2007a; Climate Group, 2007b)

21.3.1.1.4 Circumscription

Establishing a company-wide policy on energy was somewhat radical for a highly distributed worldwide company. Mandating of energy reduction projects was ambitious and put pressure on the distributed worldwide units to adjust their capital expenditure budget planning, having now to add energy projects into the mix of capital projects. There was sometimes slow progress due to each individual company having competition between regular operations and energy project units seeking budgeting from fixed capital budget.

21.3.1.2 Lap (Stage) 2 (2006-): Establish CO2 Capital Funding Process

21.3.1.2.1 Problem Definition

Johnson & Johnson's energy related projects were undertaken using capital funding budgets with attendant competition from other capital funding projects. There was a need to adjust the model of capital expenditures.

21.3.1.2.2 Suggestion

Individual company units needed infusion of capital to fund energy projects.

21.3.1.2.3 Solution Development, Evaluation, and Implementation

A clear strategy for how to allocate additional funding to capital budgets was established. As part of its new energy policy Johnson & Johnson established "an innovative CO_2 capital funding process to ensure funding for a variety of large projects that yield both notable environmental benefits and cost savings." (Johnson & Johnson, 2004)

This "capital relief" provided a standard evaluation process – ensuring that the energy projects competed on fair footing for infusion of capital relief.

21.3.1.2.4 Circumscription

Economic downturn of 2008 caused progress in the "capital relief" energy projects to fall, though perhaps the reduction was also from the effect of having addressed low-hanging fruit.

21.3.1.3 Lap (Stage) 3 (2009-): Respond to 2008 Economic Downturn and Reestablish Energy Projects

21.3.1.3.1 Problem Definition

Given the economic downturn of 2008, how to reestablish, reinvigorate, and maintain the various energy projects.

21.3.1.3.2 Suggestion

Reaffirm Johnson & Johnson's commitment and pay deliberate attention to science-based, data-driven goals and measuring progress.

21.3.1.3.3 Solution Development, Evaluation, and Implementation

A standard for reporting and measurement of policy goals related to energy was established and used. Johnson & Johnson presented its 2010

Responsibility Report consistent with the Global Reporting Initiative's sustainability reporting guidelines (Global Reporting Initiative, 2006; GRI Sustainability Reporting Guidelines, 2006) and represented the first time it was self-declaring its sustainability to be at Level B." (GRI Application Levels, 2012; Johnson & Johnson, 2010). This level of reporting included "Report on a minimum of 20 Performance Indicators, at least one from each of: economic, environment, human rights, labor, society, product responsibility." It is important especially from the perspective of transparency of a company's activities and as a dataset which can be compared with other companies' efforts.

It can be argued that part of the solution space was in how Johnson & Johnson viewed the problem of energy not necessarily as a cost, but as an opportunity. Organizations such as World Wildlife Fund and CDP were providing best practices and strategies, emphasizing the business opportunities for climate actions. (Carbon Disclosure Project, 2013)

Subsequent Johnson & Johnson reporting shows continued tracking of climate/environment sustainability. (Johnson & Johnson, 2016; Johnson & Johnson, 2019)

The 2016 report provides a "Progress Scorecard for Climate & Water," showing them both as "on track" (p. 24). The specific data for Climate and Energy (pp. 68–72) are provided and afford a level of insight that can be compared to other companies in a consistent way. For instance, it is noted that: "We do not use carbon offsets to reduce our global emissions footprint. In 2016, our combined CDP (Carbon Disclosure Project) disclosure and performance score was an A-, scoring above both the CDP program average and industry group averages." (Johnson & Johnson, 2016)

A company "Climate and Energy" web-page notes "We have set a science-based scope 1 and 2 goal to reduce our absolute carbon emissions 20% by 2020, and 80% by 2050 compared to our 2010 baseline; and to produce or procure 35% of electricity use from renewable sources by 2020, and 100% by 2050." The page invites readers "To see how we are progressing against our goals" by following a link in its 2018 Health for Humanity Report (Johnson & Johnson, 2018). It achieved 100% use of renewable energy by 2021 across its European operations. (Asad, 2021; Johnson & Johnson, 2019).

In 2019, Johnson & Johnson continued to progress with their overall energy/climate goals – both as a worldwide corporation and as a participant with others: It reported partnering with organizations like C40 Cities Climate Leadership Group—a network of the world's 90 megacities that are committed to climate leadership and action—to help fund programs that will link climate action with the benefits to air quality and human health. (Climate and Clean Air Coalition, nd)

Johnson & Johnson is a founding member of the Climate Leadership Council, a coalition of industry, NGO and thought leaders seeking to address climate issues through a carbon dividends framework. (Johnson & Johnson, 2019)

21.3.1.3.4 Circumscription

Continued progress is needed, and Johnson & Johnson is seeking out new partnerships to maintain momentum as well as to inform itself of shared commitments.

21.3.2 Diffusion

Probably the greater portion of diffusion, besides Johnson & Johnson's initiatives in establishing a corporate-wide energy/climate policy for its own worldwide organization, is Johnson & Johnson's embrace of standards organizations and Non-Governmental Organizational bodies that are involved in energy and climate. Such partnerships benefit each of the participating partners as well as the world community which can, with transparency, see how much progress is being made.

21.4 INNOVATION RESULTS

Johnson & Johnson linked itself with Non-Governmental Organizations and associations which had expertise and shared experiences that provided a framework for climate environment responses. While itself a large, worldwide organization, Johnson & Johnson recognized that, much like the worldwide Y2K effort, it would benefit from the approaches and practices of other organizations. (Borkowski, et al., 2010; Johnson & Johnson Climate Policy, 2022)

Certainly, the adoption of standard metrics is not per se an innovation, but one might argue that for such a large, private, for-profit corporation to do so with the clear intent of publicly monitoring and sharing its climate and energy efforts is perhaps an innovation.

21.5 APPLICABLE KNOWLEDGE & KNOWLEDGE CONTRIBUTION

Models/Metamodels

Unmet Social Need (Hetherington, 2008; see Chapter 1)

At the end of the last century, there was agreement on the devastating effects of climate change and the need for the industrialized and economically emerging countries to reduce carbon emissions, resulting in the Kyoto Protocol that was ratified by almost all countries in 2005. Reducing carbon emissions has thus been recognized as an unmet social need that needs to be fulfilled. Being a large international corporation with a good environmental record, Johnson & Johnson has been looked to for providing leadership in fulfilling this need.

External Partnerships

Following the adoption of the UN Kyoto Protocol in 2005, several Non-Government Organizations established initiatives to provide guidance and structure in efforts to counter climate change. Johnson & Johnson started partnerships with these NGOs and taking leadership roles in the initiatives. These initiatives include Climate Savers Business Initiative by the World Wildlife Fund, Green Power Market Development Group-Europe, and the Disclosure Reporting System for tracking climate initiatives by the Carbon Disclosure Project. (World Wildlife Fund, 2009)

Monitoring, Reviewing, and Reporting for Sustainability

Johnson & Johnson followed the Global Reporting Initiative's sustainability reporting guidelines. This is evident from its 2010 Responsibility Report published in 2010 and subsequent sustainability reports, e.g., those published in 2016, 2018, 2019. (Global Reporting Initiative (GRI, 2023)

Social Enterprise Business Model Template (see Chapter 1, Section 1.2.2)

The model, shown in Figure 21.1, summarizes the overall business model of J&J in accordance with the template provided by Figure 1.2 of Chapter 1. The eleven components of the business model are briefly described below.

Mission – Goals

The sustainability related goal of Johnson & Johnson is to address climate change by establishing a worldwide policy to reduce carbon emissions

Johnson & Johnson (Reducing Carbon Emissions) Overall Business Model				
Mission Address climate change by reducing the carbon footprint of Johnson & Johnson to fulfill its sustainability related goal.				
<u>Key Partners</u>	<u>Key Activities</u>	<u>Value Proposition</u>	<u>Customer/ Beneficiary Relationships</u>	<u>Customer/ Beneficiary Segments</u>
• Carbon Disclosure Project • Climate Group • Global Reporting Initiative • Green Power Market Development Group-Europe • C40 Cities Climate Leadership Group • Climate Leadership Council • United Nations	• Establishment of company-wide energy policy. • Establishment of CO_2 capital funding process and projects. • Adoption of standard metrics for measuring emission goals. <u>Key Resources</u> • Resources provided by Johnson & Johnson company.	• Reducing carbon emissions by reducing J&J's energy usage, using of renewable green energy • Providing leadership in reducing carbon footprint.	• Measurable reduction in J&J's carbon footprint • Leadership in helping other corporations to meet their climate obligations. <u>Channels</u> • J&J company portal • Meetings and presentations at international forums	• Society • Like-minded climate related worldwide organizations and groups • Sustainability reporting groups
<u>Cost Structures</u> • Cost of renewable energy projects • Salaries of staff		<u>Revenue Streams</u> • Revenues generated by J&J that may get positively affected by its good climate work.		
<u>Impact</u> • Achieved A- score for its Carbon Disclosure Project disclosure and performance. • Set 2050 goals of 80% reduction in emissions and 100% use of renewable energy.				

FIGURE 21.1
Johnson & Johnson (J&J) Overall Business Model summarized in Social Enterprise Business Model Template shown in Figure 1.2.

through reducing energy needs, carrying out energy projects, and setting measurable goals for reducing its carbon footprint.

Key Partners – Needed for the Social Enterprise to Work
Johnson & Johnson (J&J) engaged with standards groups and like-minded organizations to achieve its goals. It therefore partnered with the following organizations:

a. Global Reporting Initiative and used its Sustainability Reporting Guidelines.

b. World Wildlife Fund (WWF) to found Climate Savers with the specific goal of worldwide energy usage reduction.

c. Carbon Disclosure Project that helped it to reframe climate and energy efforts from that of liability and cost to one of business opportunity.

d. Green Power Market Development Group-Europe to invest in renewable energy.

e. C40 Cities Climate Leadership Group to help fund programs that link climate action with benefits to air quality and human health.

f. Climate Leadership Council to address climate issues though a carbon dividends framework.

g. United Nations for using its Kyoto Protocol as a guideline for climate obligations.

Key Activities – Performed for the Business to Function

J&J performed multiple activities to achieve its climate goals. These included establishment of a company-wide energy policy, establishment of a CO_2 capital funding process and projects, and adoption of standard metrics for the measurement of emission goals.

Key Resources – Needed to make the Business Model Work

The key resources used by J&J to achieve its climate goals were those provided by the company.

Customer/Beneficiary Segments – Served by the Social Enterprise

The beneficiary segments of Johnson & Johnson's climate work were the society all over the world that is affected by climate change. Its beneficiaries are also other like-minded climate related organizations and sustainability reporting groups who are influenced by the climate leadership of J&J.

Value Proposition – Products and/or Services that Create Value to Customers/ Beneficiaries

J&J creates value to its beneficiaries through reduction in its carbon emissions by reducing its energy usage, using, and producing renewable green energy, and providing leadership to other corporations for how climate can be addressed in a significant and measurable manner.

Customer/Beneficiary Relationships – with Customer/Beneficiary Segments

The relationships of J&J with its beneficiaries are its contributions to addressing climate change and its leadership in helping other corporations to meet their climate obligations.

Channels – to Interface with Customer/Beneficiary Segments

The channels J&J uses to interface with its beneficiaries are the company portal, meetings, and presentations at international forums.

Cost Structures – Costs Incurred to Operate the Social Enterprise

The costs incurred by Johnson & Johnson in carrying out its climate obligations are the costs of implementing and operating renewable energy projects and the cost of salaries of staff devoted to its work related to addressing climate change.

Revenue Streams – Flow Generated from Each Customer/Beneficiary Segment

The revenue streams generated are the normal revenues of the products and services of Johnson & Johnson. These get indirectly affected positively by improving the perception of J&J as a corporation that is addressing climate change.

Impact

In 2016, J&J's combined Carbon Disclosure Project disclosure and performance score was an A-, scoring above both the Carbon Disclosure Project (CDP) program average and industry group averages.

It has set specific goals for reduction in emissions—80% by 2050 and to produce or procure 100% of the electricity it uses from renewable sources by 2050.

REFERENCES

Asad, H. (2021) "Johnson & Johnson Achieves 100% Renewable Electricity Across European Operations," Annual Environment + Energy Conference: Solutions Summit '23, July 13, 2021. www.environmentalleader.com/2021/07/johnson-johnson-achieves-100-renewable-electricity-across-european-operations/ (last accessed on December 14, 2023).

Borkowski, S., Welsh, M.J., and Wentzel, K. (2010). "Johnson & Johnson: A Case Study on Sustainability Reporting," *IMA Educational Case Journal*, 3 (1), p. 2, June 2010. Johnson & Johnson: A Case Study on Sustainability Reporting. www.google.com/url?sa=t&rct=j&q=&esrc=s&source=web&cd=&ved=2ahUKEwiGnI7Wxpv_AhX3nGoFHTRCB-EQFnoECA0QAQ&url=https%3A%2F%2Fwww.imanet.org%2F-%2Fmedia%2F5ef30cdd64eb4f4d9d47d06e4370971c.ashx&usg=AOvVaw3Rb_0UVWerdV-iZFJ8O24C (last accessed on December 14, 2023).

Climate and Clean Air Coalition. (nd). C40 Cities Climate Leadership Group. www.ccacoalition.org/en/partners/c40-cities-climate-leadership-group (last accessed on December 14, 2023).

Carbon Disclosure Project. (2013). "The 3% Solution". http://assets.worldwildlife.org/publications/575/files/original/The_3_Percent_Solution_-_June_10.pdf?1371151781 (last accessed December 14, 2023).

Climate Group. (2007a). "Climate Change." www.un.org/webcast/climatechange/highlevel/2007/pdfs/climategroup.pdf (last accessed on December 14, 2023).

Climate Group. (2007b). "Green Power Market Development Group — Europe Corporate Case Studies," June 2007.

Global Reporting Initiative. (2006). www.epsu.org/sites/default/files/article/files/Naoko_Kubo_GRI_EUSSWG_Process.pdf (last accessed on December 14, 2023).

Global Reporting Initiative. (2020). "Sustainability Reporting Guidelines, 2002." www.r3-0.org/wp-content/uploads/2020/03/GRIguidelines.pdf (last accessed on December 14, 2023).

Global Reporting Initiative. (2023). About GRI, "GRI Empowering Sustainable Decisions," www.globalreporting.org/Information/about-gri/Pages/default.aspx (last accessed on December 14, 2023).

GRI Application Levels. (2012). "GRI Application Levels," 2012. https://environz.files.wordpress.com/2012/05/applicationlevels.pdf (last accessed on December 14, 2023).

GRI Sustainability Reporting Guidelines. (2006). "G3 Version for public comment," 2 January 2006–31 March 2006. www.iasplus.com/en/binary/ifac/0601g3guidelines.pdf (last accessed on December 14, 2023).

Hetherington, D. (2008). "Case Studies in Social Innovation: A Background paper," Per Capita, October 2008. https://apo.org.au/sites/default/files/resource-files/2009-01/apo-nid3954.pdf (Last accessed on December 14, 2023)

Johnson & Johnson. (2004). "Johnson & Johnson 2004 Sustainability Report."

Johnson & Johnson. (2005). "The Robert W. Campbell Award – 2005 Case Study Submittal. www.campbellaward.org/wp-content/uploads/2017/06/RWC-JJ-Application.pdf (last accessed on December 14, 2023).

Johnson & Johnson. (2010) "Johnson & Johnson 2010 Responsibility Report". www.responsibilityreports.com/HostedData/ResponsibilityReportArchive/j/NYSE_JNJ_2010.pdf (last accessed December 14, 2023).

Johnson & Johnson. (2016). "2016 Health for Humanity Report – Progress In Citizenship & Sustainability". www.jnj.com/_document?id=0000015c-ce37-df25-affd-eeb775760000 (last accessed July 14, 2023).

Johnson & Johnson. (2018). "2018 Health for Humanity Report. Progress In Citizenship & Sustainability". www.jnj.com/2018-health-for-humanity-report (last accessed December 14, 2023).

Johnson & Johnson. (2019). "Climate & Energy". www.jnj.com/global-environmental-health/climate-and-energy (last accessed on December 14, 2023).

Johnson & Johnson Climate Policy. (2022). Johnson & Johnson Position on Climate Policy. www.jnj.com/about-jnj/policies-and-positions/position-on-climate-action (last accessed December 14, 2023).

Johnson & Johnson. (2003/2022). "Climate Policy," First published in 2003, last revised in 2022, April 2022. www.jnj.com/about-jnj/company-statements/johnson-johnson-climate-friendly-energy-policy (last accessed December 14, 2023).

Reuters Johnson & Johnson Profile. (2023). www.reuters.com/markets/companies/JNJ.N/#:~:text=Johnson%20%26%20Johnson%20is%20a%20diversified,Consumer%20Health%2C%20Pharmaceutical%20and%20MedTech. (last accessed on December 14, 2023)

Schueneman, T. (2017). "WWF Climate Savers Program: Business can lead on Climate Action," February 4, 2017. https://energycentral.com/c/ec/wwf-climate-savers-program-business-can-lead-climate-action (last accessed on December 14, 2023).

United Nations Kyoto Protocol. (2020). "What Is the Kyoto Protocol?" United Nations Climate Change. United Nations Framework Convention on Climate Change. https://unfccc.int/kyoto_protocol (last accessed on December 14, 2023).

World Wildlife Fund. (2007). "The Climate Savers Programme: How Corporations Can Save the Climate," March 2007. www.collinsco.com/Library/Press/WWF-Climate-Savers.pdf (last accessed December 14, 2023).

World Wildlife Fund Climate Savers. (2009). *Climate Savers Innovation Case Studies*, December 01, 2009. https://c402277.ssl.cf1.rackcdn.com/publications/380/files/original/Climate_Savers_Innovation_Case_Studies.pdf?1345748036 (last accessed on July 14, 2023).

22

Conclusions

This chapter briefly reviews how the twenty social innovations and associated social enterprises from around the globe (discussed in Chapters 2 through 21), spread in five continents, carried out their design work. It also reviews the applicable innovation design metamodels and the contributed models/metamodels. The first section summarizes and reviews the design process followed by the design cases. The second section discusses for the design cases the applicable metamodels and the models/metamodels contributed by them.

22.1 DESIGN PROCESS

Figure 22.1 shows the social innovation design process that has been used to structure and describe all the design cases in the book.

22.1.1 Design Cases in Part I

Part I of the book has three social innovation design cases dealing with the promotion of rural economic development in different ways. The three cases are: Chapter 2: Honey Care Africa; Chapter 3: Village of Andavadoake; and Chapter 4: Buhoma Village Walk.

The first case (Honey Care, Africa) in this part of the book describes how an interesting solution was developed for promoting honey farming in Kenya in two laps (stages). In the first lap (stage) the for-profit social enterprise was established for developing and implementing the solution. The second

DOI: 10.1201/9781003479086-28

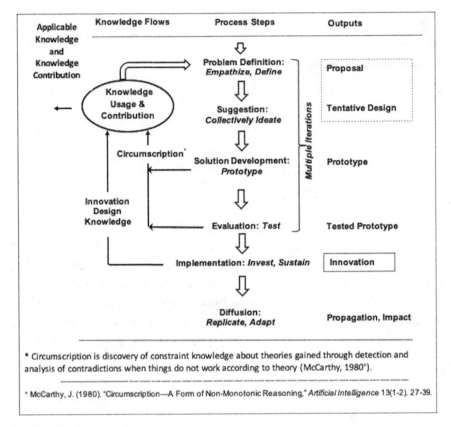

FIGURE 22.1
Social Innovation Design Process Model (same as Figure 1.1).

lap (stage) overcame some financial and logistics problems to improve the solution.

The second case (Village of Andavadoake) shows how octopus farming productivity was increased off the coast of Andavadoake village in Madagascar. The design case describes the two laps (stages) of its design journey. In the first lap (stage) an experimental solution was developed and implemented for increasing the quantity and quality of octopus catch. The second lap (stage) validated the solution.

The third case (Buhoma Village Walk) shows promotion of sustainable tourism through the development of a small-scale eco-friendly walk just outside the Bwindi Impenetrable National Park. The design case uses a single lap (stage) to develop and implement the village walk.

22.1.2 Design Cases in Part II

Part II of the book has four social innovation design cases dealing with improvement of infrastructure in different ways. The four cases are: Chapter 5: Lufumbu Village Water Scheme; Chapter 6: Husk Power Systems; Chapter 7: Waste Ventures India; and Chapter 8: Safaricom's M-Pesa.

The first case (Lufumbu Village Water Scheme) describes how the water shortage of Lufumbu village in Tanzania was offset through participative work. In the first lap (stage) the village water scheme was developed. Based on the success of this work, the water scheme was extended to cater to the additional demand of water in the second lap (stage) of its design journey.

The second case (Husk Power Systems) describes environmentally friendly generation of electricity in rural India in two laps (stages). The first lap (stage) describes how a new solution for producing electricity directly from rice husks was developed. The second lap (stage) describes how the solution successfully adapted to new realities stemming from sociological, technological, and political factors, resulting in a hybrid solution that uses both solar power and biomass sources.

The third case (Waste Ventures India) describes the on-ground development of a model for integrated waste management in India that is sustainable both environmentally and financially. The design case describes the two laps (stages) of its design journey. The first lap (stage) describes how an experimental on-ground model was developed. The second lap (stage) describes how a self-sustaining waste management system was created based on the knowledge gained from the first lap (stage).

The fourth case (Safaricom's M-Pesa) describes how a successful solution was developed for providing mobile-based financial services in Kenya in three laps (stages). The first lap (stage) describes the development and launching of M-Pesa, an electronic money transfer service. The second lap (stage) describes the linking of the accounts of M-Pesa users with their bank accounts. The third lap (stage) describes the use of the M-Pesa usage data by lenders to determine the credit worthiness of M-Pesa account holders.

22.1.3 Design Cases in Part III

Part III of the book has three cases dealing with the enhancement of healthcare in different ways. The three cases are: Chapter 9: TRACnet; Chapter 10: Aravind Eye Care System; and; Chapter 11: Rushey Green Time Bank.

The first case (TRACnet) describes the development of a dynamic information technology system for fighting pandemics in Rwanda. The design case is described in one lap (stage) of its design journey in which a phone and web-based infection monitoring system was developed.

The second case (Aravind Eye Care System) describes the design and development of a hospital network for preventing blindness in India. The design case is described in three laps (stages) of its design journey. In the first lap (stage) the initial Aravind Eye Hospitals were established to lay the foundation for the Aravind Eye Care System that provides high quality cataract surgeries free to poor people and at reasonable cost to other population segments. In the second lap (stage) the existing resources were leveraged to create a comprehensive eye care system that reaches people who would benefit from cataract eye surgery and provides cataract surgery as well as other eye care services. In the third lap (stage) the work already done was utilized to become a leader of eye care and to facilitate future growth.

The third case (Rushey Green Time Bank) describes the creation of a bank for reciprocal healthcare services exchange in the United Kingdom. The design is described in one lap of its design journey in which a time bank is established for the Rushey Green Group Practice in London that provides mental and physical health support to its patients based on offering and receiving reciprocal healthcare services.

22.1.4 Design Cases in Part IV

Part IV of the book has four cases dealing with various ways of generating or sustaining employment. The four cases are: Chapter 12: DesiCrew; Chapter 13: Infosys Global Education Center; Chapter 14: The Big Issue; and Chapter 15: WorkVentures.

The first case (DesiCrew) describes the development of rural employment in India through business process outsourcing in three laps (stages). In the first lap (stage), DesiCrew was developed and established as a rural business outsourcing company. In the second lap (stage) the training of its employees was optimized in terms of training content and training methodology. In the third lap (stage) the employee skills were upgraded to provide skills and knowledge of new technologies such as AI and machine learning.

The second case (Infosys Global Education Center) describes how the information technology company, Infosys, developed an education center that provides organization-specific, career-long multidimensional learning of its employees in a field that is changing so fast. The design case is described in one lap (stage) in which the Global Education Center was developed to provide core knowledge and to build learning agility among the employees.

The third case (The Big Issue) describes how The Big Issue magazine (newspaper) addressed homelessness by developing an income-earning model for homeless people that also builds their self-esteem. The design case has three laps (stages). In the first lap (stage), the street newspaper (The Big Issue) was developed for London, U.K. An online option for buying the newspaper was developed in the second lap (stage) and a non-cash option was provided in the third lap (stage).

The fourth case (WorkVentures) describes how WorkVentures provided skills to the disadvantaged people in Australia to make them capable of independent employment. The design is described in one lap (stage) and provides details on how WorkVentures was established and how it evolved over time.

22.1.5 Design Cases in Part V

Part V of the book has three cases offering diverse ways of transforming farming. The three cases are: Chapter 16: SEKEM; Chapter 17: Cotton Stripper; and Chapter 18: M-Farm.

The first case (SEKEM) describes how the holistic farming initiative of Dr. Ibrahim Abouleish was carried out in two laps (stages). In the first lap (stage), SEKEM company was established to promote biodynamic (holistic) and organic agriculture. In the second lap (stage), the scope of SEKEM was expanded to include other areas such as pharmaceuticals derived from plants and textiles made from organic cotton.

The second case (Cotton Stripper) describes the work of Mansukhbhai Patel for mechanizing cotton stripping in two laps of its design journey. In the first lap, the initial work on the invention and development of the cotton stripper, Chetak, was done. In the second lap (stage), the final development of Chetak and its commercialization took place.

The third case (M-Farm) describes how an information and communication tool was developed for monitoring real-time crop market prices in Kenya. The design case, M-Farm, is described in one lap (stage), in which the social innovation was developed and made available to farmers.

22.1.6 Design Cases in Part VI

The final part (Part VI) of the book has three cases all of which are dealing with climate change. The three cases are: Chapter 19: Tetra Pak; Chapter 20: Elopak; and Chapter 21: Johnson & Johnson.

The first case (Tetra Pak) describes how Tetra Pak, a world-wide producer of paper-based packages started addressing climate change in two laps (stages). In the first lap (stage), the work of reducing direct green-level gas emissions is described. In the second lap (stage), the ongoing work on reducing indirect emissions that includes emissions emanating from suppliers and customers of Tetra Pak is described.

The second case (Elopak) describes in three laps of its design journey how Elopak, among world's top-three producers of paper-based cartons, became carbon-neutral. In the first lap (stage), Elopak analyzed its business with respect to environmental standards developed in the last decade of the 20th century and made its business follow these standards. In the second lap (stage), it established an aggressive comprehensive climate policy and executed it at all levels of the company. In the third lap (stage), Elopak worked on achieving and maintaining carbon neutrality by offsetting its residual emissions by supporting a number of worldwide projects that reduce green-house gas emissions.

The third case (Johnson & Johnson) describes how Johnson & Johnson reduced carbon emissions in its worldwide operations. The design case is described in three laps (stages). In the first lap (stage), it describes how it developed a worldwide policy to reduce carbon emissions through reducing energy needs. In the second lap (stage), it established a CO_2 capital funding process for funding energy projects. The energy projects were reestablished in the third lap (stage) in response to the 2008 economic downturn.

22.1.6.1 Use of Social Innovation Design Process Model

The design work of all the twenty global social innovation design cases with different themes described in the book followed consistently the social innovation design process model shown in Figure 22.1 (also in Figure 1.1 of Chapter 1). This shows the usefulness of this model for designing social innovations and offers the innovation process model as a template for designing other social innovations.

22.2 APPLICABLE METAMODELS AND CONTRIBUTED MODELS/METAMODELS FOR THE DESIGN CASES

Figure 22.2 shows the metamodels applicable to some or all the twenty social innovation cases discussed in the book. The design cases to which a

1. Assessment of Needs, Issues, or Opportunities (Chapter 2)
2. Finding Impediments to Realizing Potential (Chapter 2)
3. Surveys and Reports (Chapter 3)
4. Adaptation and Customization of Technology (Chapter 6)
5. Technological Intervention (Chapter 6)
6. Promotion of Innovation Culture (Chapter 7)
7. Innovative Learning (Chapter 7)
8. Agent-Centric Model (Chapter 8)
9. Hub and Spoke Model (Chapters 2 and 8)
10. Micro Distribution (Chapter 8)
11. Promotion of Positive Environmental Impact (Chapter 8)
12. Leveraging Technology for Social Good (Chapter 9)
13. Continuous Experimentation & Innovation (Chapter 10)
14. McDonaldization (Chapter 10)
15. Understanding using Ethnographic Work (Chapter 10)
16. Using and Expanding the Pilot Project (Chapter 10)
17. Distributed Operations Model (Chapter 12)
18. Making Innovation Financially Sustainable (Chapter 12)
19. Global Education Center Continuous Improvement (Chapter 13)
20. Innovation Development Model (Chapter 17)
21. Overcoming Business-to-Business Barrier (Chapter 18)
22. Innovative Management for Achieving Sustainability (Chapter 20)
23. Monitoring, Reviewing, and Reporting for Sustainability (Chapter 21)
24. Exploration and Experimentation (Chapters 7 and 16)
25. Technology Empowerment (Chapters 8, 9, and 14)
26. Creating Positive Social Impact (Chapter 12)
27. Price Modeling (Chapter 6, 8, and 10)
28. External Partnerships (Chapters 19, 20, and 21)
29. Process Reengineering (Chapters 6, 7, 10, and 16)
30. Adaptive Organizational Forms (Chapters 2, 5, 6, 14, and 15)
31. Iterative Development (Chapters 2, 9, 14, 15, 17, and 18)
32. High Asset Use (Chapters 2, 5, 6, 7, 10, 12, and 16)
33. Creative Matching (Chapters 2, 4, 5, 6, 7, 8, 12, 14, 15)
34. Social Enterprise Business Model Template (Chapters 2 through 21)
35. Unmet Social Need (Chapters 2 through 21)

FIGURE 22.2
Applicable Metamodels and Contributed Models.

metamodel is applicable is shown by the chapter number(s) of such cases in parenthesis. For example, the first metamodel (Assessment of Needs, Issues, or Opportunities) in the figure shows (Chapter 2) as the chapter of the design case to which the metamodel is applicable. Similarly, #34 metamodel in the figure (Social Enterprise Business Model Template) is applicable to all the design cases discussed in the book (Chapters 2 through 21).

For each design case chapter, the applicable metamodel(s) are instantiated for the design case resulting in contributed model(s) for the corresponding design case. For example, Social Enterprise Business Model Template (#34) has been instantiated for all the design cases in the book, resulting in a contributed model (Overall Business Model) for each of the twenty design cases in the book. Similarly, the instantiation of the metamodel, Process Reengineering (#29), has resulted in contributed models (Process Reengineering) for the corresponding design cases discussed in Chapters 6, 7, 10, and 16.

All the metamodels in Figure 22.2 are either available in the literature or are based on widely used concepts and practices. The first three metamodels (#1, #2, and #3) are widely used in the problem definition phase of a social innovation design. Adaptation and Customization of Technology (#4), Technological Intervention (#5), Promotion of Innovation Culture (#6), and Innovative Learning (#7) are examples of widely used practices. Agent-Centric Model (#8) has been widely used in the real estate industry. Hub and Spoke Model (# 9) is widely used in the airline industry. Micro Distribution (#10), Price Modeling (#27), and the last seven metamodels in the figure (#29 through #35) are available metamodels described in the first chapter. Promotion of Positive Environmental Impact (#11), Leveraging Technology for Social Good (#12), and Continuous Experimentation & Innovation (#13) are variations of available concepts and models. The assembly-line model, McDonaldization (#14) is used in McDonald's (and Sears) for serving large number of customers while maintaining a reasonable level of quality and is discussed for the Aravind Eye Care System (Chapter 10) case. Understanding using Ethnographic Work (#15) uses the well-known principles of ethnography. Using and Expanding the Pilot Project (#16) uses the standard practice of using pilots and expanding them for complex projects. Distributed Operations Model (#17) uses the standard distributed system model for operations. Making Innovation Financially Sustainable (#18) is the desired goal of every innovation.

Global Education Center Continuous Improvement (#19) uses the well-known principles of continuous process improvement for training. Innovation Development Model (#20) uses the standard innovation model for developing the Cotton Stripper social innovation. Overcoming Business-to-Business Barrier (# 21) uses the standard business goal of getting rid of middlemen between buyers and sellers. Innovative Management for Achieving Sustainability (#22) uses known principles of innovative management in a novel way to get the buy-in of all the employees for reducing CO_2 emissions. Monitoring, Reviewing, and Reporting for Sustainability (#23) follows the industry guideline for sustainability reporting. Exploration and Experimentation (#24) is the standard way of discovering unknown knowledge. Technology Empowerment (#25) utilizes the practice of using technology for human benefit. Creating Positive Social Impact (#26) enunciates the goal of every social innovation. External Partnerships (#28) uses the standard practice of utilizing external partnerships with organizations that have coinciding or complementary missions and has benefited the three design cases in Part VI of the book.

Figure 22.3 shows the thirteen models and metamodels contributed by the twenty social innovation design cases of the book. Honey Care Africa Tripartite Business Model (#1) facilitates Honey Care Africa, a for-profit enterprise, to insulate small rural beekeepers from selling their honey in the market as well as facilitates the work of raising money for the needed infrastructure (see Chapter 2).

Balanced Dual Enablement Operations Model (#2) is an operations model that has been successfully used in both the Honey Care Africa case (Chapter 2) and the Waste Ventures India case (Chapter 7); see Chapters 2 and 7. It can also be used in other cases such as for rural development of businesses to create organic products or medicinal mushrooms.

1. Honey Care Arica Tripartite Business Model (Chapter 2)
2. Balanced Dual Enablement Operations Model (Chapter 2, 7)
3. Knowledge-Based Restricted Types of Farming (Chapter 3)
4. Participatory Restrictions on Fishing (Chapter 3)
5. Participatory Development of Needed Tourism Infrastructure by a Village Community (Chapter 4)
6. Participatory Development and Implementation of Infrastructure Project by a Village Community (Chapter 5)
7. Participatory Development and Implementation of needed Water Infrastructure Project (Chapter 5)
8. Husk Power Systems Business Models: BOOM, BOM, and BM (Chapter 6)
9. Deep Empathy & Compassion and its Continuous Reinforcement (Chapter 10)
10. Use of Creative Constraints to Spur Creativity in Innovation Design (Chapter 10)
11. Incorporating Multidimensionality (Chapter 13)
12. Abouleish's Decision Making Model (Chapter 16)
13. Humanistic Approach to Business (Chapter 16)

FIGURE 22.3
Contributed Models and Metamodels.

Knowledge-Based Restricted Types of Farming (#3) is a generalization of Participatory Restrictions on Fishing (#4) to other types of farming including organic and ocean farming based on the best cumulative formal and informal/ experiential knowledge that impose some restrictions to improve farming productivity (see Chapter 3).

Participatory Development of Needed Tourism Infrastructure by a Village Community (#5), Participatory Development and Implementation of Infrastructure Project by a Village Community (#6), and Participatory Development and Implementation of needed Water Infrastructure (#7), discussed in Chapters 4 and 5 are all about developing and implementing village infrastructure projects. Participatory Development of Needed Tourism Infrastructure by a Village Community (#5) is about creating a tourism product. Participatory Development and Implementation of needed Water Infrastructure Project (#7) is about creating water infrastructure project and Participatory Development and Implementation of Infrastructure Project by a Village Community (#6) is its generalization to any infrastructure project.

Husk Power Systems Business Models: BOOM, BOM, and BM (#8) are three related business models of Husk Power Systems (Chapter 6) for how the biomass gasifiers and distribution networks are built, owned, and operated. The BOOM model builds them, owns them, and operates them. BOM model only builds and owns them. BM model only builds them (see Chapter 6).

Deep Empathy & Compassion and its Continuous Reinforcement (#9) and Use of Creative Constraints to Spur Creativity in Innovation Design (#10) are from the Aravind Eye Care System design case (Chapter 10). The first model/metamodel (#9) uses deep empathy and its continuous reinforcement through eye camps to understand why rural people do not undergo cataract surgeries to prevent blindness and to develop strategies to address the issues found. The second model/metamodel (#10) develops a profound principle for spurring creativity.

Incorporating Multidimensionality (#11) is an important model for Infosys Global Education Center about imparting organization-specific career-long learning among its employees. This model can serve as a useful metamodel for training employees of any information technology company. (see Chapter 13).

Abouleish's Decision Making Model (#12) and Humanistic Approach to Business (#13) are new approaches contributed by the SEKEM project (Chapter 16) related to how social innovation businesses should be carried out.

Index

Printed in the United States
by Baker & Taylor Publisher Services